ON THE BEGINNINGS OF THEORY

Deconstructing Broken Logic in Grice, Habermas, and Stuart Mill

Peter Bornedal

University Press of America,® Inc.
Lanham · Boulder · New York · Toronto · Oxford

Copyright © 2006 by
University Press of America,® Inc.
4501 Forbes Boulevard
Suite 200
Lanham, Maryland 20706
UPA Acquisitions Department (301) 459-3366

PO Box 317
Oxford
OX2 9RU, UK

All rights reserved
Printed in the United States of America
British Library Cataloging in Publication Information Available

Library of Congress Control Number: 2005937863
ISBN 0-7618-3390-0 (paperback : alk. ppr.)

∞™ The paper used in this publication meets the minimum
requirements of American National Standard for Information
Sciences—Permanence of Paper for Printed Library Materials,
ANSI Z39.48—1984

B
1641
.G484
B67
2006

020707-2913p8

LIST OF CONTENTS

ACKNOWLEDGMENTS:

Permission to reprint material from the three works indicated below was granted by Harvard University Press, The MIT Press, and Oxford University Press:

Paul Grice: *Studies in the Way of Words* (Cambridge, Massachusetts: Harvard University Press, 1989)

Jürgen Habermas: *On the Pragmatics of Communication*. Ed.: Maeve Cooke (Cambridge, Massachusetts: The MIT Press, 1998)

John Stuart Mill: *On Liberty and Other Essays*. Ed.: John Gray (Oxford: Oxford University Press, 1991)

An 'AUB Mellon Research Grant' made it possible to complete an important chapter of this book.

INTRODUCTION

We set up a word at the point where our ignorance begins, where we cannot see any further, for example, the word 'I,' the word 'do,' the word 'suffer.'
— Nietzsche: *The Will to Power.*[1]

At the foundation of well-founded belief lies belief that is not founded.
— Wittgenstein: *On Certainty.*[2]

There are no simple concepts. Every concept has components and is defined by them. It therefore has a combination. It is a multiplicity, although not every multiplicity is conceptual. There is no concept with only one component. Even the first concept, the one with which a philosophy 'begins,' has several components, because it is not obvious that philosophy must have a beginning.
— Deleuze/Guattari: *What is Philosophy?*[3]

(i) What is Metaphysics; Nietzsche, Wittgenstein, Derrida? (ii) The Project: A Non-Defeatist Deconstructive Analytic. (iii) Two Incompatible Notions: Interpretational Instability and Structural Instability. (iv) Three Objections to the Notion of 'Interpretational Instability.' (v) The Enigma of Metaphysics. (vi) Linear Thinking Versus Repetitious Thinking. (vii) A Final Remark About Conception.

(i) What is Metaphysics; Nietzsche, Wittgenstein, Derrida? Ignorance, the point where we cannot see any further, is precisely what interests me in the following essays. And of Nietzsche's three examples quoted in the epigraph above, I have devoted a special interest to the words 'I' and 'suffer'; more precisely, the interest is here in the theories of the speaking I and the pleasure-seeking I. —I have not much to say about 'do.'

It is Nietzsche's idea that in such words, we look for and think we find a truth behind appearances, for example in the form of an 'I' behind our thinking. We 'know,' viz., experience the phenomenon of thinking, but the phenomenon is chaotic; thoughts seem to live a life of their own. They emerge and vanish according to indeterminable laws. We consequently invent an 'I' supposed to be in control of our unpredictable thinking, an 'I' understood as a small rational entity pulling the strings of our thinking. Ironically, we have now added an unknown to a known. We know 'thinking' as the experience of the phenomenon 'thinking,' but we don't know the 'I' that is supposed to explain it, and yet, we are relieved by the invention of the 'I'. We look for and believe we have found a cause, and we use this cause as a foundation.

Wittgenstein is saying the same in the quotation chosen as the second epigraph; at the foundation of something well-founded, we find something unfounded. And finally, Deleuze and Guattari are expressing the same experience of unfounded foundations in the elegant, "there is no concept with only one component."

To Nietzsche, besides the irony of explaining known by unknown, the addition of causes to our phenomenal world is utterly paradoxical, because before we can invent the cause, we have to experience the phenomenon that we will choose to see as an effect of the cause. The chronological sequence of events is thus: first, we experience a phenomenon, secondly, we choose to understand this phenomenon as an effect to which we, thirdly, attach a cause, which, finally, we interpret as preceding the initial phenomenon. We can set up the paradox of this so-called 'chronological reversal' in the following table:

> Step 1: Phenomenon →
>   Step 2: Phenomenon is interpreted as effect →
>   Step 3: Cause is attached to effect →
> Step 4: Cause is interpreted as preceding Step 1

Commonly, in a cause-effect relation, the cause is understood to come before the effect; the cause comes first, the effect comes second. If we talk about the mechanics of the physical world, the process could not easily be thought otherwise (—it is not likely that Nietzsche intends his argument to challenge Newtonian physics). In Nietzsche's phenomenalism, however, the issue is *inner experience* and *metaphysics* as derived from inner experience. Within this domain, the effect is first, and the cause is invented as secondary. The cause that is supposed to be the initial operator is reconstructed as the last step of the sequence of events; it is chronologically succeeding the effect as a fictitious addition.

In *Beyond Good and Evil*, Nietzsche gives us an example of such a chronological reversal. In a one-aphorism long passage, he deconstructs Kant's epistemology. 'How are synthetic *a priori* judgments possible,' Kant had asked himself in the *Critique of Pure Reason* and later in the *Prolegomena*, and he answered himself by referring to 2 + 12 categories that would guarantee *a priori* necessity in synthetic statements. These 2 + 12 categories would secure respectively our spatial-temporal sensation of the world and our understanding of the world. Since they are necessary parts of our cognitive apparatus, they add the—to Kant's mind—much desired *a priori* component to synthetic statements. To Nietzsche's mind, not only is the cause Kant finds in form of the categories an invention and a fiction, but also the structure of his answer is fallacious. He had asked himself, 'How are synthetic *a priori* judgments possible,' and now he answers (famously painstakingly), they are possible by means of certain categories.

> Kant asked himself: how are synthetic judgments a priori possible? — and what, really, did he answer? By means of a faculty: but unfortunately not in a few words, but so circumspectly, venerably, and with such an expenditure of German profundity and flourishes that the comical *niaiserie allemande* involved is such an answer was overlooked. . . . By means of a faculty, he said. But is that—an answer? An explanation? Or is it not rather a repetition of the question.[4]

What is it we cannot do here? —Foundations are obviously understood and designed to support what comes *after* themselves, that is, what they are foundations for. It is therefore fallacious if the foundation is a part of what it is supposed to found. To use Derridian language: in the metaphysical tradition, a foundation is a notion indicating self-presence, and it is—although it exists as a mark, or a signifier, within the metaphysical text—supposed to be located, or at least localizable, outside the text. If now we—despite our metaphysical aspirations to locate self-presence *outside*—find it *inside* and woven into the text as merely another signifier, it can no longer be understood as a foundation, because it is now woven into the text as a part of its fabric. If, as metaphysicians, we suggest it to ourselves as the ultimate cause, we believe that we have broken the spell of the text and finally found the self-presence that explains everything. But in actuality, we are caught in a circle that we cannot see when we suggest this answer to ourselves. We may imagine that the answer is outside the circle; and we may strongly desire that this must be the case, but the answer is still inside as a part of the question or, as Nietzsche says, a repetition of the question. If this is the case, then, by our answer, we have done nothing but added ignorance to ignorance. From Nietzsche's point of view, this is the comical aspect of Kant's answer. If we don't know how synthetic *a priori* judgments are possible, we know even less what a 'faculty' is. (Nietzsche's mock-answer, "By means of a faculty" is Hollingdale's translation of the original, "Vermöge eines Vermögens." 'Vermögen' is of course correctly translated as 'faculty,' but an alternative English rendition could have been, "By means of a means," to underscore Nietzsche's mockery of the repetitious pattern in Kant's answer. Coming full circle: 'by what means do we know synthetic *a priori* judgments? — By means of a means!')

To drive home his point, Nietzsche refers to the comedy by Moliere where an examiner asks a medical student about the effects of opium. The examiner asks the ignorant student why opium makes people sleepy; the student thinks long and hard over the question before he answers ponderously: *quia est in eo virtus dormitiva, cujus est natura senses assoupire*. Opium makes people sleepy 'because it contains a certain dormient faculty that has the property of making the senses sleepy'—and the examiner passes the student in admiration of such a display of profound knowledge.

As I shall argue in one of the following essays, it is basically the same fallacy John Stuart Mill is committing when in *Utilitarianism* he poses the question, how do we lead a good life, and then answers himself, by pursuing those pleasures that are considered good. Nothing has been said. It is all within the same circle. It is safe to say that pursuing a good life means to pursue pleasure, especially when one covers one's back (as does Mill) and appoints the pleasures that are good to pursue. From this point Mill's confusions begin to pile up, because it is difficult to explain the difference between a good and a bad pleasure *in principle*—that is, without moralizing before the moral theory is constituted. This is only slightly *less* difficult than knowing what pleasure *is* in distinction to pain when we are not allowed to include 'low' sensuous pleasures and pains.

(ii) The Project: A Non-Defeatist Deconstructive Analytic. The four essays I present in the following are independent of each other. This means that I repeat the same problems from essay to essay, but from different angles and perspectives, and, of course, since the essays are *readings*, according to how the problems are uniquely tackled by the author in question. I want to suggest a Deconstructive Analytic that is methodologically more rigorous than some previous attempts to do deconstruction, a deconstruction that can be seen as sharing common grounds with aspects of Pragmatism and Analytic Philosophy. I therefore refer as often to Nietzsche, Peirce, Moore, and Wittgenstein as

to Derrida. In the specific sense of Deconstruction that I am here purporting, they can all be seen as 'deconstructionists'—although of course, we gain nothing of substance by simply labeling them as such.[5]

Such a 'Deconstructive Analytic' would be, in my favored understanding, distinct from several of the current strands of Deconstruction; on various grounds. 'Deconstructive Analytic' is, for example, anti-defeatist in distinction to deconstructive practices that suspend analysis of the text for the sake of the playfulness or inventiveness of the critic. Defeatist analytical practices are exercised when one cannot engage in an analytic activity without in principle doubting the validity of one's own analytic activity. Defeatist critics resign before the text; the text or the textual phenomenon has become too complex. When, for example, in the days of Yale School criticism, Geoffrey Hartman[6] and followers were practicing deconstruction as puns on sentence fragments and plays on anagrams, the analysis became in itself poeticizing. The critic adopted the role of creator, because nothing decisive could be said about a text, which in its infinite intricacies per definition escaped any defining instance of analysis. When Stanley Fish[7] and followers are advancing the key insight that every text is infinitely readable, this insight also prevents them from engaging in any textual analysis themselves, because alternative analyses are in principle equally valid. Also if we append Fish's amendment devised to prevent interpretative anarchy, his *ad hoc* construction that any serious critic conforms to the authority of an acceptable 'interpretive community,' it is still hard to see how one could both support Fish's literary theories, and seriously perform, say, classical Marxist analysis, without involving oneself in a personal inconsistency. (One could only pose as a classical Marxist in good faith, if temporarily repressing Fish's insight that it would be merely a 'pose' among multiple other possibilities.)

Here, I argue that there are positive instances of analysis, that there is a textual object, and that there is a role for the critic. These are all claims that confront various receptionist approaches to literature (not only Stanley Fish's, but also more ambivalent, less radical, hermeneutical approaches as advanced by Gadamer, Ricoeur, and Iser[8]). However, the assertion is not here that Fish, in his radical, or Iser, in his not-so-radical, reader-response criticism is plainly wrong. It would be misleading, and ultimately nonsensical, to assert that a text cannot be 'readable,' in the sense, receptive to unexpected and surprising interpretations. (And as counter-argument to Receptionism, the assertion would be poorly chosen because we cannot know what interpretations a text can get; *a priori*, we cannot know the future universe of its receptions. We admit that texts may have *multiple* interpretations, although, strictly speaking, it could never be *infinitely* interpretable.[9]) In the present work, however, this fact is regarded as a surface phenomenon, as a fact that is only sociologically interesting, as a fact that is interesting to those whose analytical desire it is to analyze 'communities,' but not texts.

Furthermore, some proponents of 'infinite interpretability' take its conclusions beyond the defensible. A text's 'interpretability' or 'readability' can hardly have as a consequence that the text as an *identifiable structural entity* is completely suspended. A text being interpretable does not imply that there is only 'us'—as Stanley Fish has suggested—as little as our ability to view an object from multiple angles implies the non-existence of the object. Rather, we would normally say, we see an object from many angles because the object is there to be seen. But in certain strands of Deconstruction (or deconstructively inspired criticism), such a commonsensical observation is regarded as naïve or passé. We agree that the superabundance of inventive interpretations of the stars in daily or weekly horoscopes do not affect the constellations of stars, but we can no longer agree that the text is unaffected by a superabundance of different critical interpretations.

Against these 'defeatist' analytic practices, I argue for a relative stability of the text. This implies that a text has structures of, for example, thematic, narrative, and logical nature that can be identified as unique to that text. The moment of meaning of the text is therefore as important to reconstruct, as is its alleged meaninglessness. Said this, I *also* believe (with Nietzsche, Wittgenstein, Deleuze/Guattari, and Derrida) that a text ultimately cannot justify its own meaningfulness. There is no Archimedian point from where it can support itself. There is, on the one hand, nothing outside the circle; on the other hand, texts typically assert a point *supposed* to be outside. But again (to pull the carpet from under the defeatists), this *fictitious outside* can be *objectively* identified. Its fictitiousness does not produce the text as a free-flowing non-entity. A text can be objectively identified on two levels, on the level of its stability, and on the level where this stability breaks down. A text's construction can be reconstructed up to the point where it begins to vibrate, up to the point where we begin to notice its fissures and cracks, and by what superficial means the text holds together itself from falling apart. In other words, we can only deconstruct a text if we understand that there is a construction to deconstruct. A deconstructive analytic must *presuppose* belief in the text as an identifiable structural entity, because if there is no construction, neither is there deconstruction. We only perceive *instability* in something we *presume* is stable. Thus, when we analyze the objective structure of a text, there is no self-contradiction in simultaneously emphasizing its stability and instability, its play between meaningfulness and meaninglessness. (For example, there is also no self-contradiction in zooming in on what we believe is a smooth surface (indeed, *is* a smooth surface), only to discover, in the close-up view, its rifts and cracks. Indeed, only smooth surfaces, only unitary structures, crack.)

(iii) Two Incompatible Notions: Interpretational Instability and Structural Instability. We shall here distinguish between so-called 'interpretational instability' (i.e., texts are unstable because their interpretations are unstable) and so-called 'structural instability' (i.e., texts are unstable because their structure is unstable). Arguing against the notion of so-called 'interpretational instability' as advanced in contextualism, the following three essays try to locate the *structural* instability of the texts, theories, or systems in question.

An example from Wittgenstein's *Philosophical Investigations* can serve to isolate three relatively distinct levels of analysis. Wittgenstein draws a transparent cube, and comments:

You could imagine the illustration

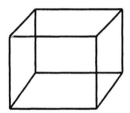

appearing in several places in a book, a text-book for instance. In the relevant text something different is in question every time: here a glass cube, there an inverted open box, there a wire frame of that shape, there three boards forming a solid angle. Each time the text supplies the interpretation. But we can also *see* the illustration now as one thing now as another. —So we interpret it, and *see* it as we *interpret* it.[10]

We have a form, and to this form we supply different meanings or contents. Every time we supply a content we see the form *as* this content, now it is a glass cube, now a box, now a wire frame, etc. The supply of content is an interpretation, because in itself, the form is sufficiently blank or empty to suggest a specific content. After interpreting or specifying the form, we see it as such specified, that is, we strongly believe that this form is a picture of an object.

If we take this example of Wittgenstein's and apply it to the situation in interpretation theory and critical theory, we notice that the example in itself is a transparent cube that can be filled in with different contents.

Immediately, Wittgenstein's example, if applied to the discussions of interpretation, would seem to illustrate the idea that a work of art is the product of its interpretation. The example is thus well chosen to bolster reader-response criticism, however not in its most radical forms. It could not support the radical claim that the reader provides *all* meaning to the text, since in Wittgenstein we have a structure that 'carries' the meaning it gets throughout the textbook. But it can support a reader-response criticism that holds that there is a work of art, an ontological and structural object, which can be concretized or appropriated in various ways, it can become an object for different aesthetic experiences. (Two strong proponents of this view would to my mind be Roman Ingarden and Paul Ricoeur.[11])

We could also go beyond Wittgenstein's intention with his example and let it illustrate the view that the work of art is a structure, which can be described in relatively definite terms. Despite the different interpretations we can attribute to Wittgenstein's transparent cube, it, firstly, cannot be seen as just anything, we can see it as a glass-cube, a box, or a wire frame, but not as a sphere, a ball, or a sun, and nobody can tell me that it looks anything like my coffee cup. Secondly, it can be structurally identified; there are eight right angles, connected by so and so many lines. If we suspend our three-dimensional view of the cube, and project it onto a two-dimensional plane the same pattern of lines appears in whichever interpretation; strictly speaking, as a two-dimensional pattern of lines the interpretations disappear. We can apply a strategy that wants to describe this pattern of lines *as such*. (A strong proponent of the view here intimated would to my mind be A. J. Greimas.[12])

Then we can finally take Wittgenstein's example to its last and ultimate level. We notice (as has been often emphasized in Gestalt Psychology) that the cube can be inverted, the front can be seen as the back of a box, and vise versa. We cannot see it in the two positions at the same time; we see it first in one position, then we invert the box and see what was its back as its front. From here, we can go on and invert the box back and forth. In each case, it takes time to invert the cube. It takes a small measure of force to see the box differently. The new image comes suddenly, as in a 'jump.' One first sees the box in bird's-eye view, this seems to be the resting-position of the box, then one makes it 'jump' and sees it now in frog's-eye view. The box is, in other words, structurally unstable. (The early work of Jacques Derrida could represent this view.)

We realize now that the example is in itself a transparent box that can have three different interpretations: (a) the box can be interpreted differently, as Wittgenstein says; (b) its structure could be abstracted from its possible interpretations as rationalist critics might well object; and finally (c), the frame of the box is structurally unstable.

In the first case, the box is unstable in Stanley Fish's preferred sense, in the second case, it is structurally stable, and in the third, it is unstable in my preferred sense. Notice now this irony: Fish emphasizes the instability of texts, as myself, but I could never substantiate instability in my sense if I believed in instability in Fish's sense, and Fish would neutralize his notion of instability if he started to believe in my notion of instability. If a text is unstable because of its readability/interpretability, then it is not possible to ascertain its breaking point, because it is too unstable for any definite ascertainment of instability. If a text is unstable in Fish's sense, then we cannot demonstrate its structural instability. There would be no objectivity to hold on to; there would be no text but merely interpretations.

These two views are mutually incompatible. If or when they are lumped together in critical theory, the reason is ideological. To paraphrase Stanley Fish (—who has a theory capable of explaining ideological formations, without seeing a problem in ideological formations), if or when the 'authority' of a current 'interpretive community' promotes a desire for 'instability,' desire, consequently, comes to override inconsistency, eschew logic, and disregard self-contradiction. When it has become ideological desirable to emphasize *instability* at any price, it is easily forgotten that one cannot consistently have it both ways.[13] Poor Deconstruction results from an ideological confusion of *interpretational* instability and *structural* instability.

(iv) Three Objections to the Notion of 'Interpretational Instability.' If a text is *structurally unstable*, the desire to found a system is perpetually frustrated, *not because* of changing contexts or because humankind historically changes its mind, but because foundationalist ambitions strand on cognitive or logical deficiencies inherent in all systematization. In order to admit research into these states of affairs, it is crucial to dismiss the notion of 'interpretational instability.' This notion must be rejected because *inevitably* it will de-legitimize all research into *objectivity*, also the *objectivity of instability*.[14] The following three objections serve this purpose.

First Objection. The problem of how a text is seen as meaningful (in an interpretation), how it is infused with (contextual) meaning, how it is (locally) stabilized, merely restarts the problem of meaning over and again. Even the wildest contextualist must believe that a given interpretation is *constituted*, since she or he believes in contextually regulated interpretations. How is this constitution explained? The problem of constitution would have to be addressed in a theory of meaning that could not be identical to Contextualism itself. The context of the context would have to be solid, like flowing water only flows relative to a ground. To know that everything is contextually regulated interpretation cannot explain the mechanism by which we appropriate an interpretation as meaningful, whether as individuals or as 'communities.' It cannot be the case that both the meaning that we appropriate and the appropriation itself are dependent on context, because 'context' then destabilizes not only the meaning which the given subject appropriates, but also the appropriation itself, implying that a given agent does not appropriate any meaning at all. In that case, contextual meaning does not exist, because meaning does not exist. If meaning cannot be appropriated, a 19th century British imperialist could not think that Arabs are irrational (to refer here to an example from Edward Said), because he could not have any meaning about Arabs whatsoever. He can only believe that Arabs are irrational if this belief is constituted, that is, if it is appropriated and stabilized, not if it is contingent upon a variety of circumstances.

Therefore, meaning (whether contextual or otherwise) must be constituted, and that constitution cannot be explained by Contextualism itself. It seems that if we want to address such a theory, we would have to take into account already existing theories of meaning. One might suggest that existing theories of meaning are so many various attempts to explain the constitution of interpretations as meaning. This problem is serious and profound; however, the problem is rarely seen, let alone addressed.

Second objection. If we are to believe Stanley Fish, interpretations are being adjusted to certain 'interpretative communities,' that is, professional communities that yield the authority to rule interpretation valid or invalid. A problem facing this explanation-model is that it is incomprehensible how we are able to adjust our interpretations to 'interpretative communities,' but not to the text, since it must be presupposed that *any* text is a passive object of interpretations. No text reads itself, says Fish, so we cannot hope to understand the *text*; we can only hope to understand the text through the *interpretations of the text*. But how do we understand an interpretation of a text, if we cannot understand a text. An interpretation of a text is also a text, and in principle, it is the object of the same exigencies as the text. If I cannot adjust my interpretation to the text, I also cannot adjust my interpretation to the authority of an 'interpretive community.'

As an addendum to this objection: if I can understand an interpretation of a text, I can also understand that some interpretations of a text are different from other interpretations. If I understand that a text has several interpretations, it is because I understand the *differential* between one interpretation and another. But if it is granted that I understand individual interpretations and the differences between them, then we must presume that I am also able to perceive whether a text's self-interpretation corresponds to the interpretation it gets by any arbitrary chosen interpreter. I understand that some interpretations of a text are different from other interpretations, ergo, I also understand when an interpretation is different from the self-interpretation of the text. Here the contextualist has painted himself into a corner. How do we understand an interpretation of a text, but not the text? Why is it that the text is an inaccessible *noema*, but its interpretation an accessible and comprehensible *phenomenon*? The interpretation of the text will have to be exactly as comprehensible or incomprehensible (*in principle*) as the text it interprets.

Third objection. In his essays, Stanley Fish repeats the assertion that 'no text reads itself.' As said, the text is regarded as passive, it cannot interpret itself, and it depends on the reader (the community of readers) who endows the text with meaning. After some reflection on our experience with texts, I shall venture the diametrically opposite assertion, 'all texts read themselves,' and argue that it makes better sense. This assertion is only absurd if we too squarely and empirically understand a text and its reader as two distinct entities opposing each other as subject to object. Phenomenologically speaking, all texts are always-already reading themselves. That is, they reach the reader partly interpreted, since they have built into their texture what we might call an *implicit interpreter* engaged in interpreting events happening in the text for the sake of easing the reader's understanding. (Concrete examples on such *implicit interpreters* could be the classical Greek chorus, the soliloquies in Shakespeare, or the inner monologues in psychological novels.) This self-interpretive activity is in other words original and primary. The work of the implicit interpreter is what we might call the *primary interpretation* or the *Arche-Interpretation* of the text. It is the Arche-Interpretation that subsequent interpretations will have to take into account if they want to document understanding of the text. The existence of the Arche-interpretation puts up limits to a text's 'interpretability.' The primary interpretation becomes a measuring rod against which certain interpretations are ruled to be 'wrong' (in cautious quotation-marks—as odd, far-fetched, strange, or silly) or simply wrong (bluntly and without caution—as misleading, incorrect, or false).

Now, also Stanley Fish would admit that some interpretations are 'wrong' (at least so in cautious quotation-marks). Lately, Fish is indeed more adamant about emphasizing the limits to interpretation than he is about the idea of 'interpretive instability.'[15] However, Fish gives a completely different explanation of this predicament than the one I am in the process of suggesting.

A simple example might illustrate the difference. If a viewer, watching a James Bond movie in which Bond joins forces with a female Russian agent, believes that she is watching the reunion of a husband and his erstwhile wife, then I suppose we would agree that the interpretation is wrong. We would probably also agree that the interpretation is possible (I think I just made it *possible*). Fish, however, would say that it is wrong because there are no 'interpretative community' to take it seriously; it is wrong for conventional reasons. The community validates or invalidates interpretation; it becomes the exclusive arbitrator, authorizing or annulling various interpretations. If there is no correspondence between the belief-structure of the community and the aspiring-to-be-accepted interpretation, the interpretation is in discordance to the beliefs of the community and is rejected.

However, this explanation-model has difficulties explaining how an interpretation is validated (or invalidated) in the first place. How does the Bond-society on its first international meeting know what it can and cannot say about Bond movies? It cannot know, in principle, that the sentimental interpretation suggested above is wrong, because there is still no authoritative 'interpretative Bond-community' established to regulate interpretations.[16] Fish's explanation-model can explain *that* a certain community has certain beliefs, but not *how* it has them.

Suggesting an 'implicit interpreter' that 'arche-interprets' the text is supposed to remedy this situation. It explains why some interpretations can be considered wrong and plainly rejected without we need to rely on and refer to the authority of an interpretive community. According to this suggestion, the interpretation of the Bond movie above is not wrong because it does not correspond to an adequate interpretive community, it is wrong because it does not correspond to the self-interpretation of the movie.

To see the difference in the two positions applied to our minimal example, one might imagine that the above interpretation is ruled to be 'wrong,' because an authoritative community has decided that it is, in some way or other, ideological incorrect. (Bond may be seen as a male chauvinist that treats women as playthings for his amusement and sexual exploits. A sentimental interpretation of the film ignores this fact and idealizes Bond, etc., and is therefore 'wrong.') But according to the theory of the 'implicit interpreter,' the interpretation is wrong because the movie has already explained or interpreted the plot to the audience. If the female Russian spy ends up in Bond's bed before they have been introduced, it is because the female KGB agent has the explicit assignment to seduce Bond. Since Bond is on an identical mission, the movie does not give him any reasons to resist (ignoring whatever other reasons he lacks for resisting that particular invitation). If language has any meaning, we *objectively* know that they do not know each other in advance, and that their encounter has been planned by authorities in whose hands they are both 'playthings.'

(v) The Enigma of Metaphysics. If all systems are *objectively* unfounded, we must draw the unsettling conclusion that there is a limit to human thinking. We cannot understand, or represent adequately, theoretical beginnings. We have perhaps a cognitive make up, perhaps a language, perhaps a logic, which makes the conception of beginnings impossible. But whether our mind, our language, or our logic is deficient, there is no possible exit. We can obviously not choose another mind; neither can we invent another language geared to explain something we only vaguely understand in the first place (besides, languages are not easily inventable). We could conceivably formulate another logic in which the problems of origins are overcome, but firmly established within the logic that we already have, it is impossible to imagine just a few ground-rules for this new logic.

The problem of origin does not come up as persistently in ordinary life as it does in philosophy; it is not 'felt' within the realm of the everyday. However, the master-thinkers—who are always metaphysicians in the sense that they are inclined to think about the ultimate and universal—are destined to strand on this problem. Since they are required—either by the community of colleagues or by themselves—to give grounds for their thinking, and (given their excruciating cognitive integrity) grounds have to be *ultimate*, they are compelled to think about what is first, original, and constituting. They are consequently bound to repeat the 'problem of origin,' even if they know that the problem cannot be adequately solved. This paradox and double-bind may then result in various ingenious solutions that the master-thinker in a spontaneous moment of exuberant creation might believe have obliterated metaphysics, but in time will prove to be merely pseudo-solutions. It seems to be the case that just as we cannot escape death except by dying, we cannot escape metaphysics except by forgetting it.

If we are to believe Kant, the master-thinker is seduced by reason into believing in foundations. By means of reason we are able to trace things back to ever more rudimentary grounds, so it seems only 'logical' that we should be able also to trace things back to the *most* rudimentary ground. The otherwise steady regression of our reason seduces us into believing that if we can go from D to C, and from C to B, what should prevent us from taking the final step to A? Yet, it is this final step that proves impossible; here the terrain becomes uninhabitable for human language and reason.

While engaging itself in taking this final step, reason makes its agent a false promise; it promises the final step to A; but that would mean to think reason's own grounding, and this is impossible. The contemporary logician asserts that this ultimate lack of logic is quite logical. We have to start our reasoning somewhere, and our start cannot be reasoning itself, since this is where we start. We are bound to start from a first axiom that cannot in itself be proved, and yet, from where all further axioms can be proved. Knowledge is necessarily based on certain indefinable fundamental concepts that are to define all subsequent concepts. Since this is the condition, the start does not need to bother us.[17] Thus, the logician is confident about the groundless ground. If only the start is intuitively self-evident, we can—in the spirit of Descartes—rest assured that the theory we build on this self-evident foundation will be solid and sound.

Given that ultimate grounds cannot be thought, what is now the status of the conceptional constructions that philosophers tend to name and understand as their 'grounds'? Philosophers typically assert a theoretical 'world,' which is reducible to, originating from, or regulated by, a certain ground. If the ground as truly grounding is a non-existent chimera, a fantasy of reason brought to a standstill, an axiom that is ungrounded in itself and therefore arbitrary, what is it now that philosophers call 'grounds'? —Here, I shall suggest that a ground is merely a *decision condensed into a word*! The ground that the philosopher supposedly reaches by inference is nothing but what in advance he holds as his favorite belief, as this favorite belief is dispersed throughout his theory. Thus, so-called grounds are typically *repetitions in miniature* of the picture we are already used to see; or, as I prefer, they are *fractal repetitions* of the already known structure. They do not add a deeper dimension to the philosophy in question, because they merely repeat the overall intention in that philosophy. Now, this intention has just been replaced to the supposed beginning of the philosophy, and, furthermore, it has been condensed and abbreviated into a single word in order to give the illusion of *point*. Metaphysics always thinks *from* the point. The origin is always simple.

If the so-called foundation is a decision already taken in the theory, the root of philosophy is nothing but a mirror of its various branches. This suggestion revises an old but persistent conception of philosophy, a conception with a long history, but succinctly captured in Descartes' metaphor of the system of thinking as a tree with its more and less fundamental divisions, starting with the root as the most fundamental, symbolizing metaphysics, running through the trunk symbolizing physics, and ending in the branches of all the various minor sub-disciplines of his day, such as law, history, mechanics, or medicine. This metaphor represented Descartes' belief in a solid foundational system from where we by systematically employing linear and deductive reasoning could develop a unitary universe of knowledge. The thinking has bottom-to-top direction. The bottom is supposed to represent the beginning, the unitary, foundational, and substantial, and the top, the end, the particular, founded, and insubstantial.

Arguing for a reversal of Descartes' allegory, we can start noticing a significant imperfection in Descartes' metaphor: the root system of a tree is anything but unitary and singular. A tree-root is not a unified whole, but a complex network of secondary roots and rhizomes branching out from a primary root. Automatically and instinctively, Descartes *reinterprets* the root system of a tree in order to adapt it to his conviction of the possibility of foundational thinking. Instead of *concretely* envisioning the root in his tree-metaphor, Descartes appropriates the customary dictionary definitions for 'root,' according to which a 'root' is an *origin*, a *fundamental principle*, a *central point*, etc. The root in Descartes' tree becomes a *word-object*. To his tree-metaphor, he applies the dictionary, and reinvents the most important part of the tree as a word-object, whereas trunk and branches are retained as *thing-objects*. Descartes is so blinded by the foundational intentions of his metaphor that it does not occur to him that anybody could take his metaphor literally. (It is appropriately ironic that Descartes' tree is supported by something as flimsy as a *word-object*. It adds new meaning to Nietzsche's dictum above, at the point where we cannot see any further, we set up a word—or rather, a *word-object*. In the beginning was the word—inserted in order to cover up incomprehensible complexity.)

In this reinterpretation of Descartes' tree, I have introduced a persistent deconstructive theme, the critical interrogation of the simplicity and self-sufficiency of origins. To the Platonist logician, origins are first and foremost simple; the simple is characterized by being that which we all know is true. The deconstructionist logician, by contrast, questions and doubts this simplicity, and is thus seen as jeopardizing universal knowledge. The Platonist logician often regards it as futile and trivial, if not outright dangerous, to further scrutinize the simple, because it implies that one qualifies its simplicity, and thus its self-evidence. This is perceived as sophistry and/or skepticism, and it is often vehemently argued by Platonist logicians (who today exist as a particular branch of Analytic Philosophy) that these positions have no *right* to question the ground.[18]

In the interpretation of the tree-metaphor above, I now suggest that the origin is never simple, or only simple in the illusory appearance of a *word-object*. The metaphor of the tree therefore has to be rethought, or rather abandoned, because if metaphysics is a belief dispersed throughout the system or the theory, but pre-consciously replaced to the 'beginning,' the notion of 'beginning' becomes an inept metaphor. According to this new perspective, we no longer have to go to the root to locate metaphysics, we can find metaphysics in a mere leaf, so to speak; that is, in seemingly inconsequential discussions of something mundane, trite, or personal.[19] As thinking, Deconstructive logic has therefore rather top-to-bottom direction; this being understood cautiously and with the proper qualifications. Especially, the distinction, bottom-to-top vs. top-to-bottom, cannot be seen as identical to the classical distinction between deductive and inductive inference. Top-to-bottom does not signify a situation where one starts out from a manifold of data that are simplified, through a number of generalizations, into single laws. At the bottom and in the top, we rather find the same. If we find a dispersion of material at the top of the tree (branches, limps, sprigs, leaves, etc.), then we find a similar dispersion of material at the bottom of the tree, in the form of the branching out of roots and rhizomes. At the bottom of the metaphorical tree, we find something that is akin to 'root' as *thing-object*, cleverly concealed, however, in 'root' as *word-object*.

This deconstructive-pragmatic conclusion is in good accordance with Wittgenstein. In *On Certainty*, we find the following remark: "I have arrived at the rock bottom of my convictions. And one might almost say that these foundations-walls are carried by the whole house."[20]

(vi) Linear Thinking Versus Repetitious Thinking. Philosophers have been convinced that they think linearly, but in reality, they think repetitiously. A crude way of ascertaining this postulate could be to carry out a simple count of how often a philosophical theme is repeated in an oeuvre. For example, one could count how often Habermas has given an account of his three validity-claims in works from the last thirty years, and with what average such an account appears in single essays.

Another, less crude, way of evidencing the postulate is to look for *fractal* repetitions of the theme, that is, repetitions of the same but on different scales, and in different contexts. One can for example compare the theory to its supposed foundation, top to bottom, and notice that the foundation is often a fractal repetition of the theory as such.

For example, Grice and Schiffer cannot resist the temptation to address the classical but intractable problem of the origin of meaning, origin of language. However, when they explain how the first word becomes meaningful in some fictitious prehistoric situation, their explanations merely repeat a formula for a certain dialectical exchange between speaker and hearer that has already been sufficiently elaborated and cultivated throughout the theory—the difference between 'theory' and 'prehistoric origin' being that at the origin speaker and hearer supposedly engage in that dialectical exchange *for the very first time.*

When Habermas lists the illocutionary force with its claim to normative rightness as one of his three validity claims, and goes on to explain that the particularly important illocutionary force has a rational foundation, then we will find *as the rational foundation of illocutionary force* Habermas' trinity of validity claims. Illocution is both part of a class and has derived or is regulated from the same class. Its rational foundation is the class of which it happens also to be a member.

Everything remains within a circle with no exit. Within this circle, philosophical thinking is fundamentally repetitious, rather than linear. It is desire or will, rather than logic, that is the *first* regulator of that thinking. According to this theoretical stance, logic must not seen as needless or superfluous—as something that we were obliged to dispense with; but it is seen as employed as secondary in the promotion of the favorite theme that the particular philosopher has a 'desire' to universalize. Logic becomes a means to talk persuasively about that which otherwise might not be immediately convincing. (One recalls Descartes' candid observation: "Philosophy gives us the means of speaking plausibly about any subject and of winning the admiration of the less learned."[21])

If this is the situation in philosophy, one notices that *diagnosing* this situation and *analyzing* certain philosophers caught up in this situation, cannot imply a *criticism* of their thinking. Essentially, it subtracts nothing from the thinking of Grice or Habermas to point out that at the foundation, the theory 'falls apart,' or, that it is here palpable that it is paradoxically supported by a decision already taken in the theory. Since this shortcoming is seen as the result of a limitation to human cognition, human language, or human logic, *it cannot be criticizable.* Here, *analysis* is not *criticism.* It may even be a misnomer to talk about the theory 'falling apart,' or about its 'shortcomings.' We could with as much right state that at the foundation the philosopher consolidates his theory in a clever and ingenious way by understanding (or intuitively sensing) what is fundamentally important in his philosophy, and replacing that to the beginning as its ground—hereby making his philosophy tautological, and with this irrefutable.

Furthermore, the strategy here offered cannot *refute* the theories in question. It cannot refute their truth-claims and cannot pretend to declare them false. The question of the truth or falsehood of the theories is suspended. Conceivably, it could be true that Habermas' validity-claims are inherent in all human communication, but, within my cognitive vista, to know whether this be the case, we would have to go beyond the circle, and that is exactly where we cannot go. Habermas' validity-claims can only be true beyond his thinking.

(vii) A Final Remark About Conception. The following essays have emerged independently of each other over the years. Thus, one can find a certain self-repetition of the theoretical stance, and especially so in the remarks introducing the essays. If nothing else, this would be performatively consistent with the theory that I have just presented. The self-repetition, however, also indicates a thinking in process, rather than the presentation of something conclusive, a thinking that is processual rather than categorical, that gropes rather than knows. When engaging in thinking, the necessity of setting off from the same point and repeating the same argumentative processes is probably to be understood as our cognitive defense against a dull memory and an indifferent self. This is how we win our way through the understanding and appropriation of a material, and how we convince ourselves about the solidity of axioms, which would otherwise evaporate in the idle interests of an unconscious self.

Therefore, although the essays have the unity of purpose, I have allowed each essay to represent a fresh start, as it was originally conceived. I have not tried to streamline the individual essays into a conclusion summarizing the diverse readings they represent, except perhaps in the present introduction that paradoxically becomes a conclusion. In the introduction, one can allow oneself the liberty of forgetting the past difficulties, the many false starts, the painful groping, in presenting one's text as the end result of a clean forward thrust.

THE SPIRAL AND THE PLANE

ON FOUNDATIONAL PROBLEMS IN GRICE'S
THEORY OF CONVERSATIONAL LOGIC

> "Now, if you will permit me," said K., "I will ask
> you a rather rude question."
> The landlady remained silent.
> "So, I may not ask," said K..
> "Oh, of course," said the landlady. "You misinterpret
> everything, even the silence. You simply cannot help
> it."
> "If I'm misinterpreting everything," said K., "then
> perhaps I'm also misinterpreting my own question,
> perhaps it isn't all that rude."
>
> — Franz Kafka: *The Castle*[1]

1) INTRODUCTION

(i) What is Deconstructive Analysis? (ii) Intention as Foundation of Meaning. (iii) A Reluctant Recourse to Conventionalist Explanation Models.

(i) What is Deconstructive Analysis? Some deconstructionists may raise an eyebrow when introduced to a Deconstructive Analytic that aspires to be, in my preferred understanding, as logically rigorous as for example the Analytic Philosophy of G. E. Moore. Among deconstructionists and sympathizers, it has been an often-repeated credo that Deconstruction is neither a theory nor a method, and that it has its strength, or rather 'charm,' by evading traditional philosophical categorization. Deconstruction is a better divine comedy, a subtle play over philosophical themes. It is best understood if taken as entertainment, rather than being taken seriously, because in the latter case we make philosophy out of an enterprise whose main aim is to tear down the building of philosophy.[2] As this is perceived as self-defeating, some deconstructionists have regarded themselves as following the program most consistently if practicing Deconstruction as puns and playful exercises over philosophical themes. Other deconstructionists—not quite

as radical—have perceived Deconstruction as rhetorical analysis of philosophy, for example in contradistinction to Analytic Philosophy's conceptual analysis. In the latter case, Deconstruction is perceived as a strategy designed to read philosophical texts as literary texts.[3]

Neither of these major approaches corresponds to the approach I suggest. It is not in the present essay my aim to define in depth what I understand by a Deconstructive Analytic (this has already been done in the preceding 'Introduction'). In this and the following essays, I will instead *practice* an analytical strategy that is, in a certain sense, contrary to these often repeated protocols for deconstructive reading, a strategy that is neither anti-philosophical ideology nor rhetorical analysis, but a method that uniquely addresses foundational problems in theoretical systems.

To give an inkling as to how such an analytic would differ from other methods with some resemblance to Deconstruction (and sometimes used more or less consistently within a deconstructive framework), one might say that if Analytic Philosophy is interested in explicating the main concepts of a text or a system, Structural Analysis in revealing the latent structures of a text or a system, Rhetorical Analysis in exposing the means of persuasion of a text or a system, Deconstructive Analytic is interested in analyzing and critiquing the foundations of a text or a system. Out of these four analytical practices, Deconstructive Analytic thus becomes the most fundamental and the most abstract; it deals with the conditions of the system itself. We notice that in G. E. Moore (and analytic philosophers like Russell and the early Wittgenstein) the consistency and meaning (or lack of meaning) of philosophical concepts is the main object of analysis. Deconstructive Analytic does not have to suspend this perspective altogether (also, it can incorporate important features from Structural and Rhetorical Analysis), but the ultimate purpose, the 'final cause,' of this analytic is—with acute awareness of the logic and argument of the text—to trace back a text to its foundations.

As such, Deconstructive Analytic is in its consequence an Anti-Foundationalism rather than a Foundationalism, but, importantly, as a *method* and by *analyzing* foundations, not because ideologically it feels obliged to follow the tenets of Post-Modernism.[4]

(ii) Intention as Foundation of Meaning. My chosen text or system in the present essay is Paul Grice's theory of conversational logic and its follow up by Stephen R. Schiffer.[5] This is an intriguing theory that has exposed features in speech acts that theorists up to then had ignored, especially the feature that some utterances are apparently 'unconventional,' since they mean something different from the

sentences they employ as their medium. Attempting to explain this peculiarity, Grice offers a theory that explains meaning in terms of intention, and understanding in terms of recognition of intention.

Here, I shall not be repeating the deconstructive criticism that belief in intention indicates a metaphysical belief in presence and a subject present to itself and its activity—that belief in intentions presupposes the notion of a self-conscious subject that after Freud and Nietzsche must be regarded as unsustainable, as metaphysical ideology, or, at least, as a naiveté. I shall also abstain from the radical claim that there 'are' no intentions. Such radical claims presume, usually falsely, that the critical author already knows what 'intention' is, what it is for an intention to *be*, since the author is able to discard it (I take for granted that to reject the existence of something presumes a foreknowledge of its mode of existence). Finally, I shall avoid entering the more precise and more valid Derridian problem, whether or not intentions can realize themselves in expressions that fully represent them, or whether intentions are radically alienated from expressions—or, at the very least, leaves a 'rest,' a 'remainder' that is inexpressible.

The type of problems above, I shall regard as of an existential or psychoanalytical nature. Whether opposing or proposing the existence of intentions, we talk about their *being*; we talk about what it is to have intentions and in what sense we have them. The problem concerning *intention* that I shall introduce is of another and more systematic nature. Here, I shall address 'intention' exclusively in the context of Grice and Schiffer's theories (this implies that it is not taken for granted that 'intention' is something we from ordinary language-use know in advance what is). Within this context, I approach it purely as a concept, and argue how, as a concept, it explains nothing, and adds nothing to our understanding of meaning. Linguistically speaking, 'intention' is a dummy that is fed into the theory without solving its problems, a *blank* operating as a *desideratum* on a deep-structural level of the theory.[6] The intentionalist theory becomes a theory of *empty-inner-mental* constitution of meaning, a theory stranding on the emptiness of its core concept.[7]

Obviously, there is in Grice and Schiffer's theory great expectations to the explicatory force of this concept, and simultaneously, it is symptomatically manifest that the concept 'intention' cannot provide the desired foundation of meaning. This simultaneity of great expectations and conceptual impotence is represented by the fact that Grice and Schiffer, confronting various objections to their theory, attempt hard to find an even deeper ground for meaning, which ironically is no more than a still deeper nested intention. The deeper nested, second-order, intention suffers from the same ailment as the first-order intention, why an even deeper nested intention is needed, and so on *ad infinitum*. As a result, we get a theory that compulsively asserts a dizzying spiral of intentions in order to save its basic insight, that intention rather than convention founds meaning.[8] It is in the pursuit of the problems of this program that it is less interesting to object that Grice's dependence on 'intention' represents a belief in the self-present subject, than to notice that 'intention' is an empty concept without qualities. It is, we notice, a concept that Grice never attempts to qualify and differentiate like predecessors in the discussions of intentionality have attempted, notably Brentano and Husserl.

(iii) A Reluctant Recourse to Conventionalist Explanation Models. Furthermore, I shall try to demonstrate that whenever Grice and Schiffer *exemplify* their intentionalist program, they cannot help but pulling in explanations of meaning that are uniquely contextual and conventional in nature.[9] The necessity of conventionalist explanations of meaning is partly recognized by themselves. Allegedly, it is not the program to abolish the importance of conventional sentence-meaning. But conventionalist explanations are added *ad hoc*, or as *supplements* to a theory that poses itself as contrary to such explanations. The result is a theory that double-binds its reader, an intentionalist theory that relies heavily on conventionalist meaning and employs explanation-types that it is designed to defeat. The final effect can only be that the intentionalist theory appears to resist its own basic axiom. It looks as if there is an inner resistance in the foundational theory to its own foundations, as if the theory tries hard to overcome this resistance, but invariably fails.

Insofar as this state of affairs seems to be a general pattern in theories, it invites the speculation that a system perhaps never had as a 'natural' feature something like a foundation; that a foundation is a highly artificial addition, which the theoretical 'immune system' attacks with all possible means until it is successfully broken down behind the back of the author. The theorist can only fool himself, but he cannot fool his theory, which for reasons that are not entirely obvious reacts fiercely against this attempt of foundational reduction.

2) GRICE'S PROJECT IN BRIEF

(i) The Distinction between Timeless and Occasion Meaning. (ii) Intending the Understanding of the Other. (iii) The Rational Foundation of Communication.

(i) The Distinction between Timeless and Occasion Meaning. Let us grant that there is a difference between what a sentence means and what

a speaker means by a sentence. Granted this difference, what is now the correlation between utterer's meaning and sentence-meaning? How is it possible for an utterer to mean something in an utterance that is not said in that utterance, but nonetheless is understood as if it had been said? Why is it that indirect speech often is understood correctly?

In pioneering articles from the fifties and in his William James Lectures,[10] Paul Grice draws to our attention this discrepancy between sentence meaning and utterer's meaning. His project is an inquiry into differences and relationships between utterer's meaning and sentence-meaning:

> My aim in this essay is to throw light on the connection between (a) a notion of meaning which I want to regard as basic, namely the notion which is involved in saying of someone that by (when) doing such-and-such he meant that so-and-so . . . and, (b) the notions of meaning involved in saying (i) that a given sentence means 'so-and-so' (ii) that a given word or phrase means 'so-and-so.'[11]

We notice that (a) and (b) imply a distinction between what a speaker has implicated and what she has said. Implicated meaning would seem to be uniquely context-dependent—dependent, thus, on 'occasion,' whereas sentence-meaning would seem to be context-independent, or so-called 'timeless.' It is therefor appropriate to set up a primary distinction between *occasion-meaning* and *timeless meaning*, as does Grice.

Someone rooted in Saussurian Linguistics (like myself), may find the term 'timeless' bothersome, why the following excursus may be in place. Grice's use of the terms 'timeless' and 'occasion' meaning indicates merely two forms of *conventional* meaning. It would be precipitate to infer that 'timeless meaning' is understood as non-conventional, context-independent, and a-historical meaning in an *absolute* sense, while occasion meaning is purely conventional and contextual (although, admittedly, the terminology *does* invite such a distinction). 'Timeless meaning' is timeless *within* a certain 'idiolect,' that is, timeless for an individual or a group of individuals. Timeless meaning is therefore (we must conclude) *a kind of* conventional meaning; it is meaning that has *stabilized* within a group, whereas occasion meaning is unstable meaning. More precisely, we can understand 'timeless' meaning as the meaning that the dictionary assigns to a word or a phrase in a language, which is shared by a group of individuals (—thus making it possible for the group to identify the meaning of a word, and, approximately, mutually understand each other), while 'occasion' meaning has no dictionary definition.

Another of Grice's terms, 'applied timeless meaning' is a derivative of 'timeless meaning.' It indicates meaning conventionally assigned to an ambivalent word or phrase dependent on a specific situation or context. A well-known example: if I say, 'I am going to the bank,' the word 'bank' is ambiguous, and its meaning depends on the situation and context in which I utter the sentence. If I am hiking in rural surroundings, far away from city life, it is understood that by bank I must mean the 'riverbank.' If I am sitting at a city café, it is understood that by 'bank' I must mean a 'financial institution.' 'Riverbank' and 'financial institution' respectively are the applied timeless meanings of 'bank.' Grice specifies the distinction between 'timeless meaning' and 'applied timeless meaning' in the following manner:

Timeless meaning: X [sentence] means " . . . "
Applied timeless meaning: X [sentence] means here " . . . "

If timeless meaning (and applied timeless meaning), *mutatis mutandis*, is the meaning(s) the dictionary assigns to words, we find no dictionary definition for occasion meanings. As a first palpable way of distinguishing utterer's occasion meaning and sentential timeless (or applied timeless) meaning, let us notice with Grice that the latter sentence-type is well and adequately specified by the aid of quotation marks, while quotation marks specifying utterer's meaning are misplaced, and are best suspended. We have consequently the following description of three forms of meaning:

Timeless meaning: X [sentence] means " . . . "
Applied timeless meaning: X [sentence] means here " . . . "
Occasion meaning: S [utterer] means that . . .

Occasion-meaning *implicates*, whereas timeless meaning *defines* or *describes*.

Although constituting an initial distinction and an important theoretical dichotomy in Gricean analysis, timeless meaning and occasion meaning are not necessary radically separate; they can coincide, as Grice notes:

> I shall be committed to the view that applied timeless meaning and occasion-meaning may coincide, that is to say, it may be true both (i) that when S uttered X, the meaning of X included "*p" and (ii) that part of what S meant when he uttered X was that *p.[12]

I take this to mean that I by conventional means can implicate something that gives reason to or motivates my conventionally uttered sentence. For example, by uttering, "I have a headache," I can implicate that I have a headache, because I have a headache. However, the crux in Grice's recognition is that this sentence does not *necessarily always* mean that the utterer has a headache. We can imagine a situation where the sentence 'I have a headache' were meant to mean 'I don't want to have sex tonight.'

If S utters, "I have a headache," the timeless meaning is that S has a painful pounding in her head. If the utterance is meant to mean that 'I don't want sex tonight,' the utterance now has an occasion meaning that is unrelated to the literal meaning of the sentence. Since there is nothing in the dictionary that relates headache and sex, it cannot be by 'conventional' means that the sentence still has a chance to be understood by the disappointed partner. Grice legitimate problem therefore is to explicate how understanding of a non-conventionally established word or phrase is possible. His answer is approximately that it is possible because the partner has understood the intention of the utterer.

In occasion meaning we notice that a substitution takes place between a conventional meaning of a word and an unconventional meaning of the same word ('headache' means suddenly 'not wanting sex' or '~sex'). Grice therefore gives the following provisional definition for occasion meaning.

> By x, S meant ϕ iff ($\exists\sigma$) {S uttered $\sigma(x)$, and by uttering $\sigma(x)$ S meant that . . . [the lacuna to be completed by writing $\sigma(\phi/x)$]}[13]

The definition looks fearsome, but it is rather simple, and, even, it makes good sense. The symbols, however, need a brief explanation: $\sigma(x)$ denotes an utterance type (σ), containing an utterance type (x) [example: σ = I have a headache, x = headache]. ϕ denotes an utterance type [example: ϕ = ~sex]. $\sigma(\phi/x)$ denotes the substitution of ϕ for x [example: '~sex' substitutes 'headache']. Thus, we see that the definition applies: By an utterance, S meant ~sex iff there exist an utterance type "I have a headache" such that S by uttering this utterance-type can mean that she is substituting '~sex' for 'headache.'

(ii) Intending the Understanding of the Other. Eventually, Grice's explicit project becomes to explain all utterances in terms of intention.

> Starting with the assumption that the notion of an utterer's occasion meaning can be explicated, in a certain way, in terms of an utterer's intentions, I argue in support of the thesis that timeless meaning and applied timeless meaning and be explained in terms of the notion of

utterer's occasion meaning . . . and so ultimately in terms of the notion of intention.[14]

Thus, Grice will claim that it is possible to derive the conventional meaning of an expression from the non-conventional meaning it has when uttered with a certain speaker intention. What is meant is not determined by what is said. So-called x-meaning (sentence meaning) is derivable from S-meaning (speaker-meaning). The meaning-content of an utterance is determined through the intention with which the speaker (S) utters the sentence (x), why speaker-intention is the most fundamental level in the analysis of meaning. At the receiver-end of the exchange, the auditor (A) must in order to understand S's utterance be able to decode the intention with which it was uttered.

Since sentential or 'natural' meaning appears to be the least problematic in Grice's project, and since his project orbits the discovery of occasion-meaning or 'non-natural' meaning, Grice introduces another definition of occasion-meaning in his seminal article *Meaning* (later he elaborates this initial definition in great detail): "For some audience A, S intended his utterance of x to produce in A some effect (response) E, by means of A's recognition of that intention."[15]

In the later article, *Utterer's Meaning, Sentence Meaning, and Word-Meaning*, this definition is abbreviated, "S intends to produce in A effect E by means of A's recognition of that intention."[16] Thus, S intends both (a) to produce an effect/response in A, and (b) to let A recognize intention (a).

There are several problems with this formula, and we shall come back to them. Let us for now first explain and exemplify the formula. The definition states that understanding a sentence depends on the understanding of two intentions inscribed in uttering a sentence: S wants x and S wants A to understand that she wants x. If S is an infant wanting its feeding bottle, and wanting mother to recognize this want, it wants two disparate things, it wants an object and it wants recognition of this want. It fuses these two interests by means of an expression; for example, it has to its disposal the ability to reach out for the feeding bottle and scream out loudly to attract mother's attention.

The question is now whether this example (which I think uniquely fits Grice's definition) is a paradigm case for all language use: is this what in general we do when we mean something? It will also be a problem how well meaning is explained by the notion of intention, and by *this* (Gricean) notion of intention. How good a foundation is 'intention' for meaning, and what characterizes this foundation?

When Grice, and later Schiffer, evoke the notion of intentionality, they do not relate to previous phenomenological analyses of intentionality.[17] Instead, they use the notion in a narrow and colloquial sense as the purposefulness of a subject pursuing or trying to realize a goal. *Intention* is, in Grice and Schiffer, approximately synonymous with desiring, wanting, anticipating, or expecting. The notion is undifferentiated and purely teleological. Being intentional, the subject *directs* itself, and specifically, it directs itself toward the other, since it wants to achieve the other's understanding of the (unconventional and semi-private) meaning of its utterances.

(iii) The Rational Foundation of Communication. In his formulae and examples, Grice invariably assumes that the subject in the remitter-end of a dialectical exchange is cooperative. If an auditor receives a message that is incomprehensible, the auditor gives the speaker the benefit of doubt, and reconstructs the utterance into a form that is understandable. Grice's auditor does not listen to the speaker's flaws; she patches together the flaws into something that is meaningful, that is, into what we may call a hermeneutical whole. Doing that, she takes for granted that the speaker is 'rational,' although the patching together may not necessarily be rational. Grice's auditor is therefore a hermeneutically active subject who 'cooperates' with the speaker by creating meaningful wholes from his patchy discourse. Grice's auditor is capable of reconstructing a flawed sentence because she expects that the sentence is meant to make sense.

Let us start our critical inquiry into Grice's thinking by questioning the assumption of this cooperative, hermeneutically active, subject.

3) GRICE'S COOPERATIVE SUBJECT

(i) Foundation and Imperative of the Cooperative Principle. (ii) Teleological Regulation of Discourse in the Cooperative Principle. (iii) How Cooperation Causes Misunderstandings; 1st Criticism: Presupposing Sincerity. (iv) How Cooperation Causes Misunderstandings; 2nd Criticism: Mis-Recognizing Speaker's Intention.

(i) Foundation and Imperative of the Cooperative Principle. Grice assumes that in conversation we obey a certain Cooperative Principle—a general principle existing as a sub-structure for all conversation. The assertion of this principle is based on an observation of ordinary speech situations. It generalizes certain empirical characteristics of dialectical exchanges. The observation justifying the Cooperative Principle is the following: "Our talk exchanges do not normally consist of a succession of disconnected remarks, and would not be rational if they did."[18]

The argument includes both a *de facto* and a *de jure* component: first, we *do* talk consistently; secondly, we *have to* (must, ought to) talk consistently, otherwise, we would not be rational. It is undecidable whether it is the *de facto* or the *de jure* component that constitutes the major in the premise—probably because there is, from the beginning, a desire to perceive speech as more rational than it is, implying that the *ought* being already enlisted in the description of an observed 'fact.' There are therefore reasons to suspect that the observational background is not as neutral as Grice takes for granted. Without offending anybody's common sense, we could with as much right claim the contrary, that ordinary non-formalized conversational exchanges consist of a succession of disconnected remarks where free association rather than rational direction guides conversation. In Grice's immediate follow-up on the passage above, this possibility is in fact (regretfully) admitted, but also downplayed. "They are characteristically, *to some degree at least*, cooperative efforts; and each participant recognizes in them, *to some extent*, a common purpose or set of purposes, or *at least* a mutually accepted direction [my emphases]."[19]

The emphases indicate that beyond a certain hypothetical rational minimum ('to some degree,' 'to some extent'), speech is exactly the opposite of what it is supposed to be: non-cooperative, without common purpose, and without mutually accepted direction. Grice half recognizes, half discards this state of affairs; or rather, his recognition of it will have no consequences for his theory. However, this discarded-recognized state-of-affairs manifests its ambivalence in the modifications with which he introduces the Cooperative Principle. Repeatedly, the principle is qualified as *tentative, provisional*, as an *approximation*, as a *rough generalization*, etc.

Despite the uncertainty of the empirical basis, the Cooperative Principle is asserted as an ideal guide for conversational exchanges that can be further broken down into four maxims after Kant labeled Quantity, Quality, Relation, and Manner. Despite the deliberate Kantian vocabulary, the maxims are not categories of the mind. They are abstracted from the pragmatics of conversation as four pragmatic rules according to which conversation (ideally) proceeds. The four maxims are explained in the following manner: Insofar as we observe *Quantity*, we do not offer more or less information than needed. Insofar as we observe *Quality*, we are genuinely sincere. Insofar as we observe *Relation*, we speak relevantly and appropriately relative to the context in which we are situated. Insofar as we observe *Manner*, we carry out our performance as clear and unambiguously as possible.[20]

How we appropriate this background of maxims in our speech is not addressed except by the 'dull' [Grice's own term] argument that they are habits internalized in early childhood. "It is just a well-recognized empirical fact that people do behave in these ways, they learned to do so in childhood and have not lost the habit of doing so."[21]

The supposedly 'well-recognized fact' that interlocutors pursue a common goal underpins the Cooperative Principle and its maxims. This goal can be explicit like pursuing a solution to a practical problem, or implicitly imbedded in the speech-situation itself as a commitment to or interest in the conversational exchange. In the latter case, it is taken for granted that there is a contractual basis for dialectical exchanges.

Again, one might object that however 'well-recognized' this 'fact' is, it fails to account for the equally well-recognized fact that there are numerous cases where it is impossible to discern a common goal. Grice knows this, and mentions quarreling and letter-writing as examples of violations of the conversational contract. We could add to this modest two-item list, the lie, the manipulation, the snub, the insult, the rebuke, the manic monologue, and the soliloquy among a whole array of cases where cooperation is absent. Furthermore, if letter-writing is a non-cooperative type of discourse, it would seem that we have to include every type of writing, since it is difficult to discern an essential distinction between letter-writing and writing in general (—writing in general, like letter-writing, being an activity carried out in solitude, thus being an inherently soliloquizing, non-social, non-cooperative activity). And if we include writing in general, we would seem also to have to include types of discourse that typically rely on a written text, such as reciting, lecturing, preaching, formally addressing, etc., since, again, it is difficult to see the essential distinction between reading a text silently and reading the same text out loud.[22]

Grice sees that when we start lining up cases of non-cooperation, his theory comes under attack. However, he fails to respond substantially to this, by himself, introduced objection:

> There are too many types of exchange, like quarreling and letter writing, that it [a quasi-contractual basis of speech] fails to fit comfortably. In any case, one feels that the talker who is irrelevant or obscure has primarily let down not his audience but himself.[23]

The last sentence indicates that the irrelevant speaker (supposedly anyone engaged in any of the alternative types of exchange mentioned above) is harder punished by failing his audience, than is his audience by him failing them. By departing from the contract of the Cooperative Principle, the speaker is guilty of an asocial behavior that returns to him as, presumably, isolation or solitude. Grice seems to be conducting an implicitly moralistic discourse, where asocial linguistic behavior represents a transgression of a discursive moral imperative. Incidentally, one notices that writing represents an asocial activity where the writer, temporarily, suspends world and other.

In order not to end up in this asocial linguistic isolation, the importance of cooperation is highlighted, and the following circular argument concludes Grice's train of thoughts on the matter:

> Anyone who cares about the goals that are central to conversation/communication . . . must be expected to have an interest, given suitable circumstances, in participation in talk exchanges that will be profitable only on the assumption that they are conducted in general accordance with the Cooperative Principle and the maxims.[24]

In other words, anyone who cares about cooperation has an interest in conducting a dialogue according to the Cooperative Principle. Or, if we have an interest in cooperation, we have an interest in cooperating.

(ii) Teleological Regulation of Discourse in the Cooperative Principle. Although the assertion of the Cooperative Principle is unfounded, or, what amounts to the same thing, is founded tautologically, the background assumption of a Cooperative Principle is necessary for Grice's system. It is only in contrast to this background that the success or failure of conversation can be determined. Thus, the Cooperative Principle represents a telos that ought to direct our linguistic actions. Grice's maxims form a categorical imperative for interlocutors that could be formulated as follows: speak only in such a way that the maxims of the Cooperative Principle become universal law of your speech. This becomes a specific Gricean 'categorical-conversational imperative.'

The recognition of the telos of the imperative impels us to reconstruct what is implied, rather than expressed, in an utterance that may not be immediately transparent. If a person by saying p, implicates q, we only understand the implication because the actual statement, p, violates some maxim of the Cooperative Principle. Since the Cooperative Principle constitutes the telos of speech, and the utterance taken literally lacks sense, it becomes necessary to reconstruct the appropriate 'implicature' in order to reinstate the authority of the telos.

It is according to this reconstruction assumed that the speaker cannot be opting out from the operation of the Cooperative Principle, and under that assumption the cooperative auditor restores the logic of the conversational dialectic by adjusting the utterance to the background of cooperative maxims. The logic is in brief: p (sentence) makes no sense; S (utterer) cannot *not* make sense; therefore p (sentence) must alternatively mean q (implicature), in which case p makes sense as a vehicle for q, in which case S makes sense.[25]

Grice offers this example: two interlocutors have a conversation about a third party X, newly employed in a bank. The utterer (S) says, 'he has not yet been to prison,' implying herewith that X potentially belongs in prison, but by his statement saying approximately the opposite. On the surface level (the sentential level of the utterance) the utterer violates the maxim in the Cooperative Principle requiring relevance ('Maxim of Relation'). Nonetheless, the auditor—convinced about the operation of the telos of the maxims—supposes that S has uttered a relevant sentence. The speaker has on one hand, "violated the maxim 'be relevant' and so may be regarded as having flouted one of the maxims conjoining perspicuity."[26] On the other hand, given the authority of the Cooperative Principle, the violation of the relevance maxim can only be supposed to be apparent, and A therefore sets out to reconstruct the relevance of the utterance.

Grice does not explain in detail how this reconstruction is carried out, but we notice that in this case it is done associatively. There are five associative stages pressing forth toward the conclusion. (i) A bank-employee handles money; (ii) people handling money have a chance to steal; (iii) some (dishonest) people desire to, or actually, steal money; (iv) these (dishonest) people are susceptible to imprisonment; (v) S must imply that X is dishonest.

I am returning to the example both in the following and later below, critically questioning the conclusions Grice draws based on this example.

(iii) How Cooperation Causes Misunderstandings; 1st Criticism: Presupposing Sincerity. It is important to notice that A, in adopting S's implication, continues to cooperate with S, since she assumes that S is not only a competent speaker, but also a sincere one. Not only relevance determines the conversational success of the exchange, but also sincerity. Otherwise, A would suspect S of violating the quality maxim (sincerity), and the trust between the speakers would break down. In that case, she would suspect S, and not bank-employed X, of dishonesty, and conclude that S for strategic (or just perverse) reasons is vilifying X.

We have said that the Cooperative Principle is supposed to secure that utterances, which are not immediately transparent, can be reconstructed into comprehensible utterances. Presupposing this principle, the hearer takes for granted that the speaker is rational, and the speaker expects the hearer to assume that. In her cooperative effort, the hearer reconstructs the absent q from the deficient fulfillment of one or some of the cooperative maxims in p.

However, if we take the above example as our paradigm-case, it is apparent that the speaker's violation of the quality maxim (sincerity) does not imply a breakdown of *meaning*. If S is sincere, cooperating-A understands that X is a potential criminal. But if S is insincere, cooperating-A still understands that X is a potential criminal, since she is deceived into that misunderstanding. Whether sincere or insincere, S conveys the same meaning to A. Also if S is insincere, A cooperates and takes for granted that S does not flout the quality maxim; on the receiver end, cooperating-A reconstructs, in both cases, the implicature *q*. Therefore, her cooperation, which is supposed to warrant understanding, gives rise to a serious misunderstanding. It is *because* she cooperates that she misunderstands.

There is therefore type-difference between violating the relevance maxim and violating the sincerity maxim. Violating the relevance maxim would indicate a temporary (or permanent) breakdown of meaning.[27] However, when speakers violate the sincerity maxim, meaning does not suffer a breakdown. If S utters 'X has not yet been to prison,' knowing that X is virtue incarnate, S (being keenly insincere) expects that A understands both the sentence *p* and the implicature *q*. If A is sufficiently alert to work out that S is violating the quality maxim 'be sincere' (discerning S's perfidy), she understands this by understanding both *p* and *q*, and by understanding that *p*, but not *q*, would constitute the real truth-content of the sentence. The utterance 'X has not yet been to prison' might now elicit indignant responses like: 'of course not!' or 'how dare you imply?'

Whether or not S is sincere, the following three steps in Grice's analysis would seem to apply:

> 1) S apparently violated the maxim 'be relevant' . . . yet I (A) have no reason to suppose that he is opting out from the operation of the Cooperative Principle.
> 2) Given the circumstances, I can regard his irrelevance as only apparent if, and only if, I suppose him to think that X is potentially dishonest.
> 3) S must know that I (A) am capable of working out step 2, therefore S says that X is dishonest.[28]

In this scheme, the question of S's sincerity would come up as a supplemental fourth step, and could be formulated: 4) S has a history of being sincere, if he indicates that X is dishonest, X is probably dishonest (or the reverse: S has a history of being insincere, if he indicates that X is dishonest, X is probably honest). But this supplemental forth step is an addition to the scheme above that does not effect A's ability to work out the implicature of S's utterance.

It is convenient to revoke Austin's old distinction between 'misfires' and 'abuses' as a distinction between *breakdown of meaning* and *breakdown of trust*. If insincere, S's utterance does not misfire, but it is abused. At most (if A discerns S's perfidy), the bonding between the interlocutors breaks down, but not meaning. If, in the latter case, S's 'competence' as a sincere speaker is put in doubt, it is not because he fails to understand conversational logic, but because it becomes apparent that he is abusing it. His *sincerity* is in doubt, but *not* his rationality. In other words, there is nothing irrational about being insincere, it is rather highly rational.

(iv) How Cooperation Causes Misunderstandings; 2nd Criticism: Mis-Recognizing Speaker's Intention. Another problem is that Grice presupposes a momentary breakdown of meaning that is immediately restored because of the operation of the cooperative maxims. The formula being (if the reader can endure yet another recapitulation), p makes no sense, ergo, S must mean q in p, in which case p makes sense. Now q is introduced as the immanent sense of the utterance, because the hearer is confident about the Cooperative Principle's teleological regulation of discourses. However, even if we for the sake of argument presuppose that the Cooperative Principle is operative, it cannot guarantee that the hearer 'hits' the right q. That is, it cannot ensure that she restores the right sense to the utterance, p. If q is supposed to fill out a *lack of sense*, there are potentially numerous ways of filling out a *lack*. Absence has many interpretations.

Let me illustrate this objection by repeating my epigraph, the small dialogue between K. and his landlady from Kafka's *The Castle*:

> "Now, if you will permit me," said K., "I will ask you a rather rude question."
> The landlady remained silent.
> "So, I may not ask," said K..
> "Oh, of course," said the landlady. . . . "You misinterpret everything, even the silence. You simply cannot help it. I do give you permission to ask."
> "If I'm misinterpreting everything," said K., "then perhaps I'm also misinterpreting my own question, perhaps it isn't all that rude."[29]

We have the conversational gesture, *silence*, being interpreted by K. as *disapproval*. The landlady, by her silence, has neglected the relevance maxim, since it is regarded as conversationally correct to respond to a question. Consequently, her want of response is by K. interpreted as her disapproval of his importunity. To her conversational gesture, p (silence), he restores q (disapproval), in which case p makes sense.

However, the problem with his restoration is that it is wrong. K. has misunderstood her conversational gesture to mean something it was not meant to mean. He has, in his eagerness to cooperate, *misunderstood*, because he does not understand what 'silence' *means*, and he does not understand what the landlady intends him to *recognize* and *respond to* by this conversational gesture. According to Grice, when S 'utters' a conversational gesture, S intends to produce in A an effect E by means of A's recognition of that intention. But in Kafka, the landlady does not intend to produce anything by her silence, nor does she intend K. to recognize any intention. K. misunderstands the landlady, because, paradoxically, he believes in Grice's Cooperative Principle. Erroneously, he believes that he has to interpret everything (restore *q* in *p*). Instead, eagerly cooperating-K. misunderstands "everything"; he "cannot help it."

For good measure, K. even misunderstands his own question; he thinks it is rude, while it is merely timid. He thinks it will offend, but it offends nobody. In Gricean jargon: S (K.) intends to produce in A (landlady) an effect E (offense) by means of A's recognition of that intention, but the landlady does not take offense, and does not recognize K.'s intention in the first place. K. instead realizes that his intention to produce effect E in A was a mistake and mis-recognition of A. (To my knowledge, Grice and followers have no formula that accounts for a speaker's mis-recognition of his audience).

My objection might be summed up as follows. K. is one of the best examples we find in the literature on a cooperating true follower of Grice, and he understands absolutely nothing.

4) RECOGNIZING SPEAKER-INTENTIONS BY UNDERSTANDING CONVENTIONS: THE PLANE.
(i) A Theory of Meaning or a Theory of Interpretation? The Theoretical Implication of Grice's Indecision. (ii) The Meaning of a Hand-Wave; Is Intention *the Origin of Meaning, or an After-Reconstruction From Meaning Already Understood? (iii) The Desideratum and the Supplement.*

(i) A Theory of Meaning or a Theory of Interpretation? The Theoretical Implication of Grice's Indecision. Having established that the Cooperative Principle constitutes a telos for conversation, Grice is in the position to suggest an expanded definition on 'conversational implicature' (occasion meaning):

A man who, by (in, when) . . . saying that p has implicated that q, may be said to have conversational implicated that q, provided that (1) he is to be presumed to be observing the conversational maxims of at least the Cooperative Principle; (2) the supposition that he is aware that, or thinks that, q is required in order to make his saying or making as if to say p . . . consistent with this presumption; and (3) the speaker thinks (and would expect the hearer to think that the speaker thinks) that it is within the competence of the hearer to work out, or grasp intuitively, that the supposition in (2) is required.[30]

A peculiarity of this definition is its oscillating perspective. We have a list of three conditions, where progressively we fluctuate from the perspective of the hearer to the perspective of the speaker. At (1) we are at the hearer-end of observation: "He [the speaker] is to be presumed [by the hearer] . . ." At (2) it is indecidable whether we talk about hearer's observation or speaker's self-observation: "The supposition [hearer's supposition] that he is aware [speaker's awareness] . . ." Finally at (3) we are introduced to the speaker's self-observation/self-reflection: "The speaker thinks (and would expect . . .)."

The oscillation of perspective seems to indicate indecision on Grice's part, namely about whether to understand his theory as a theory of *production* of meaning or as a theory of *interpretation* of meaning.[31] The oscillation of perspective also implies that the positions of remitter and receiver are interchangeable—this again indicating that Grice regards encoding and decoding as symmetrical and analogous processes. The assumption is that ideal linguistic behavior prevails in receiver and remitter in such a way that the receiver never means more (or less) than the remitter decodes, and the receiver never understands more (or less) than the remitter encodes. Accordingly, speaker and hearer are transparent to each other. This transparency-thesis is taken for granted in Grice and followers, because without it, the algorithm, supporting the equations for speaker-hearer dialectic, breaks down.

First, the hearer presumes that the speaker observes the Cooperative Principle; —consequently, if the speaker neglects any of its maxims, the hearer will insert q in order to make p consistent with the Cooperative Principle. Secondly, the speaker thinks that the hearer is able to work out that first presumption. We notice a self-immunizing and –neutralizing circularity in the argument. Ultimately, it relies on two simple premises: (a) the hearer knows that the speaker makes sense, and (b) the speaker knows that the hearer knows that he (as speaker) makes sense. Interlocutors know (and know that each other know) *that q in p is the case* (let the expression '*that q in p is the case*' indicate conversational implicature). This dialectical circle secures understanding, because interlocutors know when something has been conversationally implicated because they know (and know that each other know) that is was conversationally implicated. In this their ideal cooperation, speaker and hearer know that speech is always reasonable also when it does not manifest itself as such.

Let us formalize how respectively S encodes and A decodes messages. Initially, S would seem to enact the following relatively simple formula: S → A(E); which would read, S intends to produce in A effect E (the arrow indicating intention). A is supposed to decode this intention, according to the relatively complex formula: A(S → A(E)) = E; which would read, A recognizes S's intention to produce effect E in A, and actualizes therefore E.

However, we notice that the formula for S is simplistic and has to be further specified, since S does not merely intend to produce in A the effect E, but also intends to make A recognize his intention to produce effect E. A's position is therefore already included in S's 'thinking.' The expanded formula for S is therefore: S → A(E) → (A(S → A(E)). (Notice that I am not adding anything to Grice, but merely offering a formal rendition of Grice's theorem: 'S intends to produce in A effect E by means of A's recognition of S's intention to produce in A effect E.')

If we apply the formula to a minimalist example (originally Searle's[32]), S says 'hello!' to a colleague—expecting a reciprocal response, the response 'hello!' is now actualized in the following manner. S says 'hello!' and intends A to respond, (S → A(E)), by means of A recognizing that S intends A to respond, (A(S → A(E))—this resulting in A's response, 'hello!' (= E). It is manifest that Grice is not interested in the actual dialogue—the brief exchange: S: 'hello!' A: 'hello!'—but in the mental acts that precede S and A's utterances.

If we write the dialogue up in four steps, it is actualized in the following way.

> Step 1:   S: (S → A(E)) → (A(S → A(E))
> Step 2:   S: 'hello!'
> Step 3:   A: (A(S → A(E)))
> Step 4:   A: 'hello!'

We notice three things. *First*, only step 1 and step 3 is interesting to Grice's project; the actual speech-acts disappear. *Secondly*, 1 and 3 correspond to respectively encoding and decoding of intentions, or to *production of meaning* and *interpretation of meaning*, as inner-mental acts. At step 1, S reads A's mind, and at step 3, A reads S's reading of her mind. *Thirdly*, there is symmetry of encoding and decoding. S's expectation to A's response is by A fully satisfied. S intends A to recognize that he intends A to produce a certain effect, and A reads this intention without distortions. This symmetrical encoding and decoding rests on the assumption that the speaker and listener are transparent to each other (and to themselves). The dialectical circle of *full and pure understanding* rests of this transparency-thesis, which is made palpable, in the formula above, as formal correspondence and equivalence between step 1 and step 3.[33]

(ii) The Meaning of a Hand-Wave; Is 'Intention' the Origin of Meaning, or an After-Reconstruction from Meaning Already Understood? Since '*that q in p*' deviates from conventional meaning, knowledge of the meaning of a sentence relies, so Grice, on the ability of the hearer to work out the intention of the speaker.

There is an intention to be understood; S intends A to think or to understand *q*. Grice therefore specifies his initial definition on conversational implicature. (This time, we have a single perspective; we are consistently introduced to the hearer's observations of and reflections on the speaker's intentions.)

> A general pattern for the working out of a conversational implicature might be given as follows: "He had said that *p*; there is no reason to suppose that he is not observing the maxims, or at least the Cooperative Principle; he could not be doing this unless he thought that *q*; he knows (and knows that I know that he knows) that I can see that the supposition that he thinks that *q* is required; he has done nothing to stop me thinking that *q*; he intends me to think . . . that *q*; and so he has implicated that *q*."[34]

A is supposed to recognize that S has the intention to make her think *that q in p is the case*, with this, urging her to respond to *q*, not to *p*. But since the underlying framework for speech is an intention to be understood (at the speaker's end), and an intention to understand (at the hearer's end), conversational implicature (occasion-meaning) is only a special case of all speech. The intention to be understood is generally present in all speech; a minimum of *reason* is present in all speech.

It was Grice's initial project to understand, or rather, 'formalize,' occasion-meaning, indirect speech. Now, this project is extended to all speech, timeless as well as occasional, direct as well as indirect. The hearer not only resorts to the speakers' intentions when speech-acts are not immediately transparent, but recognition of speaker-intentions becomes a crucial feature in *all* understanding. Thus, the definition not only explains how we understand occasion-meaning (as initially it was supposed to), it explains how we understand all possible utterances. We glide from the special case of occasion-meaning to the universal case of all utterances. As such, Grice erases his initial distinction, since he erases the marks distinguishing this distinction. We are as much in the dark as to how we understand non-literal, metaphorical, indirect, ironic, etc., speech-acts as we were before, and as to how we distinguish these speech-acts from literal and direct ones. Similarly, I have not classified mammals in distinction to other animals in any precise sense by defining them as living creatures that breathe oxygen.

This tacit gliding from timeless to occasion-meaning is at stake in one of Grice's celebrated examples. Does Grice mean the following example exemplifies timeless or occasion meaning? The example is a 'hand-wave' (HW), as a speaker's way of expressing to a hearer 'I know the route.' It would seem that a hand-wave is an excellent illustration of occasion-meaning. A hand-wave has no fixed definition in the dictionary; it is sufficiently empty of conventional meaning to be uniquely dependent on the context and circumstance (in other words, the occasion) in which it is 'uttered.'

However, surprisingly, Grice uses this example to illustrate *timeless* meaning. He suggests that this hand-wave (HW), for the utterer, has the *established conventional* meaning: "I know the route."

> Initially I shall restrict myself to examining the notion of timeless meaning in its application to unstructured utterance-types. My main example will be a gesture (a signal), and it will be convenient first to consider the idea of *its timeless meaning for an individual* (within a signaling idiolect, so to speak), and only afterward to consider the extension of this idea to groups of individuals. . . . Suppose that a particular sort of hand wave (to be referred to as 'HW') for a particular individual S (within S's idiolect) means "I know the route" [my emphasis].[35]

The object of inquiry is the transition from 'private timeless meaning' to meaning realized in the intended audience.[36] During the transition-process, *timeless meaning for the speaker* is first *occasion meaning for the hearer* in order to become, finally, *timeless meaning for the hearer*. What is so far 'timeless' meaning for the speaker is occasion meaning for the hearer, because, whereas HW is part of the speaker's idiolect, it is (so far) no part of the hearer's. HW is part of the speaker's 'repertoire' for uttering 'I know the route,' but the hearer has to learn this 'repertoire' before responding as the speaker intends her to respond. In the example, it is presupposed that speaker and hearer do not belong to the same language-group (they do not speak the same idiolect).

> We are to look for an explication of the sentence "For S, HW means 'I know the route'" which will relate timeless meaning to occasion meaning. As a first shot, one might suggest something like "It is S's

policy (practice, habit) to utter HW in order to *mean that* S knows the route." . . . S, then, when uttering HW on a particular occasion, must expect A to think as follows: "S's policy for HW is such that he utters HW now with the intention that I should think that he thinks that he knows the route; in that case, I take it that he does think that he knows the route."[37]

The chance of successfully understanding S, depends on A's understanding of S's intentions. Grice lines up a whole battery of elaborate and multi-leveled formulae for how the message HW is intended to be understood:

> "It is S's policy . . . to utter HW if S is making an utterance by which S means that S know the route." . . . "It is S's policy . . . to utter HW if S is making an utterance by means of which (for some A) S M-intends to effect that A thinks S to think that S knows the route" . . . "I (that is, utterer S) shall utter HW if I intend (want) some A to think that I think I know the route." [38]

Given the thesis of symmetrical encoding and decoding of messages, S encodes HW with a certain intention, and A decodes HW for the same intention. Again, it is taken for granted that encoding and decoding are symmetrical processes—decoding mirroring encoding and being therefore self-explanatory. A 'reads' S's intention, and consequently, understands S under the tacit assumption that *meaning meant* and *meaning understood* is the *same identical meaning*. Because of the equivalence between two processes (*to mean* and *to understand*) there is, on A's part, no room for interpretation, and consequently, no risk of mis-interpretation.

How does the theory explain this eminent success? How is A's understanding of something as vague and occasional as a hand-ware guaranteed? If we envision a gesture like a hand-wave, it is impossible to think of a singular gesture that unambiguously carries the assigned meaning, 'I know the route.' It is conceivable that Grice has in mind a gesture like waving one's hand toward oneself, which means something in the neighborhood of 'come here,' 'come closer,' or 'follow me.' It is thus that simple gesture Grice interprets as expressing the complex message, 'I know the route.' This, allegedly, is what timelessly it means to S. The question is now, how can A *not fail* to understand S's meaning? How is potential misunderstanding impossible in Grice's theory? How can she *not* misunderstand S to mean, say, 'come, let's have some sex'? (I could imagine (but Grice couldn't) that instead of coming closer or following, she responds, 'no thanks, I have a headache!') In Grice's examples, the *possibility* of misunderstanding is entirely absent. A's understanding of S's intention is foolproof; how is this theoretically achieved?

Reading the example with a focus on that question, we notice that Grice attains this foolproof understanding at the high cost of abandoning the most fundamental axiom of his theory. Ultimately, he abandons the concept of intentionality, and introduces the idea that S and A share conventional foreknowledge of the timeless meaning of HW. Not only S, but finally also A, knows that HW has *timelessly* the one and only meaning, 'I know the route.' Since this is inter-subjective knowledge, there is no risk of misunderstanding.

Grice is forced, against the prevailing intention of his theory, to assert that S and A belong, after all, to the same language-group, and speaks, after all, the same idiolect. A can, in other words, only know what S means by HW if already she knows what HW means. Grice has defeated his own theory, because 'mutual' or 'conventional knowledge' is *necessary* for S and A to understand each other; it is *necessary* in order to eliminate the *possibility* of misunderstanding.

> If S utters HW, his measure of expectation of success as regards effecting the intended response *obviously* depends . . . on A's knowledge of S's procedure; and normally, unless the signal is to be explained to each A, on A's repertoire containing the same procedure. So obviously, each member of some group G (within which HW is to be a tool of communication) will want his procedure with respect to HW to conform to the general practice of the group. So I suggest the following rough definition:
>
> D3: "For the group G, utterance-type X means '*$_\psi$p'" = df. "At least some (many) members of group G have in their repertoires the procedure of uttering a token of X if, for some A, they want A to ψ^t that p, the retention of this procedure being for them conditional on the assumption that at least some (other) members of G have, or have had, this procedure in their repertoires."
>
> D3 gets in the idea of aiming at conformity and so perhaps (derivatively) also that of *correct* and *incorrect* use of X."[39]

Now, "effecting the intended response *obviously* depends" on whether A share the information of the meaning of the gesture uttered by S. 'Obviously,' Grice writes. But if that is so obvious, it is no wonder that A understands S from the beginning, and the attempt of the example to explain the transition from meaning intended to meaning understood is redundant. If they *did not* share this information, the signal would have to be either explained to A, or she would have to surmise its meaning by second-guessing S's intention.

Everything is then ultimately founded on conventional knowledge about adequate language-use within a certain language community. S has to comply with the practices or procedures of this community in order to be understood, and in order to use a sentence 'correctly.' Thus we notice that ultimately, Grice can do no better than cutting off the vicious 'spiral' of successively deeper nested intentions at the surface, at the so-called 'plane' of conventional knowledge. A no longer reads S's intentions in order to understand his utterances; A understands S's intentions by understanding his utterances.[40]

Elsewhere in Grice's work, we encounter this unsatisfactory pseudo-solution to his prevailing foundation-problem. Foundation of meaning-understanding is initially sought in the murky abysses of intention, but in the final analysis and ultimately, it is always returned to the surface of 'obvious' conventional foreknowledge. If we return to our previous example, 'he has not yet been to prison,' Grice intended by this example to illustrate conversational implicature, which the auditor is able to work out because she understands the speaker's intention. However, when we re-read the sentence more carefully, also this example defeats Grice's conclusion. Grice overlooks that the sentence has already *conventionally* inscribed its implicature. The 'yet' in the example is unfortunate, since 'yet' *conventionally* implies that 'thus far,' 'up to this point,' X has not been to prison, with this indicating *conventionally* that X is expected, sooner or later, to end up there. A understands S, because the sentence, *conventionally*, already implies that X belongs in prison.

If, for the sake of argument, we try to rescue Grice's thesis by improving on his example (it is, after all, unjust to make a 'yet' invalidate a theory), we could suggest the stronger case: S wants to imply that 'X is dishonest,' and carries out his intention this time by dryly remarking, 'that bank must have some courageous manager'— implying: the bank manager takes a risk, X is the risk, X is dishonest. Or better, S asks in mock disbelief, 'X has been employed in a bank?'— Stressing 'bank.' Or even better, S bursts out incredulously, 'a bank!'— Stressing 'bank.' Here the discrepancy and dissociation between sentence-meaning and utterance-meaning is highlighted and to the fore: 'a bank!' has the unique occasion-meaning, 'X is dishonest.'

The question is, however, whether any of these improved examples actually perform their job of rescuing Grice's line of thought. Could they be understood if we strip them, in some imagined world, of all convention and context? First, they all employ the association, bank ~ money, which is conventionally established, and which cannot be understood outside certain historical and social coordinates. Secondly, they all presuppose that we know that X is potentially dishonest. The minimal example, 'a bank!' cannot be understood except under these two preconditions: the auditor must understand the association, 'bank ~

money,' and the interlocutors must share as common background knowledge that X has a history, or a reputation, of being dishonest. This common background knowledge must accompany the exclamation before it can be properly understood as an expression of disbelief. In another context, where S and A share a different background-information, the interjection would have a different meaning. If I was told that Jacques Derrida had been employed in a bank, I could see myself exclaiming incredulously, 'a bank!' by this meaning to say a lot of things, but not that Jacques Derrida is potentially dishonest.

Provisionally, I shall suggest that in order to understand/restore an apparently flawed utterance, the cooperative auditor must engage in a hermeneutic activity that consist in gathering information from all possible contexts. We might name the *outcome* of this restoration, the 'intention of the statement,' and we may even *assign* this intention to the speaker in such a way that we *interpret* the intention of the statement to be identical to the intention of the speaker. It is evident, however, that as such, 'intention' is merely an *after-reconstruction*, and can no longer be seen as the *source* of the understanding of the statement. If we look at the examples above, it seems that it takes mutual knowledge of conventional and contextual nature to restore intention to a speaker. In other words, we only understand intentions by and through the understanding of a certain background-information—not the other way around: *it is not intentions that make us understand the background-information required to understand an utterance.*

(iii) The Desideratum and the Supplement. It must be noted here that it is not the *alleged* project of Grice to deprive sentences of their conventional meaning, although the project seems to linger as a *desideratum.* However, Grice often moderates this desideratum by introducing *supplemental* or *ad hoc* explanations that are meant to eliminate the extremism of his theory. Such *supplemental* or *ad hoc* explanations can be seen as amendments to and modifications of the theory. He slips, almost unintentionally, into conventionalist explanation-types (as above), or he generally describes how the hearer, while working-out speaker's intention, has to resort to data that is uniquely inferred from a background of conventional knowledge.

> To work out that a particular conversational implicature is present, the hearer will rely on the following data: (1) the conventional meaning of the words used, together with the identity of any references that may be involved; (2) the Cooperative Principle and its maxims; (3) the context, linguistic or otherwise, of the utterance; (4) other items of background knowledge; and (5) the fact (or supposed fact) that all relevant items

falling under the previous headings are available to both participants and both participants know or assume this to be the case.[41]

Despite marshaling the conventional knowledge required to decipher *that q in p*, Grice adheres to his favorite thesis: it is reciprocal knowledge of intentions that allows interlocutors to work out implicature. This discrepancy between declared end and ultimate justification of Grice's analysis emerges as a clash between, what I shall call, *desideratum* and *supplement*. Understanding is supposed to be explained by the understanding of intention (the *desideratum*), however, the prerequisite for understanding is mutual knowledge of convention (the *supplement*).

According to the *moderating devices* (the supplements), we must take Grice to mean that 'hello' means something in distinction to something else; for example, in distinction to 'excuse me.' We must take him to acknowledge that a word has—in Saussure's terms—*signification*, what would not prevent a 'hello' from having *value*—again in Saussure's terms. Since it has value, a 'hello' could mean everything from, 'what a nice surprise to see you' (singing) to 'don't approach me' (curtly). As well as 'excuse me' could mean everything from, 'I am sorry,' to 'what insolence' (stressing 'me'), to 'get out of my way' (in American metropolises). But since the words have signification too, 'hello' and 'excuse me' could not easily have the same values. It is difficult to imagine a context where 'excuse me' could mean 'what a nice surprise to see you.' We would expect that Grice can endorse this beginner's lesson of linguistics, but his theory in its 'raw' and unadulterated form—without modifying *ad hoc* devices—does not necessarily endorse these restrictions on word-meaning. If communication relies of intentions, and intentions are undifferentiated, then any meaning-assignment to any word is possible; the theory descends into relativism and linguistic chaos.

This poses the problem whether Grice's theory (at least beyond moderating *ad hoc* devices—intended to offset and neutralize the radical consequences of his cardinal premise) is a theory of private language. If sentences are exclusively regulated by intentions, the meaning of a sentence is relative to the intention with which it is uttered, and it is only arbitrarily related to the sentence itself. In its radical form, the claim implies a regress to a pre-Wittgensteinean notion of private language. The extreme consequence of an exclusively intentionalist account of meaning is that we no longer understand each other by means of the language in which we communicate, but as extra-terrestrial mind-readers.

Although Grice attempts to neutralize the radical consequences of his theory by (sometimes) emphasizing his belief in conventional meaning, it is clear that the theory is still vulnerable to criticisms like those sketched above. Can, for example, the sentence, *Kennst du das Land, wo die Zitronen Blühen*, mean, 'I am a German soldier,' Searle legitimately asks, in a now familiar example, and Grice's answer would have to be, 'yes, indeed.'[42]

Introducing this example, Searle's objection is that on Grice's account, any German sentence could get whichever meaning in English. Grice's paradoxical riposte is that this can happen also in French (strange confutation!). His counter-example is the following. Grice has noticed that a young daughter of a friend, receiving her first lessons in French, would take a certain arbitrary sentence in French to mean 'help yourself to a piece of cake.' Grice (obviously a person with healthy pedagogical instincts) consequently addresses her with this arbitrary sentence whenever offering her more cake. The communicative exchange succeeds since the girl's response, picking up another piece of cake, is correlated to Grice's intended response. As Grice correctly says, it does not matter whether the sentence is *actually* related to the response it produces.

> Characteristically, an utterer intends an audience to recognize (and to think himself intended to recognize) some 'crucial' feature F, and to think of F (and to think himself intended to think of F) as correlated in a certain way with some response which the utterer intends the audience to produce. It does not matter, so far as the attribution of the speaker's meaning is concerned, whether F is thought by S to be really correlated in that way with the response or not.[43]

We might say that the *institutionalized dictionary* does not matter. What Grice describes is a language beyond the dictionary, or, a language breaking away from the dictionary in the innovation of new terms and sentences. What is described is a language-community consisting of two members speaking a language where a sentence like, say, *Je suis une petit fille*, can mean 'help yourself to some cake.' Here, it does not matter, Grice says, that this sentence—according to the institutionalized dictionary—is not correlated to the meaning it got. What matters is that it is so correlated in the language of our two-member strong language-community. Now the sentence (*Je suis une petit fille*) has a crucial feature (f) that makes us expect the response (r), the girl grabs a piece of cake. It has become 'conventional' within this two-member strong language-community. In this sense, Grice is still talking about 'conventional' meaning; it is just conventional within a particularly small community.

His critics, however, do not read Grice this leniently. He is seen as reducing the importance of conventional meaning, and has been criticized by Searle in *Speech Acts* (later by Jürgen Habermas, and recently by Wayne Davis[44]) for this reduction.

> It [Grice's account of meaning] fails to account for the extent to which meaning can be a matter of rules and conventions. . . . Meaning is more than a matter of intention, it is also at least sometimes a matter of convention. . . . On Grice's account it would seem that any sentence can be uttered with any meaning whatever.[45]

In *Speech Acts*, Searle advocates a modification of Grice's theory that *de facto* only makes explicit what Grice less explicitly builds into his theory as supplemental *ad hoc* constructions. Searle does not reject the idea that intentions are at work in utterances, but he suggests a compromise-solution in the form of acknowledgment of both intentional and conventional aspects of the speech-act.[46]

> In our analysis of the illocutionary acts, we must capture both the intentional and the conventional aspects and especially the relationship between them. . . . It is this *combination* of elements which we shall need to express on our analysis of the illocutionary act.[47]

Grice also believes in compromise-solutions, albeit not with the same dedication as Searle. When he discusses Searle's objection (which thus cannot constitute a genuine objection), Grice's counter-argument (which thus cannot constitute a genuine counter-argument) reads at one place:

> Of course, I would not want to deny that when the vehicle of meaning is a sentence (or the utterance of a sentence), the speaker's intentions are to be recognized, in the normal case, by virtue of a knowledge of the conventional use of the sentence. But as I indicated earlier, I would like, if I can, to treat meaning something by the utterance of a sentence as being only a special case of meaning something by an utterance . . . and so treat a conventional correlation between a sentence and a specific response as providing only one of the ways in which an utterance may be correlated with a response.[48]

Here we see the play between the cardinal and supplemental argument at work—the passage starting with 'of course' represents the supplemental logic, the passage starting with 'but' represents the cardinal logic. (It is in worthwhile noticing that, in general, when a passage starts with 'of course' and continues with 'but,' the 'but' neutralizes the primary statement. Typically the outcome is that the *qualification* turns out to be more important than the *self-evidently true* statement.)[49] In this case, we encounter the following rhetorical logic: it is self-evidently true that intentions have to be recognized by virtue of knowledge of the conventional use of language (according to the supplemental 'of course'). However (according to the neutralizing 'but'), meaning something by uttering a sentence is only a special case of intending something in general, or, spoken language is only a special case of intending.

Despite the *ad hoc* amendments to the theory, we get the suspicion that the theory is nearly as anti-conventionalist as critics have asserted it is. In later articles, Grice has done nothing to repeal that suspicion; for example: "I do not think that meaning is essentially connected with convention."[50] (One may also note Schiffer's assertion: "I believe that it is false that illocutionary acts are conventional acts in the sense intended by Austin."[51] Only strictly institutionalized illocutionary acts like ceremonial declarations are regarded by Schiffer as conventional, not illocutionary components of ordinary language-use like *promises*, *warnings*, *assertions*, *questions*, etc.)

5) The Empty-Inner-Mental Constitution of Meaning: The Spiral.

(i) Redundant Multiple Intentions. (ii) A Spiral of Still Deeper Nested Intentions as the Foundation of Meaning.

(i) Redundant Multiple Intentions. As noted in the introduction to Grice's project, when Grice introduces his definitions of conversational implicature, the speaker's execution of two intentions is crucial. A speaker utters a sentence intending to not only induce a certain belief in an audience, but intending also the audience to recognize the first intention. The introduction of this second intention seems innocent enough; when we speak we intend not merely to utter a sentence, but also, simultaneously, to get the hearer to attend to what is uttered. We therefore discern two intentional phases in an utterance: first, S intends to introduce to A a certain belief; secondly, S intends A to recognize this intention. We could call the first intention, the *meaning* intention, and the second, the *communicative* intention. In the following quote, Grice even assumes a third intention, an intention we could call *executive*, since it presupposes that speech-acts are primarily perlocutionary rather than illocutionary.

> S meant something by uttering x is true iff, for audience A, S uttered x intending:

(1) A to produce a particular response r
(2) A to think (recognize) that S intends (1)
(3) A to fulfill (1) on the basis of his fulfillment of (2)[52]

We can break down Grice's definition into three levels of intention.

(o)   S utters x
(i)   intending a response from A
(ii)   by intending A to recognize
(iii)   that S intends a response from A

The first intention describes anticipated response. I address someone and expect some kind of response from the addressee by simply addressing the addressee. In addition to this first-order intention (i), I also intend (ii) to make A think/recognize that I (iii) intend her to respond to (i). Here it is difficult to see what exactly I do in addition to expecting a response to my utterance. Let us grant that I (i) intend a response and (ii) intend A to recognize that. However, how do I carry out (ii) that seems to be crucial in order to arrive to (iii), which is identical to (i)? How do I make A *think* that I intend a response, except by addressing A with my first-order intention? Why is a reduced one-prong formula not sufficient: S utters x, intending a response from A? What do I do beyond *speaking*? Do I look sternly at A (as long as it takes) in order to make A realize that I intend her to respond to something that I am about to utter? That cannot be, because I then intend her to produce a response before I have uttered the sentence. Do I utter x, and then in addition—and before she has a chance to answer—with vivid gestures make it clear to her that I want her to speak up?

I would suggest instead: when uttering a sentence, I engage in only one act. This one act 'always already' inscribes a remitter, the one that is determined as 'I' by pronouncing the sentence, and a receiver, the one that is determined as 'you' by the 'I' pronouncing the sentence. Furthermore, the utterance directs itself to the auditor with a certain illocutionary force, which makes A realize that S intends A to respond in a certain modus. The second-order intention is thus inscribed in the utterance-structure itself, rather than being a deliberate realization of the mental inner life of the utterer. The construction, 'I think that I want A to think that I want A to respond,' never happens, and is a superfluous and artificial complication. It is pure theory (and perhaps poor theory), because it is theory without correlate in the reality of speech-acts. If I hammer a nail in a wall, I intend to hit the nail, but I don't think/recognize that I intend to hit the nail. In the act, I don't *think* my intention or *intend* my intention, unless I (exactly) suspend or disengage myself from the act, and start engaging in some meditative practices, where I, for obscure reasons, put my inner psychological life under scrutiny.[53]

Meaning intention and communicative intention collapse into one speech act. In giving an order (e.g., 'close the door'), S's means of making A recognize the order (x) is to utter the sentence as an order. S's means of making A think herself intended to recognize the sentence as an order (x) is also to utter the sentence—because of the inscription of I, you, and illocutionary force in the *instance of enunciation*. If *at all* the utterance is supplemented by some sort of additional emphasis, I cannot see that it could lie anywhere else but in the glance. S looks at A while talking, making A thinking herself intended to recognize that the sentence is addressed to her. But if the second-order intention to make A think herself intended to recognize the sentence (x) is identical to something like a glance, then the glance in itself cannot be endowed with any meaning. It has to be filled with the meaning of the spoken sentence; otherwise, it is empty. If the glance approximately says: *'I want you to recognize that I address you,'* the uttered sentence adds the significant part: *'wanting you to close the door.'* A glance in itself says nothing. At best, it demands attention, and if not this demand is accompanied by an utterance, it becomes uncomfortable, or 'eerie,' or outright insane.

To recap, the first-order intention is that S utters x intending A to recognize x, the second-order intention is that S utters x intending A to think herself intended to recognize x. Now, doubling of intention seems to be not only an unnecessary but also a counter-productive complication of communicative exchanges. For example, what is the difference between: (i) I intend A to believe that God is dead by stating 'God is dead'; and (ii) I intend to make A recognize my intention that I intend A to believe that God is dead by stating 'God is dead.' In the first case, I may be lucky to produce by my utterance the belief in A, that god is dead. In the second case, I hardly have such luck (at least not, if we presuppose that A recognizes all folds in my convoluted Gricean self). In the second case, A is compelled to believe, rather, that I utter the sentence, 'God is dead,' not because I primarily want to her to believe me, but because I want her to understand that I intend her to understand my intention of imposing a belief on her. This implies that I do not primarily want A to believe that god is dead; I want her to understand that I am persuading her into that belief. A will now tend to think (still, given that she is able to unfold all folds in my complicated Gricean consciousness) that God exists, and that I am—for unknown reasons— trying to convince her of something that is false. (Similarly, if I think that someone has proof of the existence of God, I am convinced of the existence of God, but if I think that someone thinks she has proof of the existence of God, I am as doubtful about the existence of God as ever. There are, at least, no good reasons for me to start believing in the existence of God, since I am merely relating to a statement about S's fantasy-world.)

Instead of constituting the fundamentals for communication, it is more accurate that Grice, Strawson, and Schiffer's complications constitute the fundamentals for the breakdown of communication. They are closer to constitute the formulae for what Habermas calls 'manipulative discourse.'

Besides the redundancy and the counter-productivity in doubling intentions, intending intentions seems in general to imply an impossible complication of acts. For example, what is the difference between 'I intend to stop smoking' and 'I intend to intend stop smoking'? The first case is clear, I want to stop smoking, and I want to exert an effort to that end. The second case is not clear at all; here, it is not necessarily the case that I stop (or try to stop) smoking, since primarily I only want to intend this end. As another Descartes, I could decide to suspend the vaporous world around me, close my eyes and ears, and meditate on the possibility of intending not to smoke. My meditation on that second-order intention would be genuine and have validity whether or not I was simultaneously puffing on my cigarettes, whether or not I eventually stopped smoking, and whether or not I intended to actually stop smoking.

(ii) A Spiral of Still Deeper Nested Intentions as the Foundation of Meaning. Whereas Grice typically introduces *meaning, communicative,* and *executive* intentions into his explanatory formulae for meaning, his follower, Stephen R. Schiffer expands the formulae into complications of the nth order. One of Schiffer's illustrations on infinite dialectical regress reads:

> Suppose that you and I are dining together and that we are seated across from one another and that on the table between us is a rather conspicuous candle. We would therefore be in a situation in which I am facing the candle and you, and you are facing the candle and me. (Consequently, a situation in which S is facing the candle and A, who is facing the candle and S, who is facing the candle and A, who is facing the candle and S, who is facing ..).[54]

But, repeating and elaborating the problem already introduced above, what information does the parenthesis add that can further help to describe the initial situation: two people are facing each other? The primary scenario already sufficiently describes the dialectical relationship between S and A: S faces A who faces S (the candle seems an unnecessary complication). That S faces A again, and that A faces S again, is already described exhaustingly and sufficiently in the first sentence. On the level of perception the dialectic is simple, and only if we introduce a level of knowledge of perception, it makes sense to expand the dialectic by one or two circuits: S faces A who faces S who knows that he is seen by A who knows that she is seen by S (who knows that A knows that S sees her (A), who knows that S knows that A sees him (S)).[55] The dialectic simplified:

- S sees A / . . . /A sees S,
- S knows that he is seen by A / . . . /A knows that she is seen by S
- S knows that A knows that she is seen by S / . . . /A knows that S knows that he is seen by A

The last fold in the dialectical exchange would close the circuit. Adding a fourth, fifth, sixth, or n^{th} circuit is not only a superfluous and redundant repetition of any of the above three levels—and seems to be only a formal exercise with no equivalent in consciousness. Furthermore, such an elaboration has ontological implications which neither Grice nor Schiffer could want to subscribe to.

I could go on now to construct a further step . . . *I can go on like this forever.* . . . For example, all 'normal' people know that snow is white, know that all people know that snow is white, know that all normal people know that all normal people know that snow is white, *and so on ad infinitum.* . . . I think one would be hard put to find reasons why in the 'candle' example I could not go on *indefinitely* in the way specified [my emphases].[56]

But exactly, this circuit cannot continue *ad infinitum.* If we continue infinitely, we introduce unwarranted metaphysical assumptions about human consciousness. An nth level added to our tables above would imply the following construction: S knows that A knows that S knows that A knows that S knows that . . (etc.) . . that he is seen by A.

According to that construction, S knows not only that A knows that S is being present (which might be observed in A's behavior), but S also knows (has a mysterious insight into) A's knowledge about herself. S, furthermore, knows how his own knowledge is reflected in A (again by mysterious insight). When he knows that A knows that he knows that A knows . . . etc., then this knowledge is ultimately relying on the assumption that he has complete access to A consciousness. S and A are supposedly transparent to each other. Like mirrors reflecting mirrors they see themselves reflected in each other, and see their own reflected image in the other (and the reflected image of themselves in the reflected image of the other in the image of themselves in the other, etc.). If Schiffer's subjects face one another like two mirrors, their depth is nothing but an infinite play of their respective surfaces. This gives us, I think, a palpable metaphor on why it is unnecessary to move beyond the surface: everything reflected on any 'deeper' level is a repetition of the already well-described surface. We do not see *more* by seeing the same surface described again; we see the exact same thing.

After any one step, the formula generates itself as the same, and it is designed to perpetuate this self-generation indefinitely. At each self-generation it is as if we are deeper and deeper steeped in the depths of human consciousness, since it becomes harder and harder to follow the convolutions that the formula generates. At a sufficiently deep level, we are lost (after two or three circuits, I would say), and we have to surrender to the mere mechanics of the formula. It is this *formal rule* for infinite regress that can keep operating forever, as Schiffer asserts, but he does not note the fundamental difference-in-type between formula and psychology, between algebra and human consciousness.

6) HERMENEUTICAL TOTALITARIANISM: MEANING AS INTENDING A RESPONSE IN AN AUDIENCE

Utterances are not necessarily meant to produce intended effects, they are not primarily perlocutionary, but illocutionary, Searle has objected to Grice. The speaker typically wants to only produce understanding of his utterance.

> Grice in effect defines meaning in terms of intending to perform a perlocutionary act, but saying something and meaning it is a matter of intending to perform an illocutionary, not necessarily a perlocutionary, act. . . . The characteristic intended effect of meaning is understanding, but understanding is not . . . a perlocutionary effect.[57]

According to Grice, *S means x only if S intends x to produce e in A* (e = effect). In Schiffer, this formula is more rigorously stated: *S means x only if S intends x to produce a certain r in A* (r = response). Meaning is uttering a sentence such that the sentence is directed to a certain intended audience and such that the sentence is expected to produce a certain response from this audience. If Grice's definition implies the intention in speaker to produce *a response in a person*, Schiffer's stricter definition implies the intention in the speaker to produce <u>a</u> *response in* <u>a</u> *person*.

On Grice's view, to mean something by uttering x is just to utter x
intending to produce in some person *a certain type* of response in *a
certain type* of way. . . . One knows what S meant if, and only if, one
knows what response S intended to produce in A.[58]

According to these formulae, I mean an utterance, x, because I intend a
(certain) r in a (certain) A 'by means of'/'qua' A's recognition of me
intending the response, r. The auditor supposedly decodes my
expectation to (decodes my intended response by) her as auditor. It is
here not sufficient that A recognizes the by S intended response; A's
recognition of the by S intended response must also be 'at least part of'
A's reason to respond. The analysis of S-meaning is therefore expanded
in the following way by Schiffer:

> S meant something by (or in) uttering *x* iff S uttered x intending
> (1) That his utterance of *x* produce a certain response *r* in a certain
> audience A;
> (2) That A recognizes S's intention (1);
> (3) That A's recognition of S's intention (1) shall function is at least part
> of A's reason for A's response *r*.[59]

S expects a certain response, and encodes his utterance with a certain
intended anticipated response. A, on her part, decodes S's utterance of
the intended anticipated response. To know what S means is to know
what response S intended.

However, if conversation were actually carried out along the lines of
such rigorous formulae, all conversation would be in principle either
interrogative or *persuasive*. A paradigm example on the formulae above
could be the classroom situation, where, as an uninspired, and
uninspiring, teacher, I might ask my students a question to which there
is, according to me, only a true or false answer. For example: do you
regard Samuel Beckett an absurdist writer? The students have to answer
'yes' to satisfy my expected response. According to the definitions
above, I intend a certain response ('yes') in a certain audience (the
students).

However, as soon as I think that it is rather unimportant for students
to label Beckett as this or that, I open my questioning and do no longer
intend a certain response. I could now ask something like, 'why do you
think that Vladimir takes on and off his hat?' Since I myself have no
good answer ready-at-hand to the question, I also no longer anticipate a
certain response. —But does that make the sentence now meaningless?
In this latter situation, all I expect is that my audience recognizes the
illocutionary component in the utterance, questioning, and responds in
the appropriate illocutionary mood, answering (as also Searle seems to

suggest).

Grice and (especially) Schiffer's formulae seem therefore too rigorous to exemplify ordinary speech-situations. Elaborating on the example above: what is the feel about the following imagined dialogue between my student and me? Me: "Why do you think that Vladimir takes on and off his hat?"—Student: "Maybe just to pass time!"—Me: "No, you are wrong, *because* this is not the answer I have in mind!" and in exasperation I explain: "you see, your answer has to match the answer I have in mind, otherwise you are wrong, and I have to fail you!"

If this dialogue can pass as a model example on the requirements in Grice and Schiffer's formulae, it is evident that these artificially rigorous formulae are applicable only in cases of severe obsessive-neurotic behavior.

In general, actual conversation is too relaxed, associative, and/or distracted to fulfill these rigorous requirements. Conversation is not an intellectual Ping-Pong where the interlocutors in each instance get back the same ball they serve. If Grice and Schiffer's scenario were to apply, conversation would dry out after only two exchanges. I would ask a question expecting a certain response; the student would give me my desired answer, and expect me to confirm her answer, what I would do. After the last exchange we had both fulfilled our purposes, and would have nothing more to add—until I came up with a new question. Conversation of that type, we call interrogation.

Essentially, the exchange would not even be conversational, because in each instance, I merely receive the answer I have already in mind. Thus, the dialectical exchange would be nothing but the externalization of my soliloquizing self. Ultimately, it would be of no consequence whether, at the opposite end of this Ping-Pong table, there was an actual other person, or whether I was just playing against the wall.

If Grice's definition applies in non-pathological discourse, it would seem only to do so for the very specific type of utterances we characterize as *persuasive*. Grice introduces a definition of so-called *protreptic* utterance-types that would also describe persuasive utterance-types: "utterances by which S M-intends, via imparting a belief that he (S) has a certain propositional attitude, to induce a corresponding attitude in the hearer."[60] However, it is clear that Grice believes his definition applies to all utterances; not just to so-called *protreptic/persuasive*.

7) EXCURSUS: REVISITING THE VENERABLE PROBLEM OF 'THE ORIGIN OF LANGUAGE.'

(i) Reintroducing the Problem of 'The Origin of Language' in the 'High-Tech' Jargon of Analytic Philosophy. (ii) The Origin as the Other: Rousseau and Herder. (iii) The Origin as the Same: Grice and Schiffer.

(i) Reintroducing the Problem of 'The Origin of Language' in the 'High-Tech' Jargon of Analytic Philosophy. It is well-known that in contemporary linguistics and language-philosophy the once intense debate on the origin of language has virtually disappeared. We don't find discussions of the origin of language in Saussure and his followers; it surprises nobody that there is no entry for the 'origin of language' in Todorov and Ducrot's *Encyclopedic Dictionary of the Sciences of Language*.[61] Neither do we find any interest in the debate in the Analytic tradition, whether in Frege and Wittgenstein, or in Austin and Searle. The problem of establishing some abstract and universal pre-conditions for an 'origin' of language has rightly, and for a long time, been regarded as intractable.

Therefore, on a first look, it is surprising to find the discussion revived in the contemporary language philosophy of Paul Grice and Stephen R. Schiffer. And then again, on second thoughts, the question of the origin of language may well be seen as a logical extension of what was always the recurrent theme in Grice and Schiffer's language philosophy.

In a sense, Grice's language-theory—although addressing the problem of meaning in the abstract—was always about the 'origin of language.' At least, it seems to be less accurate to describe it as a theory of *private* language (as have some critics; e.g., Searle), than to describe it as a theory of how private language is introduced into society, and being made communal. Grice's formulae were always attempts to set up the conditions that would have to be in place if interlocutors were to acquire *mutual* knowledge of the meaning of *pre-conventional* utterances. This interest continues when Grice and Schiffer set out to determine how originally language would have had to evolve between two interlocutors; that is, set out to determine what dialectical identifications would be required to make a primitive sound (or gesture) socially meaningful. In Grice's formulation, the question becomes, how does *natural* meaning becomes *non-natural*? Differently put, when is something uttered with *communicative intent* (and recognized as such), instead of being 'uttered' simply as an involuntary grunt?

In addressing this question, Grice starts by introducing a difference between an outcry (*natural*) and an expression (*non-natural*), and surmises that the origin of language be situated at the point when the outcry turns into an expression. In the pursuit of this project, it is not surprising that both Grice and Schiffer prefer examples on utterance-types that are rudimentary and primitive (so-called 'non-composite'). *First*, primitive sounds and gestures can be seen as located on the borderline between the linguistic and nonlinguistic. As they evolve from 'natural' to 'non-natural,' we are supposedly experiencing the transition of the meaningless noise/gesture into the meaningful sign. *Secondly*, this development is also a transition from *private* to *public*, from *individual* intention to *recognizable* intention. Primitive sounds are still purely private in their intentionality; they present passionate or aggressive gestures/noises that our primordial ancestors supposedly have at their disposal for pure self-expression. Primitive sounds are not yet contaminated by convention. Thus, satisfied grunts, cries of pain, etc., are symbols of our intentional make-up *in-and-for-itself*; but eventually, they will have to be identified as meaning by other members of the tribe. Since those primitive self-expressions are primary, they are the foundation for language. We therefore understand why it is important to Grice and Schiffer to investigate the primitive 'grunt'; we understand that it is easier to argue the case for the predominance of intention in spoken language, when one replenishes one's discourse with examples on intention upon which conventional language is conditional.

When talking about 'origins,' Grice and Schiffer are obviously not interested in the actual phylogenetic and historical origins of language as were for example Condillac, Rousseau, and Herder; nor do they try (ontogenetically) to understand language-acquisition in the infant, like Jean Piaget. Still, they enter this very old, very venerable, discussion, as it has been occupying the best philosophical minds since Plato, and as it was especially thriving throughout the 18th century.[62] Grice and Schiffer are not referring to this intellectual heritage (—nor to contemporary 20th century linguistics that rejects the problem as inane). Instead, the problem of the origin of language is re-introduced in the 'high-tech' vocabulary of Analytic Philosophy as an abstract problem of the a-historical birth of meaning from meaningless noise.

As I shall argue in the following, this contemporary 'high-tech' terminology does not prevent the discussions from being as metaphysical as, for example, Rousseau and Herder's. Moreover, Grice and Schiffer's 'solution' to this problem would even seem to represent a relapse from advances achieved by their distinguished 18th century predecessors.[63]

If schematically, I introduce a list of the three most obvious 'solutions' (ways of thinking) the intractable problem of the origin of language, the *best* 'solution' would be (to my mind) to suspend and ignore the problem altogether (as in Structural Linguistics and most Analytic Language Philosophy). The *worse* 'solution' would be to explain the first word as emerging from conditions *different* from itself (as in Condillac, Rousseau, and Herder). However, this 'solution' would still be a little better than to let the first word emerge from a condition *identical* to itself (this is approximately where I see Grice and Schiffer located).

(ii) The Origin as the Other: Rousseau and Herder. Throughout the 18th century, one is in general becoming fascinated with *origins*. One ponders questions such as the origin of language and the invention of speech, as well as closely related issues such as the origin of poetry, of music, of consciousness, of knowledge, and of society. In the emerging paradigm, origins are always located in some fictitious prehistoric time. One explores origins that cannot be traced, origins that are beyond investigation because they are located in an era before humans learned to record their historical activity, therefore in an era irrevocably lost. The 18th century writers can therefore only *speculate* about this primitive constitution of language, of knowledge, and of society, and they now speculate in a language that yearns to reproduce the object it is speculating about. In its style and rhetoric, this language tries to revive its object; if it describes the first languages as figurative, this language itself becomes figurative; if it perceives later developments of language as unfortunate rationalizations of language, this language tries to rid itself of rational methodology, etc. It is a language that, when it attempts to grasp the poetry of the first languages, wants to persuade us as readers by exhibiting the tone and sound of this primordial and forgotten poetry. In this new style of a Rousseau or a Herder, one tries to compose one's language more as a 'breath of passion' (Herder) than as a rational descriptive language. One wants to get beyond 'writing' by making one's writing an echo of the voices of the first speakers.

So, origins represent a lost paradise. Certainly, writers like Rousseau and Herder would refer to even older ages; to a time *before* the first origins, but these ages 'before' the origins did not count as beginnings, they represented a past where humans were more beast than human. What was interesting was the point at which humans became civilized, the point at which the human being became a human being; that is, the interest was in the origin of civilization and not in animal prehistory, which in itself could not be traced to any origin. In the animal prehistory, there was nothing distinctive about humans for what one could seek the origin: there was neither language nor speech, neither society nor government, neither music nor poetry. In fact, there was not even a perception of an opposite sex (if we are to believe Rousseau), or a distinctive perception of the human being as such (if we are to believe Herder). This lack of distinctiveness would characterize everything 'before' the origin of society, language, and consciousness. In the pre-Romantic logic, this pre-human world was conceived as a fictitious era where all differences have imploded, and where conscious perception of the world was still nonexistent. Only subsequently, with the emergence of the first word, does consciousness awake; a distinct perception of the world arises. Finally, systems of differences and identities begin to establish themselves.

One begins a search for the 'first word': how was it spoken, why was it spoken, and what made it necessary? Origins supposedly represented human beings as they were meant to be. Understanding them, therefore, could help to criticize and correct the alienation and corruption of present society. At these beginnings, societies are still uncomplicated, speech is still harmonious and sonorous, feelings are still pure and innocent, human beings are still passionate and sensuous, etc. These beginnings were conceived in contrast to present life. If they represented a lost but happy childhood of life, present life had become alienated, unnatural, and unhappy. Thus, in these early writers there is a *political* motive behind the discussion of origins, a political motive that makes the mythological and metaphysical constructions pertinent, although, as in all theories on origins, there are insuperable logical obstacles in accounting for the origin, the beginning, or the first.

In accounting for the first word, Enlightenment philosophers were trying to account for the circumstances that make language necessary. In Rousseau, this necessity was seen as a sudden *climate change*! Rousseau speculates that pre-historic people originally—as long as the climate was warm and nature bountiful—lived dispersed in small isolated families, incestuously, and without knowing love. But with "the touch of a finger," the creator changes the obit of the globe, and climates that were once lush and fertile become dry and barren. Families that once lived isolated, without the need of other human contact, are suddenly forced to gather around the water wells with other families. Youth discovers youth, and gradually the interest in the water diminishes, and is replaced with an interest in the other sex. In Rousseau's own words.

> Girls would come to seek water for the household, young men would come to water their herds. Their eyes, accustomed to the same sights since infancy, began to see with increased pleasure. The heart is moved by these novel objects; an unknown attraction renders it less savage; it feels pleasure at not being alone. Imperceptibly, water becomes more necessary [*L'eau devint insensiblement plus nécessaire*]. The livestock become thirsty more often. One would arrive in haste and leave with regret [*on arrivoit en hâte, et l'on partoit à regret*].[64]

Slowly and imperceptibly, water is no longer the main attraction, the other sex is. This explains to Rousseau the need for the first words. Gestures are no longer sufficient, passions want to make themselves understood, and language is born out of the need to express love. (As we notice, even in this poetic (and outlandishly romantic) fable, the origin of language is something *other* than language—it is indeed difficult to conceive the issue otherwise, how could the origin of language be language?)

In Herder's more subtle explanation of the origin of language, the pre-condition, the 'other than language' is reflection. Preceding the utterance of the first word, we need to exercise an ability to reflect, Herder explains, because reflection enables a person to focus on something, namely on the object to which the word eventually may be attached, and which thus the word may eventually *represent*.

> [Man] manifests reflection [*Der Mensch beweiset Reflexion*] when, confronted with the vast hovering dream of images which pass by his senses, he can collect himself into a moment of wakefulness and dwell at will on one image, can observe it clearly and more calmly, and can select in it distinguishing marks [*Merkmale*] for himself so that he will know that this object is this and not another.[65]

Reflection halts a continuous flow of sensations. If there were no reflection but only this flow of sensations, human beings would have only pre-conscious perceptions of the world. They would not be able to fixate distinct impressions of surrounding objects in their consciousness. They would still receive impressions, but fleeting and transitory impressions, —as such ignored by the mind. In order to see consciously and attentively—that is, to *perceive* in a strict sense—humans have to *arrest* the impressions they receive. They must be able to dwell on an image, look at it again, and finally recognize it *as something* characteristically. This, according to Herder, is a reflective faculty only human beings possess. Reflection is the faculty that makes possible conscious perception of the world.

Reflection also makes possible language. In reflection, a so-called 'distinguishing mark' is established. Reflection enables human beings to see *something as something*. It constitutes identity in a flow of otherwise indistinguishable impressions. This constitution precedes the emergence and articulation of the first word. It is the pre-condition for language, indispensable to its constitution. Herder explains by an example how this formation of language occurs.

Let that lamb there, as an image, pass by under his eyes; it is to him, as it is to no other animal. Not as it would appear to the hungry, scenting wolf! Not as it would appear to the blood-lapping lion. . . . Not so with man! As soon as he feels the need to come to know the sheep, no instinct gets in his way; no one sense of his pulls him too close to it or too far away from it. It stands there, entirely as it manifests itself in his sense. White, soft, woolly—his soul in reflective exercise seeks a distinguishing mark—the sheep bleats! His soul has found the distinguishing mark [—das Schaf Blöcket! Sie hat Merkmal gefundet]. The inner sense is at work. This bleating, which makes upon man's soul the strongest impression . . . the soul retains it. The sheep comes again. White, soft, woolly—the soul sees, touches, remembers, seeks a distinguishing mark—the sheep bleats, and the soul recognizes it. And it feels inside, 'Yes, you are that which bleats.' [Ha! du bist das Blöckende!]. It has recognized it humanly when it recognized and named it clearly, that is, with a distinguishing mark.[66]

Before the reflective process, perceptions must be freed from instincts. The object must represent itself indifferently to the subject; it must represent itself solely as what it is in itself, not as in an interested perception, not as a scent, a meal, etc., but, as something 'white, soft, woolly' (Herder's idea of a disinterested view of a lamb). After this phenomenological exercise is successfully executed, reflection starts looking for a 'distinguishing mark,' that is, something which distinguishes the lamb within the disinterested impression. When the lamb finally returns, as 'white, soft, woolly,' the soul summons forth the already retained image. The lamb is recognized as this 'white, soft, woolly' creature, and when now the lamb elicits a sound, it specifically relates to and characterizes the image. The sound of its bleating constitutes a mark, something 'the soul retains,' and when the lamb bleats again, the lamb is recognized as 'the bleating.' The early human has found a name, a 'signifier,' for the lamb. This recognition enlightens the human and relieves him of the reflective struggle he has suffered in order to identify the animal as something: 'Ha! du bist das Blöckende!' The name-giving alleviates. The human being finally recognizes the lamb by its bleating, and has simultaneously found a word for the creature; "and what is the entire human languages other than a collection of such words? [eine Sammlung solcher Worte?],"[67] Herder concludes, in a conclusion that obviously would not stand up to the scrutiny of contemporary linguistics.

The condition for language is our ability to hold back images, retain them, and recollect them when they present themselves a second time. It is our ability to first *produce* a trace of impressions and then to *reproduce* the same trace of impressions. This ability to hold on to something already seen, to stop it from disappearing, and then to revoke the image when the object is seen again is, as such, an ability to *remember*. Remembrance, therefore, is a constitutional condition for language.

(iii) The Origin as the Same: Grice and Schiffer. As we have seen, Grice's recurrent problem is to describe how a 'language-community'—consisting of the usual two members in Grice's 'society': speaker and hearer—acquires mutual knowledge of meaning. When this problem is addressed in the abstract, we cannot presuppose that convention endows the agents with mutual understanding, because speakers may intend meaning 'unconventionally,' and still be understood.

When the problem is projected into the supposed prehistoric origin of language, the conclusion becomes quite the same. At the origin, at the beginning of our earliest language-acquisition, we cannot presuppose convention, since mutual knowledge of *new* meaning cannot be explained in terms of *old* meaning, that is, in terms of *convention*. However, we must assume that it has been possible for humans to acquire mutual knowledge of *new* meaning, since humans must have started to use sentences to express themselves in some way and at some point. Therefore, 'convention' is effectively out of the picture. In these speculations about the origin of language, we find a fresh attempt to reinforce Grice's intentionalist theory of language. Let us review two examples; the first is Grice's, the second Schiffer's.

In a later article, *"Meaning Revisited,"* Grice returns to the two notions of meaning he introduced in the early article, *"Meaning"*: *natural meaning* and *nonnatural meaning* (now labeled, meaning$_N$ and meaning$_{NN}$). Natural meaning is illustrated by this example: 'those black clouds meant that it would rain' (black clouds can *mean* (*indicate*) rain—without clouds having any meaning about whether it will rain or not), while nonnatural meaning is illustrated by this example: 'his remark meant so-and-so,' (the utterer is intentionally *expressing* something). Given this initial definition, also certain kinds of human behavior could be classified under natural meaning: "Among the things that have natural meaning . . . are certain forms of behavior: things like groans, screeches, and so on."[68] This type of human expressions would be characterized by their involuntariness: "In the natural sense, the production of these pieces of behavior . . . is nonvoluntary."[69]

It is now Grice's suggestion that these natural expression-types could be the primitive ancestors to nonnatural meaning. This implies that natural meaning at some non-specified (non-important) mythological point in human prehistory is modified into nonnatural meaning. The question is therefore, how is meaning$_N$ transformed into meaning$_{NN}$; or, how are involuntary outcries transformed into voluntary expressions; or, how does communication arise? An outcry has two fundamental characteristics, it is involuntary and it is not addressed to anyone. As we might expect, the specification of address becomes an important criterion for determining nonnatural meaning.

Initially pain-expressions (meaning$_N$) signal certain body-conditions. At this initial and primitive stage, it is misleading to say that the human speaks, but we may perhaps say that the body 'speaks.' However, in six stages, the human inhabitant of this body takes over, and uses the same signal (so far an empty signifier) for the specific communicative purpose to make somebody in the near vicinity realize that he is in pain.

The first two stages in this transformation are that the pain-expression is (1), uttered voluntary, and (2), that it is recognized as being uttered voluntary. "The purpose of the creature's producing the behavior voluntarily would be so that the rest of the world should think that it is in the state which the nonvoluntary production would signify."[70]

However, as Grice remarks, the whole transformation process seems so far redundant, since the bodily outcry already indicates that the inhabitant of the body is in pain. It is therefore a minor mystery what the utterer could gain by uttering a pain-expression voluntary instead of involuntary. If we have these two "creatures," X and Y, it must look to Y as if, in the voluntary pain-expression, X is merely simulating. In this sense, recognition of voluntary behavior seems to be counter-productive to X's purposes, since pain-behavior produced deliberately undermines the conclusion that X wants Y to reach, namely that X is in real and actual pain. Simulated behavior is a near neighbor to deceptive or fake behavior.

Grice therefore suggests a stage three and four. (3) X makes Y recognize that he *intends* Y to recognize that the pain-expression is voluntary. And (4), Y recognizes that X intends her to recognize that it is voluntary. This implies, at least, that X can no longer be deceiving Y, but it must still leave Y confused. "There is this creature, as it were, simulating pain, but announcing, in a certain sense, that this is what it is doing: what on earth can it be up to."[71]

Openly announcing one's deception eliminates the deception. X may be simulating pain-behavior, but he is also intending Y to realize that he is simulating pain-behavior. Grice suggests that Y is likely to believe that X is engaged in some sort of play to which Y is expected to make some sort of contribution. In order not to leave Y in this confusion, but to impel her to take the communicative effort seriously, Grice therefore needs a fifth stage, the crucial stage that will authorize and sanction X's communicative pain-expression as *serious*, not simulation and not play.

At this fifth stage, X has the task to make Y believe that the voluntary pain-expression indicates that X is *actually* in pain, and is not merely engaged in some sort of play. The success of getting Y to recognize this state of affairs depends on whether Y can regard X as "trustworthy."

> Whether Y not only recognize this [that X is in pain] but actually goes on to believe that X is in pain, would presumably depend on a further set of conditions which can be summed up under the general heading that Y should regard X as trustworthy.[72]

So, if I say 'ouch' with composed and restrained intonation, instead of screaming out in pain, I make Y think that I am really only playing a game. As such, the 'ouch' seems detached from bodily pain. Now, it is my job to re-attach it. To succeed in that task I must be so-called 'trustworthy.'

But trustworthy in regard to what reference? It does not count for trust if my interlocutor trusts me to be a playful fellow that says 'ouch' when she lightly pinches me. This is obviously not the trust Grice presupposes. 'Trust' is established when Y thinks, "X would not want to get Y to believe that X is in pain unless X really were in pain."[73] Thus, she has to 'trust' that I am *serious*, not inclined to utter fake or mock 'ouches' when using the pain-expression 'ouch.' She must consequently *know* that my ouches are serious ouches with only one possible meaning and interpretation; she must *know* that 'ouch' to me has one and only one meaning, 'I am in pain.' However, *to know* is always *to know in advance*; it is here identical to, *to know conventionally* (it is impossible to 'know' what one has never before seen, experienced, or learned). The *new meaning* has after all to be *old meaning* in order to be understood by Y.

We notice that being 'trustworthy' implies that signs when uttered are reduced to having only one unequivocal reference. Contexts that could obscure this unequivocal reference have been eliminated. When X utters a pain-expression, Y can 'trust' that there are no hidden implicatures in the utterance. Grice primordial language is as such wonderfully purified from implicatures; there are no occasion-meanings in this language. Being trustworthy is to utter, says Grice, "what is in fact the case": "Y also believes that X is . . . in general responsible, for example being the sort of creature who takes adequate trouble to make sure that what he is trying to get the other creature to believe is in fact the case."[74]

However, Grice's trustworthy and responsible language-user is now dangerously close to utter only meaning$_N$ (natural meaning instead of nonnatural meaning). By his 'ouch,' the trustworthy and responsible language-user means *pain and only pain*; —like the black cloud indicates rain, without expressing that rain is a possibility, the trustworthy language-user *indicates* pain, without leaving room for possibilities. He seems to do exactly what his primitive ancestor does when uttering 'ouch,' he indicates natural meaning. Nonnatural meaning is apparently best understood, if, ultimately, it is expressed with the same innocence as natural meaning.

In Schiffer's elaboration of Grice, the complexity and intractability of this foundation-problem of language becomes easier to grasp. Also in Schiffer's examples, we are referred to rudimentary, so-called 'non-composite,' utterance-types. Such utterance-types have to Schiffer the advantage over composite utterances that, first, they are simpler to handle than their composite counterparts since they are unstructured, and, secondary, they are evolutionary primary. Schiffer compares them to the supposed language of our remote ancestors: "It is a fair assumption that our remote ancestors communicated by unstructured grunts and gestures before they discovered the utility of language."[75]

Thus, we are introduced to a primordial 'language' made up of nothing but non-composite 'grunts' (by 'passionate sounds,' as Herder would have phrased it). The intellectual challenge is now to give an account of how this primordial 'language' becomes conventional. Our primitive ancestors utter certain grunts, yet without understanding each other, how and when do these grunts become meaningful?

Again, what is the origin of language? Since we are talking about *origin*, the problem is to account for the transition from meaninglessness to meaningfulness. As such, we can obviously not presuppose that our primitive ancestors understand each other before this transition has taken place. Here we encounter the first problem, because it seems that Schiffer's ancestors happen to have an already sophisticated understanding of their respective grunts.

> Suppose that in a certain community a certain type of sound (*nc*) means "there's a rabbit hunt today". It is clear that it is not solely in virtue of any of its physical or observable features that this sound has the meaning it has. No one could tell by simply hearing the sound that it has meaning. In another community the same type of sound may mean something entirely different or nothing at all.[76]

Schiffer's primitive sound (*nc*) (an acronym for non-composite that conveniently also abbreviates non-conventional), already means a 'whole composite utterance type' like 'there is a rabbit hunt today.' But how does one unarticulated grunt mean this much? A singular, unstructured, grunt—a grunt indistinguishable from other grunts—can hardly mean anything at all; how does it mean a complex sentence as 'there is a rabbit hunt today'—unless this sentence already exists in the linguistic repertoire of the tribe, and the grunt simply has become a short-hand expression, a label, for the sentence?

If the single, unstructured grunt were expressing a complex sentence, the 'grunt' would always-already differentiate several issues, such as the fauna of the region (a rabbit being distinct from, e.g., a fox, a deer, or a boar); or human activity (hunting being distinct from, e.g., harvesting, cooking, or sacrificing), while also establishing explicit deictic and temporal markers (here versus there; today in distinction to tomorrow or yesterday). On this stipulation, a non-composite primitive grunt cannot mean a composite complex sentence; a grunt is still not language. (Repeating our caveat from above: if a certain grunt has been *assigned* the meaning 'there is a rabbit hunt today'—like ringing a bell in a pub can mean 'I'm buying everybody a round'—then it is because a language, wherein the relevant sentence occur, *already* exists, a language then differentiating fauna, human activity, etc. Consequently, the grunt is not primordial.)

Such a grunt is in itself meaningless. It is not qua its "physical features" (its sound-image) that "it has the meaning it has" (it is already established that it has meaning), and it is not by hearing the sound that we could know that the grunt means 'there is a rabbit hunt today,' because the same grunt could mean something different, or mean nothing, in "another language" (it is established that this primordial precursor of language is in fact already a language (or part of a language)). The problem being: if these sounds in themselves are meaningless, how come that they are meaningful for our grunting ancestors? How can they take a grunt, which in itself is nothing, to mean 'there is a rabbit hunt today'?

But is this not a problem artificially created by Schiffer himself; is it not he who assigns a complex meaning to the non-complex grunt that it cannot possibly have (consequently, is not the problem non-existent in the first place)? If a grunt had meaning, the problem of *why* it has it seems to apply to all language—in a sense, language is nothing but a system of 'grunts.' That a grunt can mean something is not any more enigmatic than any word in a language can mean something. The fact that a sound means nothing in itself, and could mean something different or nothing in another language does not apply specifically to the grunt, but to all language, for example to the English sentence, there is a rabbit hunt today. In another language, it also means nothing. The sound-images, 'r a b i t,' 'h u n t,' and 't o d a y' mean nothing in themselves.

Schiffer offers another example on 'non-composite' primordial sounds. This sound is also meant to have no meaning *as yet*, although— in this case too—this new primitive sound is equipped with meaning before it logically and chronologically could have any. The new example is 'grrr.' This sound means, says Schiffer, 'I am angry,' and speaker and auditor will before having a language understand its meaning.

The example is that S and A are stranded on "a desert island without any language or other conventional means of communication."[77] They are aware of only one thing, that 'grrr' means 'I am angry,' because 'grrr' resembles the sound a dog makes when it is angry. "[S] knows that it is mutual knowledge between him and A that 'grrr' resembles the sound dogs make when they are angry."[78] They both had encounters with angry dogs, so when S growls, A—by association to her knowledge of mad dogs—infers that S is angry. 'Grrr' is a non-conventional means of communicating 'I am angry' ('I am angry' would have been a conventional means).

But how do S and A without a language know that 'grrr' means 'I am angry'? It is not enough that S as by a lucky strike of inspiration gets the idea that he could growl in order to express anger, and that A equally luckily understands the hint, remembers mad dogs, and eliminates alternative interpretations like, say, 'he must mean that he is a dog' . . . 'is something stuck in his throat?'(—granted, for the sake of argument, that she could think thus far without language).

Schiffer believes that S must also know that A knows what 'grrr' means and S must know that A knows that S knows what 'grrr' means. However, this additional requirement contravenes the attempt to explain the origin of language. It is suggested that the interlocutors have already established foreknowledge of the meaning of the first word: if S knows that A already knows what 'grrr' means, and knows that A knows that S knows what 'grrr' means, then S and A mutually always-already know the meaning of 'grrr.' So, they may be stranded on a desert island, but they have a language after all. If for a moment we believed that we were brought us back to witness the naked conception of the first word, we have been disappointed.[79]

There seems furthermore to be some uncertainty about of how strong Schiffer wants to make his assertion. Are we dealing with the origin of language itself or with a moment after the origin of language? Are we talking about the *first* utterance of a word, or about the *second* utterance of a word whose meaning has been already established as mutual knowledge in a previous first utterance? Schiffer suggests both of these two possibilities: (a) it is mutual knowledge between S and A that growling means anger, and (b) it is not yet mutual knowledge; it has be learnt or established. In citations under *Ad (a)* below, S and A already know the meaning of 'grrr.' In citations under *Ad (b)*, S and A still don't know.

> *Ad (a)*: [S] knows that it is mutual knowledge between him and A that 'grrr' resembles the sounds dogs make when they are angry. . . . It is mutual knowledge between S and A that at t_1 S meant that was angry by uttering 'grrr'.[80]
>
> *Ad (b)*: We . . . could not have predicted at t_1 [first instance of enunciation] what S would utter in order to communicate to A that he was angry. . . . we may suppose that at t_1 S was not very confident that 'grrr' would be an efficacious means of communicating to A that S was angry. . . . *Ex Hypothesi*, A managed, with difficulty, to guess that S uttered 'grrr' intending thereby to communicate to A that S was angry. The difficulty A had in figuring out what S was up to was due to A's not having prior knowledge of what S believed he could accomplish by uttering 'grrr'.[81]

The assertion of the first set of quotations is obviously the least interesting, since it ignores the problem that it is supposed to solve, and presupposes a situation where already language is born. The second cluster of quotations asserts a true origin of language, a so-called time-one (t_1) as the time for the original and first utterance of a 'word.' At time-one, the interlocutors have no established meaning of the primordial proto-word.

The theory about time-one is, however, inadequate and unsatisfactory too, since it becomes a theory about learning by means of repetition. According to this theory, meaning is established in repetition; however, nothing is being repeated. The theory asserts that the more the interlocutors utter their first word, the more certain they become of its meaning. The 'probability' of it being understood increases with the number of repetitions. It is easier for our ancestor to know at t_2 [second instance of enunciation] that growling indicates that S is angry than it was at t_1: "At t_2, however, we may suppose that S regards 'grrr' as a much surer means of communicating to A that he is angry than it was at t_1."[82] The 'probability' of knowing that 'grrr' means 'I am angry' is at t_2 "proportionally greater than it was at t_1."[83] At t_3 [third instance of enunciation], the probability increases even further, etc.

Understanding increases with use. This theory of increased probability of understanding is Schiffer's best explanation of the origin of language. We notice here that the problem of the origin of language is as intractable as ever; the theory explains how it becomes increasingly easier to understand a word at its second, third, and fourth time of use, but the theory has still not managed to explain the first time of use. It can at best suggest that at t_1 people can still not 'predict,' they are still not 'very confident,' they understand 'with difficulty' the meaning of this primordial first word. And then, nonetheless, somehow, for some reason, at some point (still in t_1) things become more predictable, the confidence is restored, and the difficulties are overcome. But how? Insofar as we aspire to explain the *origin* of language, the gist of understanding will necessarily have to happen in t_1 before we can take the next, more confident, step towards t_2. Before we can *repeat*, and in the repetition consolidate our knowledge, we need something to repeat. Repetition is always repeating something, which must have occurred at least once before; in Schiffer, however, we never encounter this first instance.

It is not the intention here to be too hard on Schiffer because he cannot explain this first instance; since my general argument is that *nobody* could. However lucid and brilliant a philosopher Schiffer is, he must strand on this problem like everybody else. Still, Herder's explanation on the origin of language seems to me superior to Schiffer's because he is offering us as foundation of language something *other* than language. Herder realizes that in order to establish an origin of language, one must introduce into the discourse something *other* than language itself. The pre-condition for the first word is to Herder the consolidation of the *psychological image of the thing in repetition*—the psychological image that today we tend to label the 'signified.' This psychological image stands out and is fixed against our floating impressions in pure perception, and it is to this image we attach a sound, Herder's 'bleating of the lamb'—a sound that today we tend to label the 'signifier.'

In Schiffer, the origin of language is language. If Schiffer's stranded islanders want to communicative meaning by means of a word, they essentially do so by employing a word they both know has this meaning. Employing Herder's example, Schiffer's word for lamb would be invented because of the *intention* to utter the word for lamb, and it would be understood because it is mutual understanding between S and A that 'bleating' is intended to mean lamb. At time-one, this may not be understood, but at time-two—miraculously—it would.[84]

A DESIRE FOR REASON

> *Vladimir*: (*sententious*). To every man his little cross.
> (*He sighs*.) Till he dies. (*Afterthought*.) And is
> forgotten.
> *Estragon*: In the meantime let us try and converse
> calmly, since we are incapable of keeping silent.
> *Vladimir*: You're right, we're inexhaustible.
> *Estragon*: It's so we won't think.
>   — Beckett: *Waiting for Godot.*[1]

(A) THE IDEAL; DETERMINING THE DESIDERATA

1) RECONSTRUCTING THE *A PRIORI* OF COMMUNICATION.
(i) Introduction to Habermas' Project. (ii) Developing Kant and Chomsky in Pragmatic Directions. (iii) Habermas' Emphatic Sense of 'Understanding.' (iv) Reconstructing the Self-Presence of the Communicative System of Rules.

(i) Introduction to Habermas' Project. According to Habermas, the purpose and telos of communication is to reach understanding and come to agreement about states of affairs. His theoretical project is to demonstrate the presence of an immanent force directed toward reason and understanding in the communicating subject. Universal reason is supposedly intrinsic in communicative actions; rationality does not depend on the arbitrary individual's strength of mind, sound judgment, self-reflective stance, etc. Rationality is a universal characteristic of the communicative behavior in mature speakers. The theoretical analysis of these universal features in communication is what Habermas calls *Universal* or *Formal Pragmatics.*

When engaging in dialogue, interlocutors allegedly meet as free and independent individuals with the inalienable right to either accept or reject the speech-offer proposed by the other. If, for example, the hearer detects inappropriateness or deception in the speaker, his speech-offer is deemed invalid and may be rejected. However, in genuine and authentic communication, the speaker does his sincerely best to make his speech-act acceptable and true, and the hearer does her sincerely best to recognize and accept the speaker's sincere and truthful effort. If a speech-act is acceptable according to a certain background of norms (a so-called 'validity-basis'), and is being recognized as such, speaker and hearer enter an interpersonal relationship where they recognize one another as responsible and accountable individuals.

The utterance of a communicating party is called a 'speech-offer' [*Sprachangebot*], since an offer can be either accepted or rejected. An 'offer' is similar to a proposal or a suggestion. Ego cannot claim success before Alter has accepted his offer. Utterances are thus dependent on their acceptance, and they have to fulfill certain conditions in order to secure this acceptance.

The dialogical exchange is in principle open to continuous criticism, since each utterance raises a corresponding condition for its success—it raises a so-called *validity-claim* [*Geltungsanspruch*]—which is in principle criticizable. The dialogical process unfolds as a perpetual, reciprocal 'check' on whether proposed validity-claims be vindicated.[2] If for example the speaker asserts something, he claims by *asserting* that his assertion is 'true'; the normative background for, or the validity-claim corresponding to, assertions is consequently *Truth*. The speaker therefore ought to 'redeem' his validity-claim; he ought to be truthful. If the speaker expresses an emotional state of mind, he claims by *expressing* that his expression is sincere; the normative background for, or the validity-claim corresponding to, expressions is thus *Sincerity*. The speaker therefore ought to 'redeem' that validity-claim; he ought to be sincere. (We notice here that the so-called validity-claims are integral parts of the definition, or the semantic content, of the corresponding illocutionary theme. According to the dictionary, asserting something is to utter a positive statement in which one declares or affirms something to be the case, or *true*. About this later.)

If the speaker in his conversation reflects and orients himself toward the imperative of validity-claims, he is presumably rational.

> The rationality of a person is proportionate to his expressing himself rationally and to his ability to give account for his expressions in a reflexive stance. A person expresses himself rationally insofar as he is oriented performatively toward validity claims: we say that he not only behaves rationally but is himself rational if he can give account for his orientation toward validity claims. We also call this kind of rationality *accountability*.[3]

Reflecting immanent communicative rationality, interlocutors encounter each other as accountable individuals, capable of sharing knowledge. Language-use is in Habermas never monological, but always dialogical. The two most important characters on his philosophical stage are obviously the speaker and the hearer. They have the precarious task to reach understanding or agreement about something. The path to this reciprocal understanding is laden with obstacles, but they will reach it if and insofar as they follow the inherent drive (thrust, motive) in language-use itself. They speak, and with this, they raise normative claims that request justification and vindication. If they actualize these normative requests, they are successful; if not, speech-offers can be criticized and/or rejected. As autonomous, individuals can respond with a 'yes' or 'no' to the speech-offer at issue. Since they can reach consensus about the validity of the claims raised in a speech-act, they are in principle able to reach understanding about and share knowledge about worldly states of affairs.

In reiterating this model, Habermas wants to emphasize that individuals are always social. They share a life-world, they share a language and the tacit knowledge of how to use it, and with this, they are able to also share their understanding of the life-world. The epistemological consequence of the theory is that the objective world is secured through the consensus that speakers reach through speech-acts. The knowledge that speakers produce about the world is social. They are not monads like Descartes and Husserl's philosophies could suggest that subjects are. In Habermas, we are not encountering the lonely Cogito's discovery of the world reflected in its own self, while situating itself at safe distance of—closing eyes and ear to—this world. We encounter a duality of Ego and Alter in their attempts to attain intersubjectively valid knowledge.

> *Communicative rationality* is expressed in the unifying force of speech oriented toward reaching understanding, which secures for the participating speakers an intersubjectively shared lifeworld, thereby securing at the same time the horizon within which everyone can refer to one and the same objective world.[4]

In their ability to reach agreement and share knowledge, speaker and hearer are able to act *rationally*. Habermas' notion of rationality is complex. The concept emerges as signifying different things. For example, it can be a ground (of regulative norms), but it also emerges as the (human) response to a ground. The notion is ambiguous probably because it constitutes one of Habermas' crucial *desiderata*. Being a *desideratum* it has several 'jobs' in the theory. It is engaged in too much deliverance.

Following Habermas, one can start noting that rationality is understood not as an inherent or substantive feature in individuals. It is not conceived as an ontological characteristic of the human constitution, like the inborn rational soul in Descartes. It rather exists because of the rational procedures of our speech-acts. It is so-called 'procedural.' It is a rationality, which Habermas believes is beyond metaphysical notions of rationality, because it can be reconstructed as the tacit and unthematized presuppositions underlying all pragmatic use of language. We might say that rationality is understood, not as a quality *in* the subject, but as a quality *between* subjects, emerging from the tacit (rational) presuppositions in normal and non-pathological language-use that silently direct us as speakers. Thus, abstractly speaking, Habermas focuses on what happens *between* entities on a background of transcendental norms. He does not locate rationality or understanding in any one entity, but 'in' the space between them. This space, we can understand as 'the social.' Ideally, rationality is realized when the response to the normative requirements of speech has been affirmative, and when agreement and consensus have been achieved between interlocutors about an aspect of the intersubjectively shared life-world. When validity-claims have been vindicated—and recognized as vindicated—understanding is achieved and agreement established.

As ground *and* response to a ground, rationality is achieved in the positive reaction to the inherent rational-normative background of speech. Speech motivates us to be rational and if we are thus motivated, we are rational. Speech raises validity-claims and humans redeem them. Speech appeals and humans respond. The human *freedom* to choose in which manner to respond also explains why there is irrationality abound; in this theology (that reminiscences St. Augustine's explanation of evil), human *freedom* implies that humans can choose wisely or poorly. They can respond to the inherent rational motive in speech, or they can deflect from, ignore, or manipulate this motive. In St. Augustine, evil does not exist except as the absence of the good; likewise in Habermas, irrational communication is the absence of a proper response to the rational norms guiding communication.

(ii) Developing Kant and Chomsky in Pragmatic Directions. Habermas' methodology has features in common with Kant and, above all, with Chomsky. We notice that as well as Kant wanted to determine the transcendental conditions for possible experience, Habermas' project is parallel in the sense that he wants to determine the transcendental conditions for possible communication. There are, however, crucial

differences between the methodologies of Kant and Habermas. Kant was led to postulate the existence of 2 + 12 categories organizing respectively our perception and understanding of the world. The categories had necessarily to be determined as universal and *a priori*; otherwise, Kant could not maintain (in contradistinction to Hume) the uniformity of certain experiences constituting scientific cognition, such as causality. Therefore, on top of being synthetic, certain experiential propositions also had to contain *a priori* components. Habermas now applies the crux of this idea to the project of communicative action. Communication is no longer perceived as an empirical and contingent fact; it proceeds according to certain transcendental conditions that always-already organize the communicative processes. Habermas does not like Kant list a total of fourteen categories, but he suggests a list of four; or, to be precise, a list of 1 + 3, since the first requirement is not strictly communicative, but linguistic (it fundamentally requires a sentence to be linguistically comprehensible and grammatically correct). Moreover, Habermas' validity-claims do not have the same cognitive status as Kant's categories. They are not categories of the mind, substantively and immanently regulating subjective perception and cognition; they are immanent rules for speech. To repeat from above, they emerge from speech exchanges, not from a subject impressing its constitutional make-up on the world; they do not appear as something *in*, but rather as something *between*, subjects, namely from the speech-exchange itself.

In working out this project, Habermas has been especially inspired by Chomsky's development of Generative Grammar. Chomsky's project was to reconstruct the grammatical rules for the formation of 'well-formed' sentences, as they were inherent in language-use, but immanently so and practiced only unknowingly by the speaker. Linguistic competency was understood as an inherent knowledge of grammatical rules enabling the adult speaker to form an unlimited number of sentences from a limited number of linguistic elements. As such, linguistic competency would rely on preconscious and pre-theoretical knowledge of a rule-system, which in the background was seen as regulating the generation of sentences. This rule-system was by Chomsky reconstructed as a general grammar.

It is this general methodological approach that Habermas applies to the formation of utterances. It is Habermas' postulate that there is not only a rule-system for the generation of grammatically correct sentences, but for the generation of pragmatically correct *use* of sentences as well. Speakers have pre-theoretical knowledge not only of how to form grammatical sentences, but also of the formation of 'correct' utterances. This implicit pragmatic rule-system can be reconstructed in a pragmatic analysis that is in principle as rigorous as Chomsky's linguistic analyses. Because of the supposed rigor, the pragmatic reconstruction is frequently described as a *reconstructive science*.

> I would like to defend the thesis that not only language but speech too—that is, the employment of sentences in utterrances—is accessible to formal analysis [*logischen Analyse*]. Like the elementary units of language (sentences), the elementary units of speech (utterances) can be analyzed from the methodological stance of a reconstructive science [*einer rekonstructiven Wissenschaft*].[5]

When we speak, we not only form sentences correctly, according to an intuitive knowledge of grammar, we also *use correctly* correct sentences. In addition to observing a grammatical rule-system, the speaker has to guarantee follow-up on the theme introduced in her speech-act, that is, vindicate raised validity-claims. A promise must be kept, an assertion must be true, an expression of emotion must be sincere, a reprimand must be justified, etc.

This 'communicative competence of rules' is as universal as is the 'linguistic competence of rules' in Chomsky; however, it expands the set of requirements a speaker needs to master. Whereas a speaker only needs to fulfill the claim of understandability in order to utter a well-formed *sentence*, a speaker must now fulfill a set of three additional validity-claims in order to utter an opportune *utterance*.

> Whereas [linguistics] starts from the assumption that every adult speaker possesses a reconstructible implicit knowledge in which his linguistic rule competence (to produce sentences) is expressed, speech-act theory postulates a corresponding communicative rule competence, namely the competence to employ sentences in speech acts.[6]

The two parallel projects investigate respectively sentences and utterances, grammatical competence and communicative competence. They perform respectively a linguistic analysis of sentences and a pragmatic analysis of utterances. It is here Habermas' insight that in actual discourse, it is not sufficient to express a sentence comprehensibly and correctly, one must express it relevantly too. The plain grammatical formation of a sentence does not situate it relevantly within the empirical circumstances for its utterance; as such, it is still in the abstract, still non-contextualized. Before it can be judged as relevant, and validated by the listener, the sentence has to be situated on three additional levels.

> In relation to (a) the external reality [*äußeren Realität*] of that which can be perceived, (b) the internal reality [*inneren Realität*] of that which a

speaker would like to express as her intentions, and (c) the normative reality [*normativen Wirklichkeit*] of that which is socially and culturally recognized. It is hereby subjected to validity claims that it need not and cannot fulfill as a non-situated sentence, as a purely grammatical formation.[7]

To the requirement of linguistic comprehensibility, Habermas therefore adds his three validity conditions, an utterance (a) has to be true, (b) has to be sincere, and (c) has to be right.

(iii) Habermas' Emphatic Sense of 'Understanding.' When Habermas reiterates—in virtually all his essays on communication—that it is the task of a theory of communicative action to reconstruct immanent principles securing understanding, his notion of 'understanding' is not necessarily coextensive with the trivially obvious notion we find in the dictionary, or in common usage.

> The task of universal pragmatics is to identify and reconstruct universal condition of possible mutual understanding [*Verständigung*].[8] . . . The concept of communicative action develops the intuition that the telos of reaching understanding is inherent in language.[9]

The conventional notion of understanding is replaced with a broader or 'deeper' notion that is also cautiously described as *possible* or *ideal* (as indicated in the quotations above: '*possible* mutual understanding,' 'the *telos* of reaching understanding'). To 'understand' is not to understand the semantics and grammaticality of a sentence in a natural language, because in that trivial sense, sentences are also understood under conditions where there is no one with whom to reach understanding, for example when read (or written) in solitary mental life; that is, in situations where Alter is absent. To 'understand' is to '*reach* understanding,' to bring about *agreement* between the interlocutors. In the realization of this agreement, the world is constituted as a communal lifeworld about which interlocutors share knowledge.[10] To *reach* or *come to* an understanding is meant to realize cooperative and mutually tolerant relations between individuals, perhaps of a private or tacit kind, but regulating joint communicative action. Habermas emphasizes the *mutuality* in coming to an understanding.

In Habermas' notion of *understanding*, we are thus talking less about *Verständigung* (usually translated 'understanding') than about *Einverständnis* (usually translated 'agreement'). 'Understanding' as *Einverständnis* is the mutual approval, acceptance, and agreement between at least two agents; I cannot reach *Einverständnis* with myself.[11]

In earlier essays, the distinction between *Verständigung* and *Einverständnis* is blurred, but in later essays, Habermas tries to draw a distinct line between these two modes of understanding. One mode of understanding is now so-called 'actor-relative,' the other, stronger, mode is so-called 'actor-independent.' One can reach agreement in a weak sense [*Verständigung*], and in a strong sense [*Einverständnis*]. [12]

> *Agreement* in the strict sense [in the sense of *Einverständnis*] is achieved only if the participants are able to accept a validity claim for the same reasons, while *mutual understanding* [*Verständigung*] can also come about when one participant sees that the other, in light of her preferences, has good reasons in the given circumstances for her declared intention—that is, reasons that are good *for her*—without having to make these reasons his own in light of his preferences [Habermas' emphases]. [13]

When justifying a validity-basis of speech, Habermas often refers to a minimum condition that (supposedly) nobody sane and sound could deny takes effect in speech-exchanges. This minimum-condition accounts for the realization of two fundamental themes in typical utterances, locutionary content and illocutionary force. An utterance typically includes these two components, it is expressed in a certain mode (as an assertion, an order, a question, a request, etc.), and it contains propositional content. This double-structure is often formalized $F(p)$—F corresponding to force, and p to propositional content.

As speakers, we enter an interpersonal relationship when we suggest something to somebody in a certain mode. The mode, in which we suggest something to somebody 'binds' us as speakers to be normatively *correct* and *sincere*, the content that we suggest obligates us to *truth*. Habermas therefore assumes that (under ideal circumstances) we are, as interlocutors, accountable and sincere; it is under that assumption, we, secondly, must assume that we can reach agreement about what we suggest to one another.

Thanks to this double-structure, speaker and hearer now enter a situation where they 'between themselves reach agreement about something'—in Habermas' formulation, '*miteinander über etwas zu einigen.*' The formulation condenses the two major moments in the speech-act: first, the '*miteinander . . . zu einigen*'—indicating the illocutionary binding and bonding between two subjects; and secondly, the '*über etwas*'—indicating the locutionary reference to a state of affairs in the world.

If minimally, speech-acts have this double-structure, Habermas' philosophy hinges especially on the 'binding and bonding' force of the illocutionary component: "The illocutionary role . . . determines the aspect of validity under which the speaker wants his utterance to be understood *first and foremost* [Habermas' emphasis]."[14] It is due to this 'binding and bonding' force of the illocutionary component that speech is essentially directed towards understanding as *Einverständnis*. *Agreement* is tacitly inherent in all *understanding* as ideal. Habermas' 'strong' or 'emphatic' sense of understanding implies the *coming to an understanding, reaching agreement,* or *securing consensus.* Proposing this emphatic sense, he adds a normative component to the speech-act. Whether explicitly or tacitly, he assumes that we not only speak to be understood (without pondering the hearer's reaction); our speech-acts are adjusted towards reaching agreement.

The abstract division of the speech-act in illocutionary and locutionary force was originally suggested by Austin, and elaborated by Searle. In Habermas, this division has now consequences beyond those envisioned by the speech-act philosophers—according to who a speech-act would have an illocutionary component whether or not the interlocutors 'bind and bond.' That is, Habermas' emphatic *miteinander* is an additional requirement that does not define the speech-act in the formulations it original has among speech-act philosophers. In speech-act theory, an utterance uttered can be adequately responded to without addresser and addressee necessarily entering any emphatic contract. It typically prompts a certain 'uptake' or 'invites response' (Austin). Speech-act philosophy would classify transpiration of agreement between speakers, beyond 'uptake,' as a perlocutionary, not an illocutionary, effect. In contrast, in Habermas every speech-act is contractual. Speakers must *accept* each other's speech offers. Besides being understood in a context, speech-acts have the consequence that speakers *bond.*

Furthermore, in Austin and Searle's sense of achieving understanding, it is not required that speakers are 'rational.' Insofar as speech-act theory in general applies to speech, it applies equally well to 'rational' and 'irrational' speakers. One must admit that also 'irrational' people speak (it is traditionally noted that they speak more than their 'rational' counterparts). But if *understanding,* in Habermas' emphatic sense, means to reach agreement and secure consensus, speech requires a fundamental rational procedure to guarantee this consensus. In Habermas' emphatic sense, we do not merely understand an utterance, we linguistically accept and embrace each other in our utterances. In these linguistic embraces, we have become transparent to each other, because in some deeper sense, we *Understand* and *Agree* (capitalized & italicized in order to emphasize the anasemic quality of Habermas' notion).

However desirable this rational ideal may be, reviewed on the background of everyday speech-situations, it appears counter-intuitive. We can marshal a host of examples on ordinary speech-situations defying Habermas' emphatic ('anasemic') notion of understanding. One example suffices: At the end of a class—students scrambling to escape the classroom—the teacher shouts: 'read from page this to page that for the next session.' We may assume that the students *understand* the illocutionary component of the utterance (i.e., as a *request* or *order*), and also that they pre-consciously *accept* that a teacher has a right to adopt this authoritative manner in speaking to students, but where is the *miteinander* in Habermas' emphatic sense; and especially, where is the *miteinander zu einigen*?

Habermas' emphatic understanding of *understanding* has the additional effect that speech-acts that are *not* aiming at *Understanding* (capitalized-emphatic-anasemic) disappear from Habermas' scheme. They of course have existence (as Habermas well knows), but they are no longer genuine speech-acts; they are difficult-to-classify hybrids; perversions of true speech. This will include all forms of manipulative, strategic, instrumental, disingenuous, insincere, etc., speech-acts—in short, 'immoral' and 'evil' uses of speech. Habermas (a professional philosopher) obviously never uses heavily loaded terms such as 'evil,' but he frequently talks about 'parasitic' uses of language. If or when *miteinander über etwas* means to embrace each other in mutual agreement, speech-acts that are *concealed* or *openly strategic* invalidate themselves as genuine speech-acts. Threats, or other 'open strategic actions,' have to be explained by adding new explanations to the theory; in this case an explanation of how some speech-acts that apparently employ the same formal components as genuine speech-acts, nevertheless are parasitic on authentic language use.

We shall return to the theory of parasitic speech-acts, for now it suffices to point out that in Habermas' strong and emphatic sense of 'understanding,' the notion is turned into an *anaseme*. An *anaseme*, I understand as a *seme* that is *ana*, beyond or besides the acknowledged class of semes, thus a seme that has no existence in any known dictionary (—we cannot look up Habermas' *Understanding* in a dictionary). It is kept alive without a conventional definition and only through its location in a conceptual grid. Referring to Grice above, the word has received an 'occasion'-meaning unique to the word, and dependent of the conceptual system of Habermas. Its 'definition' is a set of other *anasemes*, which in turn, it helps defining. (—*Understanding* has little to do with 'understanding' plainly, but is has a lot to do with 'agreement,' 'sincerity,' 'rationality,' 'equality,' and even 'democracy.')

The *anaseme* is often, we shall now suggest, the *desideratum* of the theory; it is the always-insufficient name of a desire that lives in the philosopher as a vision of the good, the right, or the necessary. *Reaching Understanding* (capitalized-emphatic-anasemic) becomes the combined foundation and telos of the theory of communicative action; it becomes a root-word that always escapes pragmatic definition.

(iv) Reconstructing the Self-Presence of the Communicative System of Rules. We read in Habermas that Universal Pragmatics performs a "reconstruction of *general and unavoidable presuppositions* of possible processes of reaching understanding [my emphasis]."[15] It has the aim of "clarifying the presuppositions of the rationality of processes of reaching understanding that may be presumed to be *universal* because they are *unavoidable* [my emphases]."[16] Despite the universalistic and essentialist motive in Universal Pragmatics, Habermas remains convinced that his philosophy represents a break with traditional metaphysics or first philosophy [*Ursprungsphilosophie*]. From the same passage as quoted from above, we continue: "Philosophy breaks with its aspirations of first philosophy (*Ursprungsphilosophie*) in any form." And yet, "this does not mean that philosophy abandons its role as the guardian of rationality."[17]

As said, Universal Pragmatics is understood as a 'reconstructive *science.*' Given the assumption that communicative rationality is immanent in language-use, Universal Pragmatics merely reconstructs, through analysis, the underlying laws for communicative rationality. Being *reconstructive*, the theory does not *add* to what already exists as an immanent system of rules [*Regelsystem*]. Neither does it speculate, since as *reconstructive*, it merely discloses and unveils the system of rules in its presence to itself, that is, in its self-presence of what already exist as unthematized presuppositions. As *reconstructive*, the theory of communicative competence uncovers the rule-system according to which it is possible for speakers to enter situations of possible understanding. Reconstruction makes explicit this background of universal rules, which, implicitly and pre-consciously, competent speakers already employ in their speech-acts.

As Habermas concedes, reconstruction must according to these assumptions make an essentialist claim [*einen essentialistischen Anspruch*]. If and insofar as the reconstruction is precise, it corresponds exactly to the essential rules that regulate actual dialogue; it discloses exactly the pre-conscious structure of the speaker's rule-competency [*Regelkompetenz*].

> To a certain extent, reconstructions make an essentialist claim [*essentialitischen Anspruch*]. One can say, of course, that theoretical descriptions 'correspond' [*'entsprechen'*] (if true) to certain structures of reality [*Strukturen der Wirklichkeit*] in the same sense as reconstructions 'bear a likeness' (if correct) to the deep structures explicated.[18]

Because *reconstruction* can hit or miss factual, albeit deep-structural, rules, reconstruction can establish itself as *science*. Since competency-rules allegedly are factual, reconstruction is falsifiable; it relates to a reality whose essence it may have, in principle, *failed* to grasp.[19] But exactly because reconstruction can grasp—or, indeed, *fail* to grasp—certain 'structures of reality' [*Strukturen der Wirklichkeit*], these structures is conceived as self-present; that is, as an universal underground they exist in and for themselves. They are unmoved by the philosopher's interpretations, which, in the best of cases, they only illuminate with the light of truth. And still, whether they become known or they remain unknown in their self-sufficient existence, they inform our speech. They are the unmoved movers of communication. As such, they represent a foundational underground for communication that is in principle immutable and universally present.[20]

According to this conception, Habermas repeats a rather common metaphysical model. The principles of communication may not have been situated *substantively* in the cognitive apparatus à la Kant's categories, but substantive allocation certainly constitutes a minor determination of metaphysics; metaphysical axioms never needed a substantive element in order to exist. Plato's Ideas also exist nowhere. Habermas' communicative principles may not be 'categories' in the mind, but they are transcendental nonetheless. However, reconstructive methodology convinces Habermas that his theory of communication is non- or *post-metaphysical*, because the mere *disclosure* of a fact cannot be implying an application of transcendental and outer-worldly principles. Reconstruction is committed to bring into the open what already exists. But exactly, bringing the already existent into the open, disclosing self-sufficient self-presence, unveiling the in-and-for-itself, has been comprehensively analyzed as a metaphysical operation *par excellance*—so, for example, by Heidegger. This metaphysical operation is by Heidegger determined as truth in the Greek sense of *Aletheia*.

Habermas' metaphysical model impels him now to perceive Universal Pragmatics as a *science*; and accordingly, the validity of the reconstructive analysis would have to be determined according to a *correspondence theory* of truth, since it is the adequacy between the concept and the reality to which it refers that defines the success of the reconstruction.

This persistently introduced conception of validity-claims as an objective and 'essential' ground underlying processes of communication cannot be consonant with the elsewhere-suggested 'fallibilism' (see later), unless the whole theory is understood as some kind of *play*. However, *play* understood then in the most general sense—subtracting associations to 'fun,' 'entertainment,' 'emancipation,' 'anarchy,' 'laissez-aller,' and theoretical kindergarten—'play,' instead, implemented as an exercise or experiment, but still as a 'serious' theoretical piece of legislation. Experimenting, the philosopher asserts an ideal well knowing that it is not necessarily actually redeemable.

In this context, it is also puzzling how the correspondence theory of truth that emerges as a consequence of Habermas' 'essentialist' assumptions is coherent with the consensual theory of truth, which is defended elsewhere.[21] To mend the two conflicting theories of truth, one would have to adopt the double-stance that truth is reached by agreement (according to the consensus theory of truth), except the truth by which we reach agreement (according to the correspondence theory of truth).

2) PHILOSOPHICAL PROFESSIONALISM: NEUTRALIZING THE EFFECTS OF ONE'S DESIDERATUM.
(i) The Ideal and the Possible. (ii) A General Notion of Play.

(i) The Ideal and the Possible. The notion of philosophy as 'play' has been advanced a good one hundred years by so-called 'post-modernist' philosophers (from Nietzsche to Derrida). Unfortunately, the notion has often been associated with theoretical superficiality, anarchy, and frivolity (as indicated above), and it is therefore no wonder that 'serious' philosophers have loathed to see their work represented as and 'reduced' to 'play.' However, at least to Nietzsche (who is often seen as the ideological father of the notion), 'play' would in general indicate merely a metaphysically creative reason, a '*dichtende Vernunft*,' necessary in any 'legislating' and 'commanding' philosopher. In this context, the term must be seen as superlative, rather than degrading. To call a philosopher 'playful' is in this context tantamount to calling him 'thinking.' It is as thinking he 'plays.' His 'playfulness' is related to the problems he confronts himself with in his thinking, and the problem-solving he accomplishes in his thinking. According to this stipulation, nothing is more important in genuine philosophy, and nothing is pursued more seriously, than 'play.' When truly absorbed, the playing philosopher appreciates the play higher than reality; he or she may for that sake adopt the same seriousness as a child at play: reality retreats and the 'play' of posing and solving problems assumes an extraordinary

reality of its own. Thus, it is only the truly serious and genuine philosopher—only those chosen few who are still capable of recovering that infantile seriousness—that plays. It is my firm opinion that Habermas belongs to those capable and exemplary few.[22]

However, if thinking is 'play' and '*Dichtung*,' it has the consequence that foundational axioms are anchored no more profoundly than in the playful mind of their author. They remain, to revive the vocabulary from the introduction, within the same circle, despite an earnest effort of their author to validate them as Real (i.e., to break the spell of the circle). This tension, this dichotomy between *Play* and *Reality*, is consequently chiseled into the core of the theory. In the theory under discussion, the dichotomy takes the form of a struggle between two poles. According to the pragmatic philosopher, asserting the (his) *Real* ought to be a small feat, and yet it slips away, transforming itself into an *Ideal* or to what is merely *Possible*.

At the core of the theory, we find *indicators* signaling that the thinking-playing philosopher is not completely capable of fixating the Real of his thinking. We pick up these indicators at the surface of the text, as they *explicitly* denounce his essentially important project. Noticing these *indicators*, arousing them from their slumber, stamping out their repression, collides with the theoretical desire of the philosopher, who receives a certain 'satisfaction' (we must presume) by living the play and living *in* the play.[23]

We have been introduced to the validity-claims repeatedly; we ask ourselves, what do these validity-claims do to actual communication, or rather, what is Habermas saying that they are doing. We run through the various answers that suggest themselves, and arrive to the surprising, the almost mind-boggling, answer that he is approximately saying that they are doing nothing, or at least, what they are doing effects nothing *necessarily* and, even, effects nothing *typically*.

What the validity-claims guarantee is not 'understanding' but '*possible* understanding' [*mögliche Verständigung*]. If they assert anything, they assert an ideal, namely the ideal that understanding *could possibly be* reached. The validity-claims exist as a rule-system of pure potentiality, pure possibility. If they exist in speaking subjects, as they do in a nondescript sense, they exist as 'idealizing capabilities' [*Idealiserungsleistungen*]. When interlocutors enter a communicative situation, they anticipate or expect that it is in principle possible to achieve understanding. Qua this expectation, it is presupposed that potential misunderstandings can be solved through further discussion. It is believed that an infinite dialectic exchange, if it were exercised, would eventually solve all misunderstandings, and establish agreement.

Thus, Habermas knows that his proposal for rational communicative action idealizes everyday communication. Admittedly, the typical state of affairs is lack of understanding and agreement. Since an endless number of examples from everyday communication can be evoked as objections to and refutations of Habermas' ideal model of communication, he admits a 'gray-area' for typical cases of either non-rational communication, or communication about matters so trivial that there is nothing to reach understanding about.

> If full agreement, embracing all four of these components [the validity-claims], were a normal state of linguistic communication, it would not be necessary to analyze the process of reaching understanding from the dynamic perspective of bringing about an agreement. *The typical states are in the gray areas between, on the one hand, lack of understanding and misunderstanding, intentional and involuntary untruthfulness, concealed and open discord,* and on the other, preexisting or achieved consensus [my emphasis].[24]

> *Formal pragmatics*—which, in its reconstructive intention . . . is directed to the universal presuppositions of communicative action—*seems to be hopelessly removed from actual language use* [my emphasis].[25]

Habermas knows that he must exclude a wide range of typical situations in everyday speech-acts, such as manipulations, rebukes, insults, quarreling, lying, intentional or non-intentional insincerity, situations of open conflicts or disagreements, misunderstandings, etc. Still, Habermas will maintain that these situations, although they are perhaps more frequent, are not more *fundamental* than the rational and justificative speech-act in which understanding is achieved. The typical situations are still *marginal* in relation to the fundamental *core*. The distinction, *center versus margin* becomes equivalent to the distinction, *essential versus in-essential communication*, which is again equivalent to the distinction, *rational versus irrational communication.*

Seduced by his own idealizations, Habermas turns the world upside-down. The world of everyday language is marginalized, and the world of highly formalized rules of communication centralized. Habermas' elite rules for good linguistic behavior are universalized, despite being (almost) universally absent.

We notice another problem in this thinking. Normativity has tacitly been *doubly* inscribed in Habermas' theory. *Essential & rational* communication is not only distinguished by constituting a background for normative regulation of speech, this background is itself a norm for language-users to adopt. They adopt as a norm a pragmatic rule-system that itself executes a norm. Habermas explains carefully and in depth how *essential & rational* communication is regulated from its background of validity-claims, but he does not explain what it would take for humans to adopt, or *why* humans should adopt, *essential & rational* communication as their norm. Neither does he explain why this norm is so frequently ignored. If humans have good and essential reasons to behave rationally, why then ignore this call of nature? This leaves an odd arbitrariness within the theory: *essential & rational* communication is the alleged exemplary model for language-use, however (as acknowledged), the model is rarely executed 'in the real.' Humans, in general, speak a language that deviates from the exemplary model that is supposed to explain language-use in its essence. What is now the status of this model if humans fail to adopt it? What is the validity of a linguistic essence, which is admittedly rarely observed?

Mutual understanding presupposes that in speech we raise validity-claims while tacitly promising to vindicate them. Since mutual understanding is an ideal that typically remains unrealized in actual communication, the expectation of the realization of this ideal is also described as 'counter-factual' [*kontra-faktische Erwartungen*]. On one hand, there is no doubt that Habermas and followers recognize that actual communication is typically misunderstood, distorted, fragmented, manipulative, etc.; one the other hand, this recognition does not influence their emphasis on the fundamental significance of the ideal. Universal validity-claims do hardly effect actual communication; still they are imperatively important.[26] Interlocutors at least 'presupposes' this ideal universality: "I shall develop the thesis than anyone acting communicatively must, in performing any speech act, raise universal validity claims [*universale Geltungsansprüche*] and suppose that they can be vindicated [*ihre Einlösbarkeit unterstellen muß*]."[27] And Habermas' commentator, Helga Gripp, internalizing Habermas' style to perfection, underlines the necessity of this ideal expectation: "Wir unterstellen im kommunikativen Handeln die prinzipielle möglichkeit eines Diskurses unter idealen Bedingungen."[28] Notice here the double modification: a 'possibility in principle' under 'ideal conditions.' Although never or rarely realized in actual dialogue, counter-factual expectations to validity-claims are still the indispensable telos and ideal for communication.

> In everyday life, we start from a background consensus pertaining to those interpretations taken for granted among participants. As soon as this consensus is shaken, and as soon as the presupposition that the validity claims are satisfied . . . is suspended in the case of at least one of the four claims, communicative action cannot be continued.[29]

Habermas is inclined to claim that without anticipating this ideal, one even involves oneself in a performative self-contradiction. That is, without this necessary presupposition, one enters a communicative situation without the desire or will to communicate rationally and to reach mutual understanding; and this is performatively self-contradictory (more about this performative contradiction in part C below). Habermas' idea can be expressed in brief, whenever we enter a dialogue, we *necessarily* anticipates an *ideal* speech-situation [*ideale Sprechsituation*] as a necessary *fiction* of immanent *foundation* for *factual* less-than-ideal speech-situations.

(ii) A General Notion of Play. The difficulties in Habermas' project is inscribed in his texts in the form of disclaimers and other stylistic devices. As such, this inscription is *not* unconscious; it is rather fully conscious; but the consciousness of difficulties will have no implications, no consequences for the elaboration of the theory, or for the persistent belief in its urgency.[30]

We notice a struggle between an Ideal-Real (the validity-claims) and a Factual-Real (actual communication), where the Ideal-Real, which in this model is the *desideratum*, is destined to miss the Factual-Real. The Ideal-Real establishes itself as a telos, but as a telos whose realization is postponed *ad infinitum* to an abstract future. Its function is purely regulative but, in the last analysis, no one is being regulated—or blissful ignorance of the regulation seems to be the order of the day. Because of this situation, Habermas' discourse is full of qualifiers, we talk about an '*ideale Sprechsituation*,' about '*mögliche Verständigung*,' about '*kontrafaktische erwartungen*,' about a '*principielle möglichkeit rationale kommunikation*,' about '*idealiserungleistungen*,' etc.: in my vocabulary, *indicators* on the philosophy's status of *play*.

Since this situation is acknowledged, Habermas is careful not to state his desideratum as concrete or actual, and professionally, he modifies his discourse by means of qualifiers like those mentioned above. It is in doing this that I suggest that Habermas 'inscribes' the impossibility of his project in his theory. It is *because of* (not despite of) his philosophical professionalism that the discourse is modified in the first place. Lesser philosophers would confuse *truth* and *reality*; they would insist that the transcendental idealizations they pronounce overwhelm patent and actual life-forms.

Still, to play on truth is the most serious of businesses. The traditional and superficial dichotomies, play vs. serious, play vs. work, do not suggest themselves here; they are suspended because the play *is* serious (philosophical) work. Playing means now, thinking about the ideal, knowing that *the ideal is not manifest*, but promising that *it will be or is becoming*, because already *it is constituted as potentiality.*

This fundamental idea of Habermas we can render as a *figure*, since it can be formalized in various ways. It is a figure that it as old as thinking itself, and since it asserts itself about the existence of idealities and essences (*truth*), we may indeed call it *metaphysical*. Several questions and objections could be raised to this metaphysical figure. Harking back to problems introduced above, we could imagine the following: Why is it that whenever engaging in deficient communication, we assume an ideal speech-situation? Why is the perfect necessary for the existence of the imperfect? How come that the ideal, despite being perpetually frustrated, still exercises influence? What exigencies, forces, or drives feed its persistent and patient optimism? Why is it that the perfect, being primary, ideal and preferred over the imperfect, did not take control over communication a long time ago? Why is it still being marred by less-than-ideal factual situations? Habermas surely addresses some of these or similar question and tries to solve them. My claim is that they are question to the *figure*, and that there is, within the geometry of this figure, *no good solution* to them.

If for example we try to formalize and concretize this figure, we might imagine the following simple model: *a circle*. We have a center and a circumference; and this is how we might envision the relationship between *Ideal-Real & Factual-Real, Truth & Real*—i.e., as center & circumference; the ideal is occupying the center, and the factual the circumference. The ideal is appropriately the center because as the ideally real, it supposedly infuses the factually real with its form, and it ought to do so from a location that is equidistant from its manifold of objects (it ought to take equally care of all speech-acts, and, so to speak, not let down any of them). Furthermore, the ideally real is the *One* (like the point of a center), whereas the factually real is the *Many* (like the innumerable points making up the line of the circumference).

So, if this is a possible formalization of Habermas' basic idea, an image of its *structure*, it is now palpable that this figure can offer *no solution* to the type of questions posed above. Asking, for example, why is the ideal counter-factual, why is it not realized, why does it not control communication in the first place, etc., is now similar to asking, why is there a distance between center and circumference; why is the center not equal to its circumference; why is not the center encircling the circumference; why is not a point equal to many; (etc.)? As is evident, such questioning is impossible within the geometry of a circle; within this geometry, these questions have no solutions. The figure itself prohibits a solution.

Similarly, metaphysics consists of figures of thought that are constructed in such a way that they cannot be further reduced, analyzed, or broken up. Metaphysical 'logic' seems to defy logic, but we have no logic by which to rectify this situation. Because we cannot help ourselves out of this situation, there is therefore something equally absurd in requiring the philosopher to explain himself, and in the philosopher trying to explain himself. When we address these last grounds or justifications, we ask questions to a figure that offer no possible solutions beyond its unsatisfactory self-repetition, and we bestow upon the philosopher the impossible task to resolve the irresolvable.

(B) THE INSIDE AND THE OUTSIDE

1) THE LEGITIMATE INSIDE
(i) Within the Text, and Beyond. (ii) The Inside of Three Validity-Claims; The Meaning of the Number Three in Habermas.

(i) Within the Text, and Beyond. There seem to exist a class of distinctions, which are—as much as the text will assert them as distinctions—*secretly* characterized by identity. They behave as both distinctions and identities within the same text. This class of distinctions renders a formula that in the next section I shall call a 'logic of illogicality.' When formalized the logic is necessarily nonsensical:

$$[\exists: p, q | (p \neq q \cap p = q)]$$

In other words: there exists a class of oppositions for which it is the case that the oppositions are both different and identical. This nonsensical 'law' says that certain oppositions—that perhaps initially suggest themselves as intuitively clear, obvious, and harmless—tend to collapse when the author, in his obligation to explain, elucidate, and justify the distinctiveness of the distinctions, puts them under explanatory pressure.[31]

The most radical conclusion we can draw from this insight is the remarkable one that *difference does not really exist.* We have here to insert a (vague) 'really,' because, *practically,* in our actual cultural life-world differences are constantly asserted, and, *theoretically,* in its material manifestation, the text is nothing but an endless series of differences. However, this inherently discriminatory universe evaporates under scrutiny. *Beyond* our conventionally erected life-world, and *beyond* the text, we live in a world without differences.[32] Our universe is inherently non-discriminatory. At the bottom of our reality, there is no (theoretical, cultural, political, or psychological) difference between inner and outer, good and evil, man and woman, black and white, Jew and Arab, etc. However, differences are perpetually being produced. This radical view may *de-objectify* (*de-naturalize*) discriminations, but it evidently *cannot rid them of their reality.*

Also in Habermas we notice an inside and an outside, and although the distinction is fundamental and important, it is ultimately impossible for Habermas to prevent his 'outside' from borrowing the guises of his 'inside.' Drawing up a clear line of demarcation is as always a problem. As the 'inside,' we have the authentic use of language directed towards understanding; as the 'outside,' a strategic or instrumental use of language that is merely parasitic on the original and authentic understanding-oriented use. When we analyze what the parasitic use of language is doing in distinction to the authentic use of language, there seems to be exactly no discernible distinction.

(ii) The Inside of Three Validity-Claims; the Significance of the Number Three in Habermas. It can escape nobody that Habermas repeatedly introduces the number three in his theory. This number is so profusely displayed that it is not completely off the mark to claim that the theory is constructed around tripartition as Habermas' basic schematizing principle.

In the history of philosophy, the number three has always had importance. It perhaps never had the importance of 'two,' which designates the distinction, or of 'one,' which designates self-presence, but especially within a German tradition from Kant, over Schelling, to Hegel, a tripartite division of the 'world' is crucial, and frequently exercised. Now, Habermas is also adopting the number three, but not as a dialectical figure. The two first terms do not stand opposed as thesis to anti-thesis resolved in a synthesis introducing a third term. In Habermas, we typically encounter three terms existing in a non-dialectical relationship, but complementing each other, and in their complementarity exhaustingly describing a certain realm, or a 'world.' The three terms or components abstractly divide a 'world' in such a way that, supposedly, the 'world' is fully accounted for; ideally, there are no remainders existing outside the 'world' thus divided.

We talk of course about the world of communication in which we will find exactly three validity-claims corresponding to three types of knowledge: knowledge about the external world as set forth in propositions, knowledge about the social world of norms and conventions as set forth in interactive language-use, and knowledge about the internal world as set forth in expressions. (The fourth validity-claim, *linguistic comprehensibility*, is taken for granted as underlying the three specifically *communicative* validity-claims.) We find introductions to these three validity-claims in virtually every essay Habermas has written on the theory of communicative action during the last forty years.

> A successful utterance must satisfy three validity claims: it must count as true for the participants insofar as it represents something in the world: it must count as truthful insofar as it expresses something intended by the speaker; and it must count as right insofar as it conforms to socially recognized expectations. . . . The three general pragmatic functions of an utterance—to represent something in the world using a sentence, to express the speaker's intention, and to establish legitimate interpersonal relations—are the basis of all the particular functions that an utterance can assume in specific contexts.[33]

Habermas presents these three pragmatic validity-claims in a diagram, which is often reproduced with slight variations in his essays. Three modes of communication represent three different types of speech acts, emphasizing three different themes, and corresponding to three different validity-claims. The themes of the three types of speech-act represent the different kinds of knowledge that is accentuated in the respective speech-acts.

Mode of Communication	Type of Speech-Act	Theme	Validity-claim
Cognitive	Constative Locutionary	Propositional Content	Truth
Interactive	Regulative Illocutionary	Interpersonal Relation	Rightness
Expressive	Representative Speech	Intention of Speech	Sincerity

Introducing any of these themes, the speaker raises a validity-claim, that is, prepares herself to validate her speech along the lines of either truth, rightness, or sincerity.

I shall introduce some problems in this tripartition of the world of possible communication, some of which Habermas is well aware of, and addresses and amends in the course of developing his philosophy. Obviously, I introduce these problems from another perspective (with another cognitive interest) than Habermas. I am interested in the problems related to *the formal principle, tripartition*, and want to demonstrate the relative arbitrariness in how this formal principle interprets and 'slices up' the 'world.'

We start noticing that tripartition *as formal principle* has, to paraphrase Habermas, a validity-basis of its own. The formal principle is bound to follow a certain rule, a certain logic, constituting also the regulative norm of the principle. One fundamental rule is that when a realm is tri-partitioned, the components of the trinity must necessarily be seen as belonging to a *class of the same*. We do not have complete freedom to tripartite everything, for example, we cannot tripartite, 'slice up,' a 'world' in the laws of physics, the rules of grammar, and Australian fauna, because it is impossible to organize the entities under a class of the same. Entities must be aspects of a class of the same; that is, they must be identical in type or category.

Furthermore, they must be seen as exhausting this class, and dividing this class with approximately equal weight. One could imagine an early schematizer tripartite his world into mammals, fish, and birds, and with this postulate that the same entities in type, namely animals, can be exhaustingly and equally divided between animals living on land, in water, and in the air. According to the definition of this tripartition, mammals cannot live in water. Per definition, a whale would have to be a fish (—that today we know, according to other principles, that this is false is not important; it is here important that the formal principle has been observed). In comparison, one cannot divide the world into mammals, fish, and sparrows, since the division cannot be perceived to exhaust or complete the class that it divides. It excludes all birds not being sparrows from the world, leaves them—so to speak—hanging in the air, as remainders outside the scheme.

Finally, the entities must mutually exclude each other in such a way that A complements and excludes B and C, B complements and excludes A and C, and C complements and excludes A and B. The entities have to be identical in type but different in kind, they must belong to a class of the same, but mutually exclude each other. It must not be possible for a mammal also to be a fish; and it must not be possible for birds or fish to be seen as sub-categories of mammals.

This is then the law for tripartition: the entities must belong to a class of the same as aspects of the same type (*identity*), and they must mutually exclude each other as different kinds of that same type (*difference*), in such a way that they complete or exhaust the described world. Expressing the difference of parts in the identity of the whole, we say for shorthand that they are *mutually complementary*. This is thus the 'norm' or the 'law' that regulates Habermas' table; he will have to argue that the entities in his trinity are aspects of the same, mutually excluding each other, but completing the world of communication.

Initially we notice that Habermas' 'world' is the world of language-use in the speech-act. This world is contrasted to linguistics by being a world of activity. Linguistics describes the passive rule-system for sentence formation, whereas Habermas' world describes rules for utterance formation. Linguistics describes a language-system independent of any speaker; pragmatics studies speech-acts as performed between speakers. Thus, we have an initial contrast between descriptions of passive and active language, linguistics being passive, pragmatics active.[34]

In this initial determination of a 'world' of language-use as activity, Habermas is already excluding rival examples of language-use: on one hand, soliloquy and writing, and on the other, purpose-rational, strategic, or instrumental language-use.

It is not difficult to see what is the problem with soliloquy and writing. In both of these 'silent' linguistic activities (if they are activities in Habermas' sense), the interaction between speakers is absent. There is no speech-act being performed. The crucial encounter between Ego and Alter is not actually taking place; all linguistic performance is retained in the unreal internal forum of the self. Furthermore, neither as soliloquizing nor as writing does the individual need to *reach understanding* of the meaning of what she says/writes to herself, since in the monologue, she is supposed to have immediate access to the meaning of her utterance. It is presupposed that the soliloquizing/writing self is transparent to itself. It does not have to vindicate validity-claims in order to prove to itself its own accountability. It does not take a 'yes' or 'no' position to the utterances in its own inner monologue. Since understanding and agreement pre-exist in inner monologue, to *reach understanding* and *come to agreement* are redundant operations within the internal forum of the soliloquizing self.

On a first look, the purpose-rational or strategic speech-act could be a better candidate for Habermas' world of speech activity, since it is actually performed between two interlocutors, being an activity that carries concrete consequences. However (as we have seen), it is a crucial qualification of Habermas' anasemic notion of understanding, that speech-acts aim at mutual agreement. Purpose-rational and strategic language-use forfeits this stipulation, since it includes persuasive, calculating, manipulative, etc., speech-acts. It flouts a crucial requirement for belonging to Habermas' trinity, because it is not aimed at agreement between free agents.

The determination of Habermas' 'world' of communication must now be, *language-use in the concrete speech-act with the aim to reach understanding/agreement between free agents*. From the beginning, we have two language-uses that are outside diagram. One (soliloquy/writing) because it does not to realize itself in the public sphere of speakers. It has a certain *embryonic* status. Another (purpose-rational/strategic) because, although it *does* realize itself in the public sphere of speakers, it perverts the immanent telos for authentic communication. It has a certain *parasitic* status. Authentic communication, captured by the diagram, we find situated (1) in contrast to the language-system and (2) between the *embryo* and the *parasite*.

The diagram is thus from the outset narrowly defined against a threatening outside that has no viable place within the diagram. The diagram is drawn up as a 'world' with borders that subsequently has to be defended against a host of perpetrators. The criteria for belonging to this world are identical to the rules that this world is set to define as constituting communicative competence; —as if the 'world' depicted by this diagram is an exclusive club with the purpose of discussing the possibility of rationality in discourse, but only admitting entrance to those members that are already considered rational.

The danger of tripartition, and of all schematization, is that that which cannot be captured by the scheme can only be classified as a non-belonging outside. Using the example above, my early schematizer draws up a world consisting of mammals, birds, and fish, but produces to himself a new difficulty in how to explain the existence of, say, insects and reptiles. Now he has to employ all his ingenuity to explain away the existence of such sub-groups. And insofar as my early schematizer is a mere example on the typical philosophical operator, he might go about his task by dividing the universe into good and evil. The first set of creatures is now created by God, whereas insects and reptiles are the work of the Devil. Instead of a universe of indifferent and equal classes, we suddenly have a universe divided between a radical inside and a radical outside—a universe that is inherently discriminatory. The radical outside is as dangerous and disturbing, as the radical inside is desired.

This early schematizer is not operating in a manner fundamentally different from Habermas. Also Habermas will divide the universe of communication into authentic and inauthentic, good and evil uses of speech. At the inside of the three validity-claims, we find explicitly what it *right*, what is *true*, and what is *truthful* (it cannot be hazardous to conclude that this represents *The Good* in Habermas' universe). At the outside, we find the parasitic, manipulative, deceptive, strategic uses of language. This moral distinction between language-uses, we do not find in Austin and Searle, and since Habermas is using the analytical apparatus of speech-act theory, he creates for himself a new quandary, namely, how in principle one determines 'strategic' uses of language in distinction to 'understanding-oriented' uses of language (to this we return in the next section).

We noticed initially that entities in a scheme must mutually complement and exclude each other. The entities have to be identical in type but different in kind. It could not be possible for birds and fish in the example above to be perceived as sub-categories of mammals. However, Habermas' scheme does not honor this requirement, here we notice that one type of speech-act is superimposed on the other two, namely illocution. Cognitive and expressive speech-acts must necessarily be interactive, that is, directed toward an interpersonal relation, and they must necessarily contain an illocutionary component. *Asserting* something to be true, or *confessing* something sincerely are also illocutionary acts. The illocutionary interactive use of language is therefore overlaying the two other uses of language.

We also notice that the illocutionary speech-act is type-different from its two complementary categories. Whereas the validity of cognitive and expressive utterances are established insofar as the contents of the utterances are proven true or truthful, the illocutionary, interactive utterance does not report about a content that can be either true or truthful. It can only be correct (Habermas) or felicitous (Austin). Cognitive/propositional and expressive/emotional utterances refer to or report on a content, let it be empirical or emotional, while the illocutionary utterance is self-reflexive. There is therefore *a not very rigorous* distinction between the proposition and the expression, while there is *a very rigorous* distinction between, on the one hand, proposition/expression, and on the other, illocution. Thus, the three speech-act types are not completely analogous cases, and they are not evenly weighted regarded their importance in the scheme.

2) THE ILLEGITIMATE OUTSIDE
(i) Reinventing the Perlocutionary Component of Speech-Acts as Strategic Use of Language. (ii) Concealed Strategic Use of Language. (iii) Open Strategic Use of language.

(i) Reinventing the Perlocutionary Component of Speech-Acts as Strategic Use of Language. In *How to Do Things with Words*, Austin ends up suggesting three components of the speech-act: the locutionary, the illocutionary, and the perlocutionary.

Although Austin in distinction to Habermas has no schematizing desires (whenever a scheme suggests itself to him, his next move is typically to erase it again), he obviously produces this famous trinity. We notice, however, that there is no overlapping between Austin's trinity of speech-act components and Habermas' trinity of validity-claims. The perlocutionary act is absent from Habermas' scheme; it is instead transformed into a technical description of instrumental and parasitic use of language. (In later essays, Habermas ambivalently tries to restore 'perlocution' in approximately the sense it originally had in Austin, without giving up his re-interpretation of the term. About this shortly.)

From Austin's scheme, Habermas retains locution and illocution; to these two components, he adds the *expressive* utterances expressing intention. In Habermas' rewriting of speech-act theory, perlocution comes to play a much more sinister role than in both Austin and Searle.

In Austin and Searle, 'perlocution' describes an entirely innocuous and value-neutral aspect of speech-acts. It indicates that speech-acts typically produce effects in the addressee; we *do* things with words, prompt people to act on what we say, or produce mental changes in auditors by our utterances. Austin and Searle give the following accounts of the perlocutionary effect.

> We may also perform *perlocutionary acts*: what we bring about or achieve *by* saying something, such as convincing, persuading, deterring.
> [. . .] For clearly *any*, or almost any, perlocutionary act is liable to be brought off, in sufficiently special circumstances, by the issuing, with or without calculation, of any utterance whatsoever.
> [. . .] The perlocutionary act . . . is *the achieving of* certain *effects* by saying something [Austin's emphases].[35]

> Correlated with the notion of illocutionary acts is the notion of the consequences of *effects* such acts have on the actions, thoughts, or beliefs, etc., of hearers. For example, by arguing I may *persuade* or *convince* someone, by warning him I may *scare* or *alarm* him, by making a request I may *get him to do something*, by informing him I may *convince him* (*enlighten, edify, inspire him, get him to realize*). The italicized expressions above denote perlocutionary acts [Searle's emphases].[36]

According to these accounts, illocutionary acts typically have perlocutionary effects. By asserting something, I make the hearer believe something; by requesting something, I make the hearer act on something; by promising something, I make the hearer trust something, (etc.). Thus, it seems that illocution and perlocution indicate a distinction between utterances and their consequences. This would simplify the picture: the utterance is uttered by the speaker, and it takes effect in the hearer. Illocution and perlocution, at a first look, seem to indicate a difference between speaker vs. hearer *as between* cause vs. effect.

As he proceeds in his work, Austin complicates this picture. Also illocutionary acts have effects, he concedes. The difference between illocution and perlocution can consequently not be construed along the line of the familiar cause-effect distinction. Illocutions have effects in the sense that they "secure uptake, take effect, and invite response."[37] In the dialogical situation, uttering a sentence with a certain illocutionary force typically invites a specific, thus *conventional*, response. Asking a question invite the response 'answer'; giving an order invite the response 'obedience,' etc. These effects Austin calls 'conventional,' since they seem to be conventionally contained in the typical response-pattern brought about by the utterance.

In contrast, the perlocutionary effects are *not conventionally* contained in the utterance. "Illocutionary acts are conventional acts: perlocutionary acts are *not* conventional."[38] Perlocutionary effects are reactions in the hearer that the speaker may not have anticipated; at least, they are typically extrinsic to the speech-act itself. Asking a question could in some circumstances cause anxiety in the hearer. ('Where were you on the night of the murder?' The police officer asks the intimidated witness.) 'Anxiety' would now constitute a perlocutionary effect.

The perlocutionary effect is thus *different* from the illocutionary effect. The distinction between illocutionary force and the perlocutionary effect is *exactly not* a cause-effect relationship, since there is no *logical nexus* between illocution and perlocution. The perlocutionary effect deviates from—and could be intended to deviate from—the explicitly performed illocutionary theme. Austin believes that the distinction is sufficiently demarcated through the use of 'in' and 'by.' '*In* saying x, the speaker was doing y,' would then illustrate *illocution*, while '*by* saying x, the speaker was doing y,' would illustrate *perlocution*.

We may make the distinction more transparent by applying a variation over the Kantian distinction between analytic and synthetic judgments. We may then suggest that the effect of the illocutionary act is analytically contained in the act itself, while the effect of the perlocution 'synthetically' adds something to the illocutionary act. A *question* is defined as an interrogative mode of speech that is addressed to someone in the expectation of a reply. If the effect of the question is that the hearer replies, then *her replying* is analytically coextensive with the definition of the particular illocutionary component of the speech-act. The effect is analytically contained in its definition. If she becomes nervous, 'nervousness' is no part of the definition of the speech-act; it is an external and synthetic addition to the effects that per definition questions are supposed to have. Along the line of this new distinguishing principle, we might also say that illocutionary effects are *speech-act intentional*, since they are intended effects embedded in the speech-acts themselves, whereas perlocutionary effects are not. In contrast, perlocutionary effects *may be speaker-intentional* (but not necessarily), insofar as the speaker could be *intentionally using* his speech-act to produce an effect in the hearer other than the effect the speech-act conventionally has (the criminal investigator could *intend* to make his witness nervous). We can finally say that the perlocutionary effect is always a *side-effect*, insofar as it is an addition to the effect of the speech-act itself.

This brings us back to Habermas. Habermas adopts Austin's distinction between illocutionary acts as conventional and perlocutionary as non-conventional. "The possible perlocutionary effects of a speech act depend on fortuitous contexts and are not fixed by conventions, as are illocutionary results."[39] However, Habermas dissociates the perlocutionary effect from authentic speech, and sees it as a *perversion* and an *abuse* of speech. In Habermas' prism, perlocution becomes the technical label for strategic and instrumental use of language. In this reading, the perlocutionary effect is not only exterior to the speech-act, it also represents a perversion of language by being parasitic on 'original' understanding-oriented language-use. Whereas in Austin, the introduction of the perlocution is meant to underscore that speech-acts may have and normally have unintended or intended *side-effects*, in Habermas, these perlocutionary *side-effects* are, first, always intended and, secondly, always manipulative or exploitative.

(I briefly mentioned that Habermas in later essays corrects this reading. After having been criticized by commentators (by Searle, Apel, Skjei, and others) for distorting and misreading Austin and Searle on these grounds, Habermas amends his initial misreading by setting up a distinction between two kinds of perlocutionary effects. There are those that are unintended results from the illocutionary theme of the speech act (similar to Austin's), and those that have achieved independent status, are intended, and are strategic. Despite this correction, it is still the case, however, that even in his definitive and authoritative work, *The Theory of Communicative Action*, Habermas *prefers* to see the perlocutionary effect as strategic action. Perlocutionary effects in Austin/Searle's less dramatic sense are acknowledged, but they are also quickly dismissed as obvious and trivial. "Speech acts, like actions in general, can produce side effects that the actor did not foresee; these are perlocutionary effects in a trivial sense, which I shall not consider any further."[40] On this background, I think we are justified in remarking that *perversion* of discourse indicates the *favorite* notion of perlocution in Habermas. The innocuous situation is not what interests Habermas. 'Perlocution' is primarily coextensive to *intentional language-abuse*.)[41]

Granted the existence of an 'inside' and an 'outside' in the theory of communicative action, it is important to separate the outside from the inside, and to produce convincing criteria for the demarcation between the respectively 'good' and 'bad' uses of language. The distinction between illocution and perlocution offers Habermas this demarcating principle. Habermas loads these two principles with attributes that seem to stand in an antithetical relationship to each other. 'Conventionality' becomes one such attribute: illocution being 'conventional,' perlocution being 'unconventional.' Another attribute is 'openness': Illocutions are expressed openly, while perlocutions are secret—they secretly use the illocution as a means to their end. "A speaker, if he wants to be successful, may not let his perlocutionary aims be known, whereas illocutionary aims can be achieved only through being expressed. Illocutions are expressed openly; perlocutions may not be 'admitted' as such."[42]

(ii) Concealed Strategic Use of Language. Instrumental or strategic language-use influence or effect a listener, whereas understanding-oriented language-use only requires accept and approval from a listener. To influence or effect is a non-illocutionary aim that necessary employs illocutionary speech-acts. However, the pursuit of non-illocutionary aims in the guise of illocutionary speech-act is a deception, and a deception that is only successful if concealed. It engages the speaker in a so-called 'concealed strategic action.' (Habermas' other example of strategic action, so-called 'open strategic action,' is analytically different; and below, we shall deal with it separately.) In 'concealed strategic actions,' we encounter a discrepancy between appearance and being; the speech-act appears to be something it is not. The hearer is taken in by the appearance, and is deceived. She has not been treated as an end in herself, but as a means to an end. One problem in deceptive speech-acts is that the autonomy of the hearer has been offended.[43]

Since 'concealed strategic language-use' disguises itself in understanding-oriented language-use, it is parasitically dependent on the latter.

> *Language oriented toward reaching understanding is the original mode of language use upon which* indirectly reaching understanding, giving to understand something or letting something be understood—in general, *the instrumental use of language—is parasitic. . . .* What we initially designated as 'the use of language with an orientation toward consequences' is not an original use of language but the *subsumption* of speech acts that serve illocutionary aims under conditions of action oriented toward success [my emphases].[44]

> *The latently strategic use of language lives parasitically on normal language usage* because it functions only if at least one of the parties involved assumes that language is being used with a built-in orientation toward reaching understanding [my emphasis].[45]

Let us just briefly recall the definition of *parasite*. From original Greek, it indicates a professional dinner guest sitting at another person's table, eating up his provisions without offering a return (*para* = beside, *sitos* = grain, food). In contemporary usage, a parasite is defined as an organism living on or in another organism, obtaining part or all of its nutrients from the host without contributing anything itself. In many cases, parasites damage the host, cause disease, or even death.[46]

The distinction between *Understanding-Oriented-Language-Use* (hereafter UOLU) and *Concealed-Strategic-Language-Use* (hereafter CSLU) imitates a classical distinction between 'seeming' and 'being.'[47] If CSLU is parasitic on UOLU, it must be because it as parasite lives *inside*, and *disguised* as, UOLU. Parasitic language 'seems' but 'is' not, but insofar as it 'seems,' it necessarily has the exact appearance of UOLU. CSLU creates the illusion that it is playing by the rules of UOLU, but it is mere pretense; in the instance of enunciation, it has secretly flouted these rules. These rules we have already introduced, they are the rules being actualized in the reciprocal agreement about redeeming validity-claims; the speaker raises validity claims, and gives the hearer reason to believe that he is ready to vindicate them. The rule of UOLU is thus, speaker-S's intention to redeem, and to make hearer-H believe that he intends to redeem, validity-claims.

Karl-Otto Apel has given the following description of what happens in strategic use of language:

> Let us take the case of someone wishing to achieve a 'perlocutionary' effect in a manipulative way when speaking to another, so that the conversation partner has no opportunity first to *understand* the speech-act (*illocutionary effect*), and then either to accept it or not accept it, on the basis of the *validity claims* which it raises. If the speaker wishes to do this, he must not allow the other to become aware that this is his aim. In other words, he must use language in such a way as to create the *illusion* that he wishes to give the other the opportunity to 'reach agreement about validity claims' which is in fact being withheld.[48]

The description of Apel is precise in the sense that it precisely summarizes the idea in Habermas' notion of manipulative action (which may be Apel's sole purpose). However, it is imprecise in the sense that it seems to suggest that *language itself* is manipulative. The hearer has 'no opportunity to understand the speech act'; she is not given the opportunity to 'either accept or not to accept it' based on the raised 'validity-claims,' etc. But this description needs at least to be clarified. The manipulation is only effective because the hearer *understands* the speech act, because she *accepts* it and *agrees* on the validity-claims it raises. The formal requirements for communication, as described by

Habermas, are implemented to the same extent and degree in manipulative as in genuine speech. Apel is right in saying that language has been used to 'create an illusion'; the illusion being that the speaker to the hearer looks as if he *adheres* to and feels *obligated* by a speech-act that contains the same components as any authentic speech-act.

Given that the hearer is a victim of this illusion, she does not and cannot understand the 'will' or 'intention' of the speaker. More precisely, the tacit negations, which the speaker in his inscrutable inner mental life has added to the validity claims that he explicitly raises, cannot be understood by the hearer (—except perhaps from *experience*: the hearer may have learnt from experience that this particular speaker is, for example, a compulsive liar.) We may formalize it in this way. A speaker utters, 'If you do x for me, then I'll do y for you; and this is no lie.' This utterance is the same whether or not the speaker means it. If he does not mean it, he becomes an impostor because he *tacitly* adds negations to his utterance, for example: 'If you do x for me, then I'll ($\sim$)do y for you; and this is ($\sim$)no lie.'

The hearer obviously cannot understand the ($\sim$)'s since they are not pronounced. The hearer is necessarily naïve, and must perforce believe that the speaker is not lying, since he tells her that this is what he is not. In UOLU, S would not be lying about not lying; but in CSLU, S is lying about not lying. However, whether S is lying or not about lying, we notice that the speech-acts in respectively UOLU and CSLU are identical, as well as the *speech-act intentions* are the same. On the linguistic surface, a manipulative action is therefore identical to a non-manipulative action. It is only uttered with another 'will.' Let us characterize this secret 'will' the *speaker-intention* distinctive from the *speech-act intention*. In non-manipulative action, the 'will' is the expression of the speech-act; it is coextensive with *speech-act intention*, while in manipulative action, *speech-act intention* is replaced with a *speaker-intention* that negates the intention expressed in the speech-act.

Exactly because a manipulative speech-act is the same as a non-manipulative one, the grievance and sense of injustice in having been deceived is intensified. The deceived is not only disappointed in the deceiver, but rightly, she feels fundamentally wronged because she was never given a fair chance to perceive and counter the deceit. Language *itself*, the *linguistic surface*, can *a priori* not give her that chance. Thus, there is no parasitic language *as such*, and so-called 'parasitic' language-use does not follow a set of formal rules different from the formal rules for 'original' language-use. Parasiticality is inscribed in all language as its always-present *possibility*. However, if parasiticality is an always-present possibility, no language is more parasitic than other language. In other words, all language is *potentially* parasitic; depending on whether or not the speaker secretly promises himself to follow the promises of his utterances. Language *itself* cannot have an intention that is opposite to the intention it expresses.

Thus, if we are reluctant to give up the metaphor of the 'parasite,' we can at best say that 'parasitic language' does not constitute any specific mode of language, since the 'parasite' at best lives '*in*' language as the secret 'will' of the speaker. The 'parasite' is a *speaker-intention* that secretly defines itself as contrary to the *speech-act intention* that it expresses.

The demarcation between UOLU and CSLU is further blurred, because even when a speech-act is recognized by the hearer as potentially deceptive (as CSLU), there is still room for argumentative and justificative discourse. UOLU may be inscribed in so-called parasitic language, insofar as CSLU may follow justificative and argumentative procedures that are identical to language-use aimed to reach agreement. To our speaker above, adamant about not lying, the hearer could respond: 'I don't believe you'; whereupon the speaker would have to provide further reasons: 'I would never let you down,' 'what could I possibly gain from lying,' (etc.). The discussion would continue like this until they reach an agreement about whether or not the speaker is lying. If finally the speaker succeeds in convincing the hearer that his insincere motives are sincere, they have reached such an agreement. The agreement has been reached through reason and rational argument. UOLU has been incorporated into CSLU to the extent that the two language-uses are formally indistinguishable.

Habermas might respond that a hearer accepting a speech-act on false grounds has been manipulated, and the reached agreement between speaker and hearer is therefore invalid. In other words, in Habermas' emphatic sense, they have not reached *Agreement* (capitalized-emphatic-anasemic).

We are now able to see why not. To Habermas' emphatic sense of *Agreement* corresponds an equally emphatic sense of *Sincerity* in the speaker. In order to prepare the ground for true *Agreement*, the will of the speaker must be completely absorbed in the expressed speech-act intention; there must not be a shred of doubt that he 'wills' what he says.[49] In the emphatic sense, the speaker must therefore be *Sincere* (capitalized-anasemic), because if the speaker's speech-offer is not *Sincere* (capitalized-anasemic), the hearer cannot *Accept it* (capitalized-anasemic), and they have not *Reached Agreement* (capitalized-anasemic), even when on appearances they have reached agreement (i.e., non-anasemically).

However, introducing these emphatic senses into communicative theory is merely to set up ideal requirements for communicative behavior, it is to add ideal and hollow constructions to a theory that wants to understand itself as pragmatic. It is clear that such ideal and hollow constructions, which I call anasemes, are meant to safeguard the prominent desiderata of the theory: first, that true and genuine communication is possible, and second, that true and genuine communication is also the original or primary mode of language use on which other modes are parasitic. In order to eliminate strategic language-use from UOLU, or to argue for its parasitic dependency of UOLU, Habermas loads his concept of understanding with ideal requirements that presuppose that interlocutors, transparent to themselves and to each other, embrace in *Agreement*.[50]

The notion of UOLU is further compromised as soon as we introduce *unconscious* motives into the speech-act. If *Agreement* requires *Sincerity* in the speaker (this requirement eliminating manipulative motives), such motives could *conceivably* be obliterated as long as they are *conscious* (anybody *conscious* about his insincerity, could modify his behavior and *command* himself to be sincere). But if insincere motives are *unconscious*, UOLU is further complicated to an almost infinite degree, because even in the most rational moments of a speech-act, it is doubtful whether the speaker can erase all traces of unconscious 'interests' and 'desires.' If in pursuing the interest of the hearer, the speaker is unconsciously pursuing the interest of himself, is he now completely sincere?[51]

With the introduction of unconscious motives, UOLU is immediately converted into CSLU. We have a situation, where speakers, on the dialogical surface and in own self-understanding, may be pursuing UOLU, but 'beneath' that surface act concealed strategically. However, they do not act with a 'will' to conceal; they do not secretly promise themselves to negate the promise they carry out in the apparent speech-act. They act unconsciously-concealed-strategically (or *concealed-concealed-strategically*). As soon as this monstrosity is introduced into Habermas' speech-act theory, it is no longer possible to distinguish UOLU from CSLU. Now, UOLU is transformed into Unconsciously-Concealed-Strategic-Language-Use, which is by the speaker (since unconscious) seriously understood and believed to be straightforward, upright, and frank use of language. As a form for concealed strategic language-use, it even works more efficiently after having been repressed, since the speaker no longer has to take upon himself an act. Now, it is no longer concealed only from the hearer, it is concealed also from the speaker himself. It has become *concealed-concealed-strategic*.

Since this type of linguistic action appeals to reason and advocates tolerance, goodwill, and sincerity—and therefore dress itself in the guises of UOLU—we can finally determine this construction by the monstrous title: *Unconsciously-Concealed-Strategic-Understanding-Oriented-Language-Use*. Its acronym would be the equally unhandy, UCSUOLU.

Here I shall suggest that the unhandy UCSUOLU is the *typical* use of language. It is according to this formula that people *speak*, and—while mutually understanding the linguistic act—simultaneously 'misunderstand' each other in the sense, 'misunderstanding' their unconscious motives. At the very least, although I would insist that people typically understand the linguistic act, they necessarily *Misunderstand* (capitalized-anasemic) each other on Habermas' normative background of emphatic *Understanding*, since it is conditional upon a notion of an ideal, artificial, and non-existent *Sincerity*. Habermas' theory thus has an odd and counter-intuitive consequence. *Mutatis mutandis*, it has this formulation: if as the aim of communication we require *Understanding* (capitalized-anasemic), then all communication can be nothing but *Misunderstanding* (capitalized-anasemic). However, if the more modest aim of communication is that we understand, then we rarely misunderstand each other—and only for peripheral reasons, we didn't hear or were not acquainted with a word, and misunderstood (non-capitalized non-anasemic).[52]

(iii) Open Strategic Use of Language. According to Habermas, there are two strategic uses of language: *Concealed-Strategic* and so-called *Open-Strategic* Language-Use (hereafter OSLU). My monster-construction above has no existence. (Habermas is not completely unaware of unconscious language-uses, but these belong to the pathologies, and come under the label 'systematically distorted communication.')

As well as CSLU, also OSLU is parasitic on UOLU, but less obviously so. In Concealed-Strategic-Language-Use it can be argued that language is used parasitically on UOLU, since the speaker uses language as disguise for a manipulative *will* that is undetectable to the hearer. This analysis does not apply to OSLU, because in this case, we do not find a 'speaker-intention' in conflict with an explicitly expressed 'speech-act intention.' Since the speech-act is 'open,' the intention of the speaker is there for the hearer to see and to understand. This, however, does not make the speech-act 'understanding-oriented,' because the open strategic speech-act does not fulfill the requirements for reaching *Understanding* in Habermas' anasemic-emphatic sense. The open-strategic speech-act may be *open*, but it is still 'strategic' or so-called 'success-oriented' (in contrast to 'understanding-oriented'). It is performed for the purpose of, for example, gain and profit; or for other egotistical purposes that exclude the hearer from understanding-oriented dialogue. The speech-act is not directed towards achieving the hearer's accept. Speaker and hearer are not supposed to reach understanding about or arrive to any consensus about the speech-act, because the speech-act does not offer any validity-claims to be vindicated. It deprives the hearer of the possibility of accepting or rejecting the speech-act; it excludes the hearer from adopting the 'yes' or 'no' position to the speech-act—which it is, in understanding-oriented dialogue, so crucial to grant her.

The paradigmatic example of the *Open-Strategic-Language-Use* is *the threat*. Habermas offers these examples of OSLU (from a bank-robbery situation): "Hands up!" or "Hand over the money, or I'll shoot!"[53]

Karl-Otto Apel cites the examples and adds the problematizing commentary:

> At first glance, it is difficult to see in what sense the bank robber's use of language is not oriented towards 'understanding.' After all, the robber give the cashier the chance to *understand* his intentions and then—admittedly at lightning speed—to *consider* whether there are *good (rational)* reasons of self-interest to accept the robber's demand.[54]

If we presuppose a semantic, non-emphatic (non-anasemic) notion of understanding, this objection of Apel must be correct. In the situation described by Apel, understanding has been achieved; misunderstanding would indeed be fatal. Also, there is no parasitic relationship between a bank-robber's language and language in general. (Although one of course may argue that there is a parasitic relationship between a bank-robber and society. But, crucially, the bank-robber is not abusing language, he is abusing society.)

As Apel correctly indicates, if Habermas wants to argue that the bank-robber is still abusing language, he can only do so by committing the fallacy of a *petitio principii*. He has to presuppose a notion of language where threats per definition and from the beginning are excluded from language-use. His argument is consequently begging the question; it runs approximately: 'according to my rules, language does not include threats, so therefore, if somebody is making threats, he is not following the rules for language-use in my sense.'

Habermas *is* presupposing, of course, his anasemic notion of *Understanding*, and according to this notion, threats are excluded from proper language-use. This is asserted explicitly in an article where Habermas states: "Threats do not have proper illocutionary force at all."[55] If they do not have illocutionary force, they cannot raise a validity-claim, and the hearer is not free to take her 'yes' or 'no' position to the speech-offer. There is nothing to accept or reject. Threats, Habermas will argue, do not appeal to vindication or validation of validity-claims, they appeal to 'sanction-conditions' in form of power or violence. Sanction-conditions replace the validity-claims that in 'proper' discourse would confer authorization to the speaker.

Thus, threats belong to speech-acts that are type-different from, and radically outside of, speech-acts in UOLU. Habermas wants again to establish a demarcating principle that initially seems evident, but under scrutiny collapses. Initially it seems evident because he can rely on the following distinction: in UOLU, the participants express goodwill, whereas in threats they express hostility. Hostility seems contrary to the orientation towards understanding—hostility connotes antipathy and hatred, whereas understanding connotes sympathy and love. But although the distinction, hostile vs. friendly, hate vs. love, is easy to the mind, it cannot establish a philosophical rule for language. It cannot establish two radically different formal characteristics for respectively 'friendly' language and 'threatening' language. I shall argue for this view by listing six objections, which cumulatively, I believe, are sufficient to deconstruct Habermas' distinction.

Firstly, if threats have no 'proper illocutionary component,' what about speech-acts that have family-resemblance to 'threats,' like the 'order' or the 'request'? Especially the order seems to belong to the same class as threats—the class Searle calls 'directives.' Using Habermas' example, the order would have the form, "Give me the money!" or elaborated, "I order you to give me the money!" The request is weaker, "I request you to give me the money!" And the supplication is weaker still, "I beg you to give me the money!" However, we notice in the three cases that as soon as the sentence is followed up by an 'or y' or an 'otherwise y,' the order, request or supplication is transformed into a threat. If Habermas is right that in 'threats' sanction-conditions are replacing claims to validity, then they do so explicitly and by means of the addition 'or else . . .'—adding emphasis and urgency to the directive. Alternatively, but achieving the same effect, the threat can be expressed by an 'if-then': 'if you don't do x . . . then y.'

Threats or 'open-strategic-language-uses' have now these two basic communicative forms ('y' being the sanction that follows if the hearer fails to do 'x'):

(1) Do x, or/otherwise y
(2) If you don't do x, then y

This, however, implies that speech-acts that clearly have an illocutionary component are transformed into *threats*, not because of a unique communicative structure that set them off against UOLU, but because a sanction is promised should the hearer fail to carry out the directive at issue. Under that condition, orders, requests, and supplications are easily transformed into threats.

(a) I order you to give me the money, otherwise your are fired!
(b) I request you to give me the money, otherwise I'll inform my lawyer!
(c) I beg you to give me the money, otherwise I'll commit suicide!

Secondly, are threats necessarily explicit? What happens to the speech-act if a threat is implicit or implied? Is an utterance *implying* a threat a threat or is it defined by the illocutionary mode in which it is uttered (in which case it is not a threat, since threats have no illocutionary mode)? Do threats necessarily have to be spelled out and followed by an "or else . . ."?

Frequently, threats are implicit and subtle. What about "I don't know what I would do to myself, if you left me"? Reformulated into one of the communicative forms for threats, she is implying, "If you ever leave me, I'll do something to myself." However, this is not being said. Or what about this typical Hollywood scene: The mobster tells our hero, "you have a nice family, beautiful wife, nice kids . . ." and our hero responds, "are you threatening me?" —Not so according to Habermas, we can tell our hero. However, on the street, people develop subtle uses of language; and threats may be uttered disguised in compliments and shows of concern. Or what about: "Do you want to know the truth, are you sure you want to know what's going on . . . ?" Another threat that reformulated implies (perhaps), "If you don't stop nagging, I'll tell you the truth!" However, the illocutionary force of the utterance is a 'question.' (We notice here that sanction-conditions are not only determined by the potential for inflicting violence; one can threaten another person with *truth*.) Moreover, the 'question' implies a 'threat,' and threats are, according to Habermas, paradigm-cases of open strategic action and success-oriented dialogue; but it is not intuitively evident that the last example displays this type of action. Toward what 'success' is the speech-act oriented? (To make her stop nagging, one might respond, but only because we can stretch language in all possible directions—like we can possibly say, "Didi *succeeded* in buttoning up his fly," because the word, as the minimal semantic unit, has considerable flexibility and elasticity.)

Thirdly, why is not the 'order' an implicit threat? The commander screams to his soldiers "Attack!" It is implied that if they do not follow order, they will be court-martialed and shot. If the commander's "Attack!" is an order, and his "Attack, or I will have you shot!" is a threat, it is hard to discern the substantial difference. The first case is an order, whose authority is ultimately backed by a threat of absolute violence. The last case is an order, followed by a threat of absolute violence if disobeyed.

According to Habermas, there is a substantial difference between the order and the threat. The order is still raising validity-claims, because the hearer can question whether the speaker, giving the order, is supported by the appropriate authorizing norms or institutions. Supposedly, this gives the hearer the possibility of either accepting or rejecting the utterance. If the hearer disputes that the speaker has the authority to command anything of her, she has the possibility of responding, "No, you cannot order me to do anything."[56] But this possibility is obviously only there when the authority of the speaker is in doubt, and it is authority that constitutes the validity-claim of the 'order' or 'command' in the first place. If the authority of the officer is intact and unchallenged, the private cannot respond, 'No, you cannot order me to do anything'—and count on surviving his mutiny (ignoring for now that certain modern armies permit troops to dissent from an order). The foot soldier has as much a gun to his head as the victim of the bank robber.

Fourthly: Habermas believes that this situation is radically different under a threat. But that he can only argue because he is using an extreme example, and even then the argument is doubtful. "Give me the money, or I'll shoot!"—Supposedly, with a gun to her head, the cashier does not start to debate the bank-robber's 'right.' In order to make his case, Habermas does, what is sometimes seen in Analytic Philosophy, making generalizations based on sentence-fragments of simplified English. We are supposed to believe that no debate is possible, but debate in Habermas' example is exactly as possible or impossible as in the case of the private disputing the command of his officer. 'No, I don't think you have the guts to shoot me,' the cashier could possibly respond, with this disputing the bank robber's readiness to carry out his threat—with this disputing the bank robber's *sincerity* and *seriousness*. *Sincerity* is one of the three validity-claims!

Fifthly, Habermas' extreme case, "Give me the money, or I'll shoot!" prejudices us unfavorably against the class of speech acts that we call threats. In the exemplified utterance above, there is no other claim than a claim to power and violence. But what about the 'threat' in general, that is, any sentence of the form, 'Do *x*, or I'll do *y* (*y* will happen),' or 'If you don't do *x*, I'll do *y* (*y* will happen).'

Notice that threats are sometimes made out of love. It is out of his infinite love of mankind that the preacher promises his congregation: "If you don't worship our lord, you shall be damned and burn eternally in the fires of hell!" And threats are not necessarily irrational declarations of violent sanctions conditional upon a certain course of action. Sometimes threats can be rationally motivated; sometimes a threat is implied in a piece of beneficial information; sometimes threats can be politically correct—like in these three cases:

(a) The doctor tells his patient: "If you don't stop smoking, you'll develop lung cancer."
(b) The scientist tells representatives from industrialized nations: "If you don't reduce the emission of carbon dioxide, the world will experience dramatic climate changes."
(c) The political advisor tells the autocrat: "If you close down the free press, you can expect more corruption on government levels."

The threat of cancer, of climate change, or of corruption urges the hearer to reconsider a pattern of behavior. Now the threat is a catalyst for rational behavior. In the face of penalizing consequences, the hearer starts contemplating and rethinking a previous decision that has had a certain appeal, but may have unwanted repercussions. There are no formal pragmatic differences between these (benevolent) threats, and Habermas' preferred case:

(d) The bank-robber tells the bank secretary: "If you don't hand me the money, I'll will shoot."

Finally, *sixthly*, a threat may have a propositional content that is in principle no different from the propositional content any other speech-act may have. "Hand me the money, or I'll will shoot!" has a propositional content identical to, "I'll shoot those, who don't hand me the money!" which is identical to, "I'll not shoot those, who hand me the money!" The first utterance has the force of a threat, while the last has the force of a promise. This is not merely a repetition of the second objection, that certain threats are implicit.

Habermas wants to argue that there is a radical and fundamental difference between threats and (for example) promises, according to distinctions such as: the former is success-oriented while the latter is understanding-oriented; the former relies on sanction-conditions while the latter relies on vindication of validity-claims; and the former contains no illocutionary component while the latter does. Habermas thus wants to argue that the threat is *type-different* from the illocutionary speech-act. I would counter this by claiming that there is precisely no type-difference between (in this case) threats and promises, there is only *token-difference*. The same can be said, the same result can be aimed at, by two different linguistic tokens or components. The tokens used are relatively indifferent to the pragmatic realization aimed at in the speech-act.

Western governments may threaten with sanctions if a rogue state does not dismantle its capability to produce weapons-grade plutonium, or they may promise funding for the building of safe nuclear reactors without this capability. The promise of funding is not 'understanding oriented,' whereas the threat of sanctions is 'success oriented.' Whether the stick or the carrot, the threat or the promise, the governments aspire to achieve the same end, a halt on the production and proliferation of weapons-grade plutonium. The diplomatic initiatives taken to achieve this end are oriented toward success. And in the same breath, we must admit that in the actual process of negotiation, language is understanding-oriented. In an utterly explicit and pragmatic sense, the parties have to *reach agreement, come to an understanding,* and *achieve consensus* about the issue in question. The distinction that Habermas wants to draw between understanding- and success-oriented language breaks down again. The idea that on one side we can isolate a pure and uncorrupted understanding-oriented use of language, and on the other, an equally clean success-oriented use is as such artificial and contrived.

Especially if politics and business constitute the preeminent realms where we find success-oriented language-use, language seems here, more than in dull ordinary language-use, understanding-oriented since *agreement* is inscribed in the negotiation-situation as the telos of its success. Now, does this imply that success-oriented language use is in fact understanding-oriented in Habermas' strong anasemic sense? Is acute and brilliant Habermas guilty of some sort of fundamental unconscious error that has impelled him to confuse understanding-oriented language with success-oriented language?

In some sense, yes, it seems to be the case! From the outset, Habermas seems to take (tacitly and perhaps unconsciously) for granted that in using language we are involved in negotiations. Rational and accountable speakers are negotiating their utterances, offering them up for acceptance, agreement, and applause. If this from the outset is presupposed, it is no wonder that the image of the political negotiation can be superimposed on understanding-oriented ordinary language-use as its natural extension. Habermas (desiring to describe in ever-more distinct language a vision that is out of focus and blurred on the edges) is in the grip of a belief that we are all *Politicians* (capitalized-emphatic-anasemic).[57] (However, within this stipulation—his theory of communicative action is political theory that applies to the supposed rational behavior of politicians—who would not agree with Habermas, and root for his project as pertinent?)

3) AT THE INSIDE OF THE INSIDE
(i) The Intrinsic Anaseme of the Theory of Communicative Action. (ii) Recursive Definitions and Self-Reference.

(i) The Intrinsic Anaseme of the Theory of Communicative Action. It is of major importance to Habermas to distinguish *illocutionary* from *locutionary* and *perlocutionary* speech-acts. 'Illocution' becomes the most important 'anaseme' in the theory. As *anaseme*, it condenses a series of concepts that are prerequisite for evidencing how rationality is intrinsic in speech. It has no ostensive definition as its meaning, but a structure. To put it in the terminology of structural linguistics, it is a *signifier whose signified is a complex structure of other signifiers.*

Just as the meaning of this anasemical signifier is a complex structure, the meaning of the concepts to which it is contrasted is also a complex structure. These concepts are opposing or juxtaposing the anasemic desideratum; in this, they outline its structural borders. Because of this intrinsic complexity, defining and isolating the anaseme is not only a difficult task, but an infinite one too—and, in the final analysis, an impossible one. It becomes an impossible task to *completely stabilize* the meaning of a concept '*A*,' whose meaning is determined by another concept '*B*,' to which the concept '*A*' already contributes meaning. When concepts are mutually defined qua their reciprocal relationships, their signification cannot be exhaustively and rigorously determined.

This understanding of philosophical concepts as 'anasemes' has several implications, of which only three shall be mentioned. *First*: theories are regarded as *artificial* systems; they are interweaving both the theoretical desire of the author and the state of affairs they supposedly express themselves about. *Secondly* (as a consequence of the first implication): systems are not expressing 'facts' about the reality they take upon themselves to elucidate—in this case, the reality of communication—*except within a language-game* that is already shaping the presentation of such 'facts.' *Thirdly* (as a consequence of the two first implications): if theoretical systems are fundamentally self-referential, it appears to be the case that in theory one is able to 'prove' only what one believes in advance. This 'proof' will always appear insufficient because it represents merely a 'smaller version' of what it is meant to prove. Assertions at the macro-level of the system are substantiated by means of identical assertions at the micro-level of the system.

This position does not result in general skepticism, but rather in a *theoretical pragmatism*, whose principal idea is that theories are not mirrors of the reality they express themselves about. In expressing themselves about a reality, they *produce*, rather than *discover*, that reality.

(ii) Recursive Definitions and Self-Reference. Let me try to exemplify the idea outlined above in regard to Habermas' definition of his core notion, *illocution*. I shall here only address the early essay, *What is Universal Pragmatics?*, in order to demonstrate the absence of any convincing closure of the text.

In order to understand rational conditions for communicative action, *illocution* is particularly important, since it is in the illocutionary act that interlocutors address each other in the attempt to secure understanding. It is of major importance to offer a cogent and consistent determination of this term. In the pursuit of this determination, we learn that the specific validity-claim for illocutionary speech-act, *rightness*, is not sufficient. Besides *rightness* as the corresponding validity-claim for illocutionary discourse, we must also presuppose, says Habermas, the execution of the validity-claim, *truth* (which was originally corresponding to the constative speech-act).

> *The validity claim of constative speech acts is presupposed in a certain way by speech acts of every type.* The meaning of the propositional content mentioned in nonconstative speech acts can be made explicit through transforming a sentence of propositional content, 'that p' into a propositional sentence 'p'; and the truth claim belongs essentially to the meaning of the proposition thereby expressed. *Truth claims are thus a type of validity claim build into the structure of possible speech in general. Truth is a universal validity claim* [my emphases].[58]

Truth over-determines its neighboring validity-claims, since it regulates all speech-acts. If *truth* is a universal validity-claim, the *illocutionary claim to rightness* must in addition be regulated by the superior *claim to truth*. So, if *rightness* regulates the illocutionary speech-act according to the following notation, *rightness → illocution*, in an extended model, we get this notation: *truth → rightness → illocution*.

After introducing 'truth' as a new validity-claim, the conditions under which communication can be judged as true and right still need to be determined. It is not sufficient that an utterance is understandable and true; it must be *acceptable* to the hearer too. And according to Habermas, an utterance assumes acceptability "if the speaker not merely feigns but sincerely makes a serious offer."[59] Consequently, a new *sincerity-claim* is added in order to determine the opportune and felicitous utterance. We notice now that the all-important illocutionary speech-act is not simply regulated by its *corresponding* validity-claim, *rightness*, nor by the universal validity-claim, *truth*; it is *also* regulated by the validity-claim, *sincerity* (which originally belonged to the expressive speech-act). According to this new stipulation, we now have the following series of validity-claims regulating illocutionary speech: *sincerity* → *truth* → *rightness* → *illocution*.

Because of the anasemic status of the term 'illocution,' because its meaning is a structure of other anasemes, it always evades explicit and unambiguous definition. A speech-offer is no longer simply *right*; furthermore, it must be *true* too; and finally, it must be *sincere and serious*. But this final requirement needs further definition and explanation, because, what is exactly a 'sincere and serious' speech-offer? In order to explain this requirement, Habermas sets up a condition outside his familiar diagram, and asserts that a 'sincere and serious' speech-offer depends on a certain *engagement* of the speaker: "So far as I can see, previous analyses of speech acts have been unsatisfactory, as *they have not clarified the engagement of the speaker, on which the acceptability of his utterance specifically depends* [My emphasis]."[60] And later in a sentence highlighted by Habermas: "*The illocutionary force of an acceptable speech-act consists in the fact that it can move a hearer to rely on the speech-act-typical commitments of the speaker* [Habermas' emphasis]."[61]

The criterion is still sincerity, that is, the correspondence of speaker-intention and speech-act intention. But how does the hearer trust the sincerity of the speaker? Habermas' answer, by gauging the speaker's *engagement*, appears to be a new recursion. This new recursion creates a new problem, because how, as Habermas asks, do we determine, at a meta-communicative level, *engagement*? "If illocutionary force not simply has more than a suggestive influence, what can motivate the hearer to base his action on the premise that the speaker *seriously intends the engagement* she indicates [My emphasis]?"[62] How can the hearer know whether the speaker is serious in her engagement?

As we have seen, the communicative concord is violated if an apparent illocutionary speech-act is a manipulation in disguise, and if, in the instance of speech, we are unable to detect this. However, as Habermas explains, the single speech-act cannot be understood as an isolated fact, since in reality speech-acts elapse as a series of exchanges. In the course of such exchanges, the parties experience whether or not speech-act obligations are met or ignored over a longer series. The acceptability of the utterance, therefore, depends on the *repeated* success of an exchange of speech-acts, and success is achieved if the speaker *repeatedly* obeys cognitively controllable validity-claims.

Since as listeners, we have the possibility of testing whether or not typical speech-act obligations are respected in the long run, speech is seen as having inherent rationality: "*In the final analysis, the speaker can illocutionarily influence the hearer and vice versa, because speech-act-typical commitments are connected with cognitively testable validity claims*—that is, because the reciprocal bonds have a rational basis [Habermas' emphasis]."[63] Habermas again chooses a notion outside his scheme as a final criterion for the rational foundation of communication: speech-acts are 'testable' or 'controllable.' In this schematic illustration on recursion, we observe how the author regresses to a seemingly unending series of anasemes in order to explain how rationality is implied in communication. I outline the series discussed up to now: *testability → engagement → (sincerity → truth → rightness) → illocutionary force.*

It appears as if Habermas could always take another recursive step back, as if this recursive structure of his system is just another example of the *regressus infinitum*. However, this is not exactly the case. There is a halt to Habermas' deliberations, and in the present essay we stop at the notion 'testability' (or 'controllability'). Beyond this term Habermas goes no further. But we notice that this term is in itself a *complex structure* made up of three components insofar as *test* or *control* implies, 1) an utterance, 2) a background whereupon the utterance can be controlled, and 3) a controller. This implies that the controller is supposed to test or control the utterance against a certain background, and that background is, obviously, the background of the already mentioned three validity-claims. The term is supposed to close the discourse, but it only opens a new structure, apparently the same as the one we have just been discussing—the one we thought we had left behind. However, it opens the same structure *in miniature. The closing term repeats, at a micro-level of the text, what is already represented at a macro-level.*

The explanation of the rational ground of communication relies, in the final analysis, on a control by which a controller controls the rational foundation of communication. The controller controls whether or not communication actualizes the background of validity claims, *truth, rightness,* and *sincerity.* Controlling speech against this rational background is simultaneously an explanation of the same background. As we control the speaker against a background of validity-claims, we *substantiate* and *explain* the legitimacy of the same background. Thus, the background *substantiates itself* (it validates the validity-claims of truth, rightness and sincerity; the validity-claims, *truth, rightness,* and *sincerity* validate the validity-claims, *truth, rightness,* and *sincerity*). Consequently, '*control*' is a concept composed of concepts that are identical to those that the term is supposed to explain. The terms it explains are presupposed in its own structure, according to the following, and final, schematic representation: *((truth → rightness → sincerity) → test/control) → engagement → (sincerity → truth → rightness) → illocutionary force.*

Therefore, the recursive definition is not identical to infinite regress; it is rather defines something on its own terms such that *the definition is represented as a smaller version of the system it is defining.* The recursive definition is in other words a *fractal repetition* of the system it is defining. It is a kind of *recurrence of the same* on the level of theoretical systems; but 'recurrence of the same' *on a smaller scale*—the system ultimately defines itself, the same defines the same. In the present *Habermasian* system, illocution is both part of a class and is derived or regulated from the same class. Its rational foundation is the class of which it happens also to be a member.

(C) STRATEGIES OF SELF-IMMUNIZATION

(1) CHIASMATIC CRITICISM
(i) The Fallacy of Escaping a Fallacy. (ii) Who is Collapsing What and How Much. (iii) A Critique of Reason must Employ Reason. (iv) The 'Pre-Postmetaphysical' Assumptions Behind the Critique of Metaphysics.

(i) The Fallacy of Escaping a Fallacy. In his work, *The Philosophical Discourse of Modernity,*[64] Habermas believes he detects in Derrida's thinking an application of the so-called 'performative contradiction,' and he considers him, together with Heidegger and Adorno, as guilty of this paradox. Habermas also notices that they all develop strategies to escape the paradox. The late Heidegger, for example, "flees from this paradox to the luminous heights of an esoteric special discourse, which absolves itself of the restrictions of discursive speech generally and is immunized by vagueness against any specific objections."[65] Heidegger can in other words criticize the foundations of logic by writing in a style that abandons the requirements of discursive logic, a style that is semi-private and elitist, with this, inaccessible to the critique of the uninitiated.

Derrida chooses another strategy; he "does not place himself in lordly fashion above the objection of pragmatic inconsistency, but renders it *objectless.*"[66] He does so by denouncing the authority of logical consistency-claims. Logic becomes the depreciated term in the classical hierarchy, logic versus rhetoric. The focus on rhetoric, style, and literature replaces the traditional focus on logic, argument, and philosophy. Derrida turns the world upside-down, says Habermas. Philosophical texts are read as literary texts. This cancellation of a classical distinction implies that the all-important 'genre-distinction' between literature and philosophy breaks down. Derrida avoids the performative contradiction by employing a strategy that is more dubious than the performative contradiction itself. Habermas admits that, "there can only be talk about 'contradiction' in the light of consistency requirements, which lose their authority . . . if logic loses its primacy over rhetoric."[67] In that case, "the deconstructionist can deal with the works of philosophy as works of literature and adapt the critique of metaphysics to the standards of literary criticism."

(ii) Who is Collapsing What and How Much. The paradox of the 'performative contradiction'—also the so-called 'self-referential critique of reason'—is that reason is being criticized in a discourse itself employing reason. The philosophical author is using logic to criticize logic, with this producing an inconsistency between 'performative' and 'constative' level: reason is being 'performed' while simultaneously critique of reason is the theme and content of the discourse.

Instead of logic, Derrida makes rhetoric the theme of deconstruction; and in this, he abandons discursive obligations in his style. As such, the rigorous distinctions between the following oppositions is collapsing under the deconstructive reading:[68]

TERM I	TERM II
Logic	Rhetoric
Argument	Text
Philosophy	Literature
Critique of Metaphysics	Literary Criticism

Derrida collapses,' 'undermines' or 'erases' these distinctions, which Habermas finds indispensable for the continuation of his so-called 'unfinished project of Modernity.' However, when Habermas talks about 'collapse,' he tacitly implies three different definitions of the term.

Derrida is guilty in them all, but some are more severe than others. In the first definition, 'collapse' means that the distinction between the two columns in the table above breaks down. As such, it implies a leveling of a classical hierarchy where traditionally logic has had primacy over rhetoric. This leveling, neutralization, and equalization describe what Deconstruction typically employs as *one* of its reading-strategies; it describes a procedure that we encounter in much of Derrida's work. 'Collapse' in this sense is a deliberate analytical strategy of Deconstruction.

However, 'collapse' gets a stronger sense in Habermas. In this sense, 'collapse' means that the hierarchy above is not only leveled, but it is also turned upside-down. Derrida instates a new hierarchy where Rhetoric has primacy over Logic, Literature over Philosophy, etc. As Christopher Norris has pointed out, this is an objection that might characterize certain early American receptions of Derrida's work, such as the Yale School Criticism or the Neo-Pragmatism of Richard Rorty, but as an understanding of Derrida's work, it is distorted.[69] It is nevertheless this sense of collapse, Habermas chooses to argue against. "The frailty of the genre distinction between philosophy and literature is evidenced in the practice of deconstruction; in the end, *all* genre distinctions are submerged in one comprehensive, all embracing contexts of texts. . . . This is the ground of the primacy of rhetoric."[70] From this point onwards, Habermas establishes that Derrida's project is to assert "the primacy of rhetoric over logic." The assertion is repeated several times. It becomes Habermas' favorite critical conception of Derrida.

Finally, in the strongest sense of 'collapsing,' Derrida is guilty of collapsing all discourses whatsoever under the heading of an all-encompassing aesthetic dimension of language. This implies that not only does Derrida neutralize the genre-distinction between philosophy and literature, he also neutralizes distinctions between ordinary language and philosophical discourse, between ordinary language and literature, and between philosophical discourse and scientific. According to this charge, everything is to Derrida the same. There is no difference between ordinary language, poetry, theory, and science, because everything is organized under the same poetical-creative register of language.

> For Derrida, linguistically mediated processes within the world are embedded in a world-constituting context that prejudices everything; they are fatalistically delivered up to the unmanageable happening of text production, overwhelmed by the poetic-creative transformation of a background designed by archewriting. . . . Because Derrida overgeneralizes this one linguistic function—namely the poetic—he can no longer see the complex relationship of the ordinary practice of normal speech to the two extraordinary spheres, differentiated, as it were, in opposite directions. The polar tension between world-disclosure and problem-solving is held together within the matrix of ordinary language. . . . Derrida holistically levels these complicated relationships in order to equate philosophy with literature and criticism.[71]

It is under the hegemony of this single poetic-creative dimension that Derrida subsumes discourses that are problem-solving, productive, and educational. In doing so, Derrida demotes discourses by which we interact in the world and with the world, and linguistically understand it.

However—apropos of collapsing genre-distinctions—we notice the irony that Habermas himself, while criticizing Derrida of collapsing genre-distinctions, condenses different genres such as literature, poetry, aesthetics, criticism, and rhetoric into one comprehensive dimension of language, a so-called 'poetic-creative.' This is done intuitively and without appending qualifying remarks that could possibly explain the distinction between one (good) kind of collapse and another (bad) kind.

This constitutes a first simple example on what I shall call *chiasmatic criticism*. The criticism becomes a mirror of its critical object; and the critic repeats what he criticizes. He is as if trapped in-between the level of his content and the level of his performance, but only able to oversee his content, while his performance is 'overseeing' him (or, is 'working behind his back,' to resort to a more familiar metaphor).[72]

(iii) A Critique of Reason must Employ Reason. To Habermas, the problem is not that Derrida suggests the existence of a poetic-creative dimension of language, but that he subsumes all alternative language-games, or 'modes of communication,' under its authority. Habermas readily defends the existence of such a poetic-creative dimension, also labeled *world-disclosing* (—since supposedly poetry discloses to the subject the world as an ever-open realm of possibilities). A poetic-creative dimension of language has the capacity of suggesting life-forms different from and more authentic than those which reside in the stagnant routines of daily life. With this, a poetic-creative dimension has an emancipative and transgressive-liberating potential, and it becomes (at least from *The Theory of Communicative Action* onwards) an important addition to Habermas' diagrams of indispensable language-games. In later essays on communicative action, it is typically added as a forth row to Habermas' tables over essential language-games.

However, to over-generalize the poetic-creative dimension of language, as allegedly Derrida does, deprives the theorist-philosopher of intervention in the world, because the world has been reduced to playful text-production. The philosopher has become poet, or at best, literary critic. Philosophy's role as custodian and guardian of reason has been thwarted. Therefore Habermas must object to this one-dimensionality; if we follow Derrida's (so-called) 'recommendation,' "philosophical thinking were to be relieved of the duty of solving problems and shifted over to the function of literary criticism, it would be robbed not merely of its seriousness, but of its productivity."[73] By requiring philosophy to be 'serious,' Habermas implies that it has an obligation to disclose, criticize, and transform existing repressive life-forms.

This is why Derrida's self-immunization *against* the paradoxical 'self-referential criticism of reason' is in itself paradoxical. His self-immunization against performative contradiction overwhelms rational consistency-claims by overemphasizing style, rhetoric, and creativity. This has the consequence that the critique of reason becomes itself blunted. "Whoever transposes the radical critique of reason into the domain of rhetoric in order to blunt the paradox of self-referentiality, also dulls the sword of the critique of reason itself."[74] If it is philosophy's task to criticize repressive forms of reasoning, such a critique can only be exercised by reason itself. However, if Derrida relinquishes all appeals to reason, if he turns upside-down the hierarchy between rhetoric and logic and prioritizes rhetoric, then he obstructs this task. He has reduced philosophy to mere play and poetry, with this, suspending its 'serious' social obligations. Instead of acting as a socially responsible adult, he has cast himself in the role of a playful child. Emphasizing rhetoric over logic is to be playful instead of serious, but such an attitude is to Habermas counter-productive, because—although the playful philosopher aspires to criticize reason—the result is a weak and impotent critique. Philosophy has become 'unproductive,' it is no longer problem-solving; it is no longer potentially directed towards relieving society of repressive life-forms. Therefore the paradoxical outcome: if one criticizes reason *universally* and demotes its superiority, one has blunted the only available tool by which one could criticize reason.

The collapse of the genre-distinctions between literature and philosophy, implemented in order to devaluate the authority of reason and escape the performative self-contradiction, is seen as a new aporia that Derrida unwillingly gets caught up in: "The false pretense of eliminating the genre distinction between philosophy and literature cannot lead us out of this aporia [radical critique of reason dulls critique of reason itself]."[75]

Hence, Habermas regards Derrida's totalizing criticism as a new 'aporia'; it becomes a new paradox, which Habermas sometimes seems to confuse with the paradox of 'performative self-contradiction.' Habermas' critical position is ambivalent. In various other contexts, Habermas cannot resist the temptation to characterize Derrida as propagator of the fallacy of the performative contradiction—although Habermas' reasoning in the present excursus strictly should prevent this.[76] Derrida cannot *both* be guilty in the 'performative self-contradiction' *and* in immunizing himself against it by his topsy-turvy emphasis on rhetoric.

Several writers have questioned and criticized Habermas' reading of Derrida,[77] and I shall not repeat these criticisms at this point. Here, we shall instead expand on a certain irregularity in Habermas' reasoning indicated above. We notice two oddities: first, we notice as already indicated that neither Heidegger nor Derrida are in fact guilty in the performative contradiction, which is, at least, *threatening* their thinking insofar as they to Habermas' mind belong to a skeptic, anti-foundationalist, and postmodern trend in continental philosophy. It is as if they as *skeptics* (Habermas' blanket-word for irrationalists, anti-cognitivists, etc.) *ought to have been* guilty in performative contradiction; as if the desire involved in the *ought* blinds Habermas to the otherwise expressed state of affairs. Secondly, we notice that Habermas ends up *recommending* performative contradiction as the proper remedy against their *evasion* of the 'performative self-contradiction.' How do we *properly* criticize reason, Habermas retorts to Derrida's totalizing criticism? —Not by abandoning reason, but by employing reason! In other words, we employ a tool with the purpose of destroying the efficacy of that tool.

Here, we have a particularly strong example of *chiasmatic criticism.* We notice how positions are being reversed as in a *chiasm* or *decussation.* That is, positions are crossed and inverted in the form of an 'X'. The auxiliary object in the critical position, and the hostile object in the criticized position change places during the argument, in such a manner that if at the beginning of the argument, 'performative contradiction' is a hostile object, it is at the end of the argument turned into an auxiliary object. Antagonist becomes protagonist. This, however, happens without full awareness of the author, who continues to believe that he is criticizing 'performative contradiction.'

(iv) The 'Pre-Postmetaphysical' Assumptions Behind the Critique of Metaphysics. Heidegger and Derrida's abandonment of rational consistency-requirements rests on a general misunderstanding, Habermas claims, and he ends his excursus on Derrida's 'leveling of genre distinctions' by adding a long footnote explaining what has given rise to this misunderstanding. Surprisingly, in unrelentingly critiquing metaphysics, Derrida &co. have not grasped the postmetaphysical condition of contemporary thought. Ever since Hegel, philosophy has given up 'status claims' to truth. To proceed as if truth is still at the heart of philosophy is to knock down already open doors. Paradoxically, the Heideggerian 'destruction' and the Derridean 'deconstruction' of metaphysical notions of truth assume that strong concepts of truth and theory are still the order of the day. They mistakenly proceed as if universalizing notions of philosophy, dreams of ultimate foundations, of unconditional validity, and of absolute truth were still dominating philosophical discourse.

However, these notions of philosophy have long ago given way to more local, more humble notions of the task of philosophy. It is no longer philosophy's task to communicate the 'World-Spirit'; philosophy is no longer 'usher' [*Platzerhalter*] but 'stand-in' [*Platzhalter*]; it is no longer 'judge,' but 'interpreter,' Habermas writes in another essay, correcting Kantian-Hegelian ideals of the role of philosophy.[78] Long ago, the 'fallibilistic' consciousness of the sciences caught up with philosophy too. Philosophy learned that there is no universal and absolute truth; consequently, the endeavor to 'deconstruct' such constructions is futile and redundant. However, as Habermas goes on in this note, an important amendment is added to his claim.

> With this kind of fallibilism, we . . . do not by any means eschew truth claims. Such claims cannot be raised in the performative attitude of the first person other than as transcending space and time—precisely as claims. But we are also aware that there is no zero-context for truth claims. They are raised here and now and are open to criticism. Hence we reckon upon the trivial possibility that they will be revised tomorrow. Just as it always has, philosophy understands itself as the defender of rationality in the sense of the claim of reason endogeneous to our form of life. In its work, however, it prefers a combination of strong propositions with weak status claims; so little is this totalitarian, that there no call for a totalizing critique of reason against it.[79]

Habermas introduces a double-bind in regard of the raising of truth-claims. We must both raise them (in the 'performative attitude of the first person'), and simultaneously criticize them/expect them to be criticized (since there is no 'zero-context for truth claims'). Philosophy is, on the one hand, a defender of rationality, but, on the other, it defends a rationality with 'weak status claims.' Finally, since the 'no zero-context' and the 'weak status claims' of truth is taken for granted by everybody in today's philosophical environment, there is 'no call for a totalizing critique of reason against it.'

Here we notice a third example on *chiasmatic criticism*, or alternatively, *chiasmatic reasoning*. We notice again that chiasmatic reasoning is not governed by the argumentative logic that Habermas so eloquently elaborates in several essays. It is rather a defense-mechanism employed to protect a theory from a criticism that the author knows would be potentially devastating. Below, I shall suggest that it is the metaphysical assumptions in Universal Pragmatics that stimulates Habermas' chiasmatic criticism. Habermas has (correctly) 'felt' that a school of anti-metaphysical philosophers (such as Nietzsche, Heidegger, and Derrida) threatens the metaphysical foundations of his theory, and he is reacting by turning around the criticism in order to confront the threat. Chiasmatic reasoning is well-adapted to that task, because it *decussates* the positions in question. Now (*first decussation*), the anti-metaphysicians have not understood the post-metaphysical condition of contemporary thinking; they are still 'pre-post,' they are still breathing within a metaphysical tradition, giving metaphysics importance by spending energy defeating it. Now (*second decussation*), Habermas' metaphysical thinking is truly post-metaphysical, since he knows that it is no longer worthwhile to argue against metaphysics. We are so far beyond metaphysics that we can relax our defenses against it, and re-employ its most typical gestures.

The argument is pure magic. Habermas can now reproduce all the traditional operations and make all the traditional theoretical choices of metaphysics, and still claim that he is 'post' metaphysics. That there is no manifest difference between metaphysics and Habermas' post-metaphysics causes no disturbance, because it is already decided that we know that we are 'post.'

2) THE NOTION OF 'FALLIBILISM' AS SELF-IMMUNIZING STRATEGY

(i) A Postmetaphysical Theory Making Universalistic Truth-Claims. (ii) First and Third Person. (iii) Habermas' Double-Bind. (iv) The Superficiality and Necessity of the Concept 'Fallibilism.' (v) 'Fallibilism' as a Self-Immunizing Stratagem.

(i) A Postmetaphysical Theory Making Universalistic Truth-Claims. Habermas *interprets* his philosophy as 'fallibilistic' and 'post-metaphysical.' He is convinced that it participates in a 'modern' project of gradually suspending universalistic and substantive truth-claims, in order to replace them with provisional and regional truth-claims. Rationality is neither inherent, eternal, nor objective, Habermas contends; however, this is contended in the face of a theory of communication, which *admittedly* makes 'essentialistic' and 'universalistic' truth-claims.

Habermas' so-called *universal* pragmatics is allegedly *post-metaphysical* since from Marx, and Historical Materialism in general, Habermas has inherited the notion that theories are never final and absolute (what exactly seems to imply that they are never *universal*). Theories are no longer infallible and static explanation-models of the universe; they are instead 'fallibilistic.' They are subjected to the better refuting argument, in a sense analogous to how Karl Popper's scientific theory is subjected to refuting experiments or observations. Thus, fallibilistic theories recognize their provisional and historical status, and accept refutation, as do Popper's falsifiable scientific theories.

Habermas' *fallibilism* is thus to the humanities what Popper's *falsifiability* is to the sciences. This idea of fallibilism is supposed to replace the ambitious project in classical, medieval, and pre-modern thinking of founding a *primae philosophia* explaining all aspects of the world once and for all.

When situating himself as post-metaphysical, Habermas typically presupposes a specific classical notion of metaphysics, as expounded in ancient philosophers like Plato, Aristotle, and Plotinus. Accordingly, metaphysics is understood as absolutistic, universalistic, and unitary. Metaphysics asserts *One* principle that supposedly explains, participates in, and informs the *Whole*. Classical metaphysics explains what is first, always has been first, and always will be first; it is determining the *One* unitary principle that is eternal, and as such informs the finite *Whole* of changing events and objects. This eternal unitary first principle is paradoxically both world-present and world-transcendent. It is supposed to be potentially present in all changing things and it is supposed to transcend the world of changing things. As the unitary first principle gives identity to the particulars of inner-worldly things and events, they can now be perceived as parts of a *Whole* informed by the *One*. Evidently, classical metaphysics is a-historical in this aspiration to explain (1) *once and for all* (2) *everything* by (3) *one transcendental principle*. Habermas underscores especially the a-historicism of metaphysics.

Habermas believes that he has defeated these metaphysical aspirations if he *says* that he does not believe that his theory of communicative action is a-historical; if he *says* that he believes that his theory is fallibilistic and subject to the better refuting argument. If this from the outset is declared, Habermas believes that he has earned the license to construct a theory that aspires to determine the first principles that inform the world of communication. As long as Habermas holds in mind that he is a product of history, his construction of a theory that transcends the historically contingent is no longer metaphysical. (It is perhaps a detail of some significance that Habermas, despite smaller adjustments of his theory, has not so far accepted any refutation of his theory of the rational constitution of communicative action. Habermas remains deeply convinced that language is orientated towards reaching understanding. The response to refuting arguments is typically to explain the theory once more. One wonders; is it now a mere coincidence that the fallibilistic theory does not seem to accept refutation?)

(ii) First and Third Person. Of course, it cannot take us by surprise that Habermas does not see his philosophy refuted. It is safe to presume that he has a bias in favor of his own theory. But exactly because this insight

is trivial and truistical, the notion of 'fallibilism' needs some further clarification and qualification.

How is the following schism resolved? On the one hand, one's theory is accepted to be fallible—at one point certain to be refuted. On the other hand, any philosopher worth his name tends to be biased in favor of his theory, and ready to defend it against objections. That is, he will naturally perceive it as infallible and do his best to immunize his theory against refutations. For example, he will not perversely construct a theory, and thereupon declare that this was merely some private game, which nobody ought to take seriously.

Habermas solves this schism by splitting himself into two subjects. In the footnote quoted above, the first person poses, in his 'performative attitude,' truth claims that transcend 'space and time.' But in addition to this attitude, we have another attitude—which we might call the 'transcendental attitude' of the 'third person'—recognizing the historical character of truth. Further elaborating on other remarks by Habermas on this split, we can suggest a distinction between a first-person and a third-person Habermas.

> In posttraditional societies, or under conditions of postmetaphysical thinking, all knowledge—from the stance of a third person—is deemed fallible . . . even though in the performative stance, that from the perspective of a participant, we cannot avoid unconditionally regarding the asserted knowledge as true.[80]

Ergo: we have a performative and a reflexive stance, a first person and a third person! The first-person Habermas is identical to the historically situated Habermas that responds to the context of present philosophy (and to the community of present philosophers) by offering theoretical solutions to contemporary philosophical difficulties. To the first-person Habermas these solutions evidently have a certain stability and reliability—he proposes them in good faith. The first-person Habermas is humble enough to understand that as situated in time, he responds to his time by constructing what he must regard as solid and genuinely rooted knowledge. That is, he constructs what he must regard as (so far) infallible knowledge. Here, the humble philosopher acknowledges that in the cognitive development of his work, it is impractical and self-defeating to simultaneously reiterate to himself that his work is fallible. Because he is a mere fleck in the flood of history, because he is overpowered by his time, he can only tell the truth.

Third-person Habermas realizes something (which in fact first-person Habermas already realized—but humbly pushed aside), namely that 'Habermas' is a product of history. This implies that his theory of communicative action is fallible, and in the course of history will be refuted or replaced. As third person, Habermas reflectively fathoms the historical, fleeting, and provisional character of his theory. Third-person Habermas is Habermas as Absolute Spirit; he perceives everything from the perspective of eternity. Under that scrutinizing gaze, first-person Habermas cannot survive, and it is from that perspective that his theory is fallible.

Whereas, ultimately, third-person Habermas is right about the historical character of theories, this rightness is not practical in everyday life. We can adopt a reflexive attitude (a third person attitude) to our decisions, but in everyday life, we cannot practically perform this attitude. Here we must adopt what here I call the 'humble' attitude, we must tell the truth and believe that what we tell *is* the truth. We recognize thus that we are no absolute spirits; we resign ourselves to our historical fate, and renounce the attempt to perceive the world from the perspective of eternity.

> Although when we adopt a reflexive attitude we know that all knowledge is fallible, in everyday life we cannot survive with hypotheses alone, that is, in a persistently fallibilistic way. . . . Certainly, we have to make decisions in the lifeworld on the basis of incomplete information. . . . At any rate, the performative need for behavioral certainty rules out a reservation in principle with regard to truth.[81]

We notice the following paradox emerging. The first-person Habermas that toils to secure the infallibility, or truth, of what he is doing is the *historical* Habermas, and the third-person Habermas that asserts the fallibility of his own effort is the *a-historical* Habermas. As historical, Habermas must emphasize his own infallibility, but as a-historical absolute spirit, he knows that all theoretical validity is fleeting and bound to fail. Paradoxically, it is a-historical Habermas who knows that he is a product of history.

(iii) Habermas' Double-Bind. The notion of 'fallibilism' is supposed to enter the current debate about foundational and anti-foundational theories. With this notion in hand, Habermas situates himself as an anti-foundationalist in a theoretical stance that seems counter-factual to both his polemical engagements in *The Philosophical Discourse of Modernity*, and to his inherent philosophical project. First, in *The Philosophical Discourse . . .* Habermas situates himself in opposition to philosophers that traditionally are regarded as anti-foundationalists— Nietzsche, Heidegger, Foucault, and Derrida—in a criticism that objects to the perspectivism, subjectivism, and aestheticism in their anti-

foundationalist positions. Secondly, although Habermas labels the theory of communicative action 'fallibilistic,' the project is still to account for the universal rational features of communication. These universal features are *a priori*, and account for our ability to form a world of historical and changeable knowledge. As such, the features themselves cannot easily be conceived as historical.

By adopting 'fallibilism' as a meta-theoretical stance in a theory that admittedly makes 'essentialistic claims,' Habermas double-binds his reader. It becomes unclear how universal features can also be historical, how necessary *a priori* concepts are also contingent and fallible. (If we take this double-stance seriously, we are inclined to believe that Habermas' is merely gambling on the universality of his validity-claims; it is only in a gamble a thing can turn out to be the case or not to be the case. However, modest knowledge of Habermas' work will assure us that gambling he is not; the universality of validity-claims does not hinge on a toss of the dice.) That Habermas sometimes gets around this problem by adding the adjective 'weak' as a characterization of his specific brand of universalism—a 'weak' foundationalism making 'weak' universal claims, etc.—obviously only repeats the schism. It is a purely linguistic remedy; it condenses the unthinkable paradox, necessity vs. contingency, into one handy phrase.[82]

Because the notion 'fallibilism' creates such binds, and because it seems at odds with the inherent project of the theory, the emphasis on the notion appears to be symptomatic, and should be treated as a symptom of a deeper seated problem. As symptom, the notion performs another job than the job it says it performs. It seems to indicate a regress from Habermas' strictly philosophical project (which is also a metaphysical project) to an *ideological obfuscation* of that project.

(iv) The Superficiality and Necessity of the Concept 'Fallibilism.' When we re-think this notion, we also start to notice several problems in its invocation. That the theory of communicative action is fallibilistic seems, *first* (as already mentioned), discordant with the entire immanent motive (desire) of the theory to found universal rational characteristics of speech. *Secondly*, if fallibilism implies the fact that all theory is historical—according to the so-called third-person attitude introduced above—this fact is trivial and self-evident and hardly worth mentioning. It is a knowledge that theories can afford to ignore, because the disregard of the insight does not subtract from their inherent historical constitution. Whether one is a stout foundationalist or a flimsy anti-foundationalist, the foundational and anti-foundational theories alike are products of history. It does not change anything in the theory to know or to say that it is historical. In that light, *thirdly*, the claim seems strangely superficial

and superfluous, and the urgency of making it seems futile. The notion 'fallibilism' does not perform any 'job' in Habermas' theory. Whether or not the theory is regarded as 'fallibilistic,' it does not change anything in the immanent structures of the theory. For example, if the theory is seen as fallibilistic (as supposedly it should), this insight does not change anything in the concrete analytical project. The insight has no consequences; we can be certain that the theory will continue to analyze or 'reconstruct' the *a priori* validity claims of conversation. The only job the notion 'fallibilism' here performs is to call this reconstruction 'fallibilistic.' It has no other job than being a label. *Fourthly*, if 'fallibilism' simply implies that one can adopt a third-person attitude with which to judge theoretical engagements and decisions in the current life-world as historical, changeable, and replaceable, then all theory is fallible. Fallibilism is not a distinctive feature of Habermas' Universal Pragmatics, and the notion does not distinguish the theory in any which way, since Habermas must mean that it applies with equal pertinence to, for example, Searle's Speech-Act Theory or Derrida's Deconstruction. The only thing distinguishing Searle or Derrida from Habermas on that count is that they have not adopted the label.

It is these problems and redundancies inherent in the notion that make me suggest that the notion is 'symptomatic.' In other words, there must be a *reward* for introducing the notion; something that gives (or is seen as giving) Habermas an important advantage; something that helps the survival of his theory in the competitive community of contemporary philosophy. Within the framework of Habermas' theory, it is for several reasons expedient to be perceived as a fallibilistic, rather than a foundational, philosopher. *First* (not to forget the obvious), the notion that theories have provisional and historical status is well rooted in Habermas' theoretical heritage from Marx, Lukacs, and the Frankfurt School. Since deriving from his personal intellectual heritage, Habermas' introduction of the notion is not without integrity. *Secondly*, within the current paradigm of Continental Philosophy, and in some quarters of Anglo-Saxon Philosophy, it has become increasingly difficult to defend foundational philosophical positions. If one successfully can label one's theory as anti-foundational, the theory is immediately brought up to speed with the current victorious paradigm. *Thirdly* (most importantly, I believe), within Habermas' theoretical paradigm, the acknowledgment of the theory's fallibility is *performatively consistent* with deep-structural motives of the theory. The theory of rational communicative competence emphasizes the value of rational dialogue, discussion, and argument. If the theory itself is open to dialogue and argument, the theory is proving the point that it is asserting in its content. Habermas is consequently performatively consistent. If Habermas asserted his theory authoritatively, professing the existence of an immutable ensemble of laws governing speech,[83] he would be vulnerable to criticism for performative inconsistency. He would then assert a theory emphasizing rational dialogue that could not be discussed any further. It is therefore seriously important to underscore the 'fallibilistic' character of Universal Pragmatics. That the theory is fallible now implies that it can be discussed, that it can accept the better refuting argument, and that, eventually, it *will* be refuted, revised, or replaced.

(v) 'Fallibilism' as a Self-Immunizing Stratagem. The attitude seems open-minded, it invites discussion and counter-argument, it adopts Popper's criticism of 'immunizing tactics,' but now in the realm of philosophy. On a first look, the gesture displays generosity and magnanimity towards criticism (and we have no reason to doubt that this is a genuine reflection of the author's personal attitude). It is only under scrutiny, when we critically reflect, re-think, and in some sense, deconstruct the gesture (what we are invited to by the theory—as we just read), that we detect another motive.

First, it is not without problems to apply to philosophy Popper's criticism of 'immunizing tactics' or 'stratagems' in the sciences. Falsifiability in the sciences and fallibility in the humanities are not analogous cases.[84] In Popper, falsifiability indicates that a scientific theory, in order to pass as science, must be constructed in such a way that it is *in principle* possible to *falsify* the theory, that is, it must be constructed in such a way that it is possible to *test* the theory. If a theory is so constructed, it is falsifiable and earns the distinction *scientific*. 'Fallibility,' on the other hand, can add no distinction to a philosophical theory. There is no way we can construct a philosophical theory to be *in principle* 'fallible,' if 'in principle fallible' here indicates that it would be possible to test the philosophical theory, and prove it wrong (or true). We have nothing to test the philosophical theory against, no external court of appeal that once and for all could decide philosophical questions about truth, beauty, or the good.

In Popper, scientificality is attained if a scientific theory is in principle falsifiable, but calling a philosophy 'fallible' attains nothing—fallibility could not warrant a certain 'philosophicality.' Thus, *fallibilism* cannot constitute a notion parallel to Popper's *falsification*. A philosophical theory that does not accept the requirement of 'fallibilism' doesn't demote itself to non-philosophy, and a philosophical theory that accepts the requirement doesn't promote itself to 'philosophy.' In the context of philosophy, it is even a misnomer to talk about 'falllibilism' as a 'requirement' (or worse, a 'formal requirement'), because the modest 'formal requirement' for *fallible philosophy'* is that it exists within a historical context in which it is discussed, criticized and eventually replaced with other explanation-models. But since philosophy is *subjected* to this 'requirement' as a condition, it cannot constitute a *requirement*. We cannot *require* something to be what it already is. We cannot ask a red thing to turn red. Therefore, there is no difference between a philosophy accepting and a philosophy not accepting its fallibility.

When talking about 'immunizing tactics,' Popper's intention was originally to describe the means by which pseudo-scientists attempt to avoid falsification. For dogmatic or ideological purposes, pseudo-science tends to reject refuting observations by employing certain speculative devices. These devices could be, for example, 'ad hoc' explanations—adding 'another part' amending, excusing, or modifying the 'main part' of the theory by explanations not themselves falsifiable. Or, they could constitute tautological theoretical constructions that can never be proven false to begin with, and therefore escape the fundamental scientific requirement, falsification. When scientists started to adopt these strategies, the science would degenerate to ideology, religion, or metaphysics. It would at best be an interesting theory, but it could no longer be called scientific. It would in other words have become philosophy.

Let us finally notice that whereas a scientist must be sufficiently open-minded to accept a refuting experiment, evasion of refuting arguments has in the history of philosophy never constituted a problem. It is *comparatively* (compared to philosophy) difficult for a scientist to adopt (or at least *sustain*) Popper's 'immunizing tactics,' since an argument refuting the objectivity of an experiment or an observation is futile, and eventually becomes the object of ridicule. If an object does not behave as a scientific theory has predicted, no amount of ingenious argumentation can change that fact. In a scientific community, arguments meant to refute facts are looked down upon as 'ideology' or 'philosophy.' In philosophy, on the contrary, counter-argumentation is the order of the day, the rule of the game, and expected from all in the community. When Descartes' *Meditations* were met with several objections from his contemporaries, some of them penetrating and devastating, it never subtracted from Descartes' reputation as philosopher that he was able to evade criticism. When Diagones in refutation to Zeno's arguments for the impossibility of motion, stood up and started vigorously pacing the room, Zeno was, as far as the anecdote goes, unmoved in his conviction of the infallibility of his theory. Philosophy, we can say as a rule of thumb, *invites* immunizing strategies and *counters* attempts of falsification.

Paradoxically, this rule of thump applies exactly to Habermas. Under scrutiny, when we re-think Habermas' gesture above, we notice that he has done exactly what he does not want to do (or what, at least, he believes he does not want to do), namely to immunize himself against criticism. The notion of 'fallibilism' is paradoxically a very effective (because concealed) immunizing strategy. It is applied in order to escape the overwhelming perception that the theory is inherently universalistic, essentialistic, a-historical, and metaphysical. If now such criticism is mounted, it cannot gain any foothold because *another part* of the theory is asserting that the essentialist aspirations of the theory are ultimately historical and fallible. If a critic raises a critique of the essentialist and metaphysical aspirations of the theory without further qualifications, he reveals that he is not aware of the *other part* of the theory. As such, his critique will be deemed inadequate and incompetent; and as such neutralized. However, the problem is exactly that the theory has 'another part,' incongruent with the immanent motive of the theory, but introduced in order to immunize the 'main part' from criticism. The notion 'fallibilism' is precisely an 'ad hoc' construction. It constitutes 'another part' devised to ideologically obfuscate the 'main part.' In a specific 'habermasian' context, 'fallibilism' is ideology; it has another 'job' than it says it has. It says that it allows the theory to be criticized, but it is designed to avoid criticism.

3) THE METAPHYSICAL FOUNDATIONS OF REFUTING STRATEGIES.

(i) Philosophical Style and Self-Immunization. (ii) Performative Contradiction as Philosophical Defense-Mechanism. (iii) The Anatomy of the Performative Contradiction. (iv) The Performative Contradiction and Its Phono-Logocentric Foundation.

(i) Philosophical Style and Self-Immunization. Typically, Habermas sees self-immunization as a question of adopting a certain esoteric style. When philosophers like Heidegger or Derrida immunize themselves against criticism by means of emphasizing style, style becomes like a smokescreen produced to conceal the content of their philosophy (or lack of . . .), and avoid argument.

The charge appears arbitrary for various reasons. For one thing, different readers have different opinions about the understandability of a theory (it is not exactly beyond our imagination, for example, that some readers may find Habermas' style dense and esoteric). More importantly, rather than applying the charge to a small group of (post-modern) philosophers, the criticism would seem to apply to the entire philosophical community. Philosophical style (and perhaps all professional language) will always be esoteric and with this, adopt self-immunizing tactics. In philosophy, the relative complexity with which to describe abstract topics, the introduction of sub-distinctions to plain distinctions, or of sub-sub-distinctions to sub-distinctions, are devices that raise the level of difficulty, and thus 'immunize.' Introduction of ad hoc devices—such as modifications of, amendments to, or qualifications of the theory—'immunize.' The 'promises' of philosophy 'immunize'; that is, the author's 'promise' that problems, which in the present treatise are *as yet* unsolved, *shall* be solved (philosophy is always in *debt* to its reader). The display of erudition immunizes[85] ('name-dropping' in the novice). These and other devices are meant to prevent spontaneous and uneducated criticism—or simply, to 'scare off' as large a group as possible of potential critics. To a certain extent, philosophical style is an *inoculation against aggression*, an *outer layer of protection*.

Habermas typically situates self-immunization in the rhetorical register of the theory, as a question of style. Given his belief in a strong division between logic and rhetoric, logic is not as obvious a means of self-immunization, as is rhetoric. I shall venture the claim that self-immunization (while performed in or as philosophical style) is inscribed also in the very core of a theory, that is, in its so-called 'logical'—understood as its methodological, meta-theoretical, or metaphysical—register. Thus, philosophy have multiple layers of protection, not just easy-to-cognize *outer*, but also *inner* layers.

(ii) Performative Contradiction as Philosophical Defense-Mechanism. We notice that at the core of Habermas' theory of communication, it is immune to criticism because it is constructed so sufficiently ingeniously that it *cannot* be refuted—or (to say the same thing) it can only be refuted by someone seriously adopting Habermas' validity claims. These claims are therefore not radically falsifiable, because the critic who wanted to falsify them could do so only in a discourse that observes rational dialogue (—or, in a discourse that can be at least *interpreted* as following Habermas' validity-basis). I could not criticize Habermas' validity-claims in a manner understandable to Habermas, without entering a critical dialogue that would utilize the validity-basis I criticize. In other words, the potential critic of Habermas' validity-claims would be guilty in *performative self-contradiction*.

Over years of rigorous argumentation for his theory of communicative action, Habermas has produced a circle that hermetically closes off any attempt to criticize his theory—this, of course, in stark contrast to the alleged status of the theory as in principle 'fallible,' in principle open to criticism. The fallacious 'performative self-contradiction' (or 'self-referential criticism of reason') articulates the formal impossibility of criticizing the theory of communicative action. Those who endeavor to criticize communicative reason have contradicted themselves in the process—with this opting out of the community of accountable and competent speakers.

In other words, Habermas has constructed a defense mechanism that entraps his critics in incontrovertible contradictions. If they criticize him, they destroy themselves; they opt for a 'Robinson Crusoe' existence, Habermas says in the essay, *Discourse Ethics*; they adopt the semi-private language of the loner, the anti-social, or the schizophrenic.[86] The circle that closes off all further discussion of Habermas' theory of rational communication can now be reconstructed.

(a_1)   It is *only* possible to argue while conforming to validity claims that are latently present in all dialogue.

(a_2)   It is *not* possible to argue except by conforming to validity claims that are latently present in all dialogue.

(b_1)   If a critic criticizes the existence of communicative validity claims (or the possibility of rational dialogue), she is guilty in a formal and incontrovertible logical fallacy, because she relates and conforms to latently present validity claims in her criticism.

(b_2)   If a 'consistent' critic (e.g., Derrida) nonetheless criticizes communicative validity claims, in his performative attitude shunning also validity claims latently present in all dialogue, he has opted out of the communicative community. His attitude is self-destructive: solipsistic, schizophrenic, or suicidal. In his lack of conviction about the power of rational dialogue, the *consistent skeptic* is threatened by autism or death.

(c)   The critic realizing b_1 and b_2, is *formally* obliged to return to a_1 and to accept a_2 as the unavoidable performative attitudes in speech-acts.

As such reconstructed, the notion 'performative self-contradiction' stops all further discussion. It functions as what Samuel S. Wheeler in a recent work has called an 'interpretation-stopper.'[87] It stops further interpretation. Wheeler's 'interpretation-stopper' is a reformulation of Derrida's notion of 'self-presence'—philosophy's reference to a principle that also stops all further discussion, because as 'self-present,' it is also self-given and self-evident (it is never necessary—it is even perverse and absurd—to debate the self-given and self-evident). In the tradition of Western Thinking, which Derrida has labeled 'phono-logocentric,' self-presence finds a special form. It becomes the point-zero where *voice* 'meet' *reason* and amalgamate into a unit that resists further differentiation; the word infused with reason becomes the final guarantor for the self-present subject, the metaphysical guarantee for our rational potential.

Given the suggested chain of associations: performative contradiction ~ interpretation-stopper ~ self-presence ~ phono-logocentrism, it is pertinent to ask whether these associations are merely accidental, or whether 'performative contradiction' as notion masks but carries the germ of self-presence in its most primitive assumptions. I shall argue that this is indeed the case, but since the claim is not intuitively self-evident, it is necessary to dissect the anatomical structure of Apel and Habermas' notion, and try to understand it in more detail.

(iii) The Anatomy of the Performative Contradiction. Following Karl-Otto Apel,[88] Habermas gives the following definition of performative contradiction: "A performative contradiction occurs when a constative speech act *k(p)* rests on noncontingent presuppositions whose propositional content contradicts the asserted proposition *p*."[89]

Apel and (subsequently) Habermas give as example Descartes', *Cogito, ergo sum*—or rather (as we must take them to imply), the preparatory arguments leading up to this conclusion. That is, Descartes' introduction of his hyperbolic doubt, which we can abbreviate into the statement, *I doubt that I exist*—written according the formula above, *I doubt(I exist)*. The proposition *p* (*I exist*) is contradicted in the pronunciation of the performative attitude (*I doubt*) presupposing existence.

(Allowing a brief digression at this point. It is obviously not Apel and Habermas' purpose to analyze the finer fabric of Descartes' text. In the *Meditations*, it is on the first pages clear that Descartes is mindful that his doubt is only hypothetical and provisional; explicitly, he warns us against taking his preparatory arguments literally, since that would compare him to the deranged that his readers could observe in the Parisian asylums. It must also be noted that Descartes' argument is exactly opposite to Apel and Habermas' use of it. This argument runs briefly, *I doubt therefore I think therefore I exist*. Descartes' conclusion is obviously not, *I doubt that I exist*. Apel and Habermas create a statement out of Descartes' philosophy that is contrary to its explicit intentions. In the *Principles of Philosophy*, Descartes is even more explicit when he asserts, "it is not possible for us to doubt that we exist while we are doubting," and he explains in the same paragraph, "it is a contradiction to suppose that what thinks does not . . . exist."[90] Now, we can of course feel confident that philosophers of the stature of Apel and Habermas are aware of such elementary scholarship. However, this level of argumentation does not have their interest. They have an interest in the *skeptic's argument*[91] reproduced by Descartes as a hypothesis and as contradistinctive to his deliberate project. "Descartes" is merely a label on something that is not his product, but has a vague association to that product.)

It is the skeptic's, *I doubt that p*, which urges on refutation. However, it is not any expression of doubt that forces a performative contradiction. We can doubt all kind of things without being guilty in performative fallacies; we don't commit performative contradictions by doubting the existence of ghosts, doubting the effectiveness of certain conflict resolutions, or having doubts on the sincerity of a politician. To be effective as a performative contradiction, the formula, *I doubt that p*, needs additional specification. Thus, the contradiction is committed when, *a skeptic expresses doubt on p, where p can be replaced with any proposition being tacitly presupposed in the first person present expression of doubt*. Before a performative contradiction is committed, it must be possible to return the rejected proposition in the utterance to the enunciating subject as a condition for his enunciation. Hence, a performatively contradictory statement is not specified by the form, $k(p)$ (which can designate any statement), but by the form, $p(k(p'))$, construed in the following manner: any constative speech-act that asserts a doubt regarding (p') is a performative contradiction if (p') is identical to, resembles, or is a variation over p as the indispensable condition for the utterance. Accordingly, the preparatory Cartesian argument, 'I doubt the existence of myself,' is performatively contradictory. The Heideggerian/Derridian, 'I doubt the existence of rational dialogue' is performatively contradictory as well (this may not be immediately evident, but shortly we will realize that within a Habermasian framework it cannot be otherwise).[92]

(iv) The Performative Contradiction and Its Phono-Logocentric Foundation. Ever since the groundbreaking essay on communicative action, *What is Universal Pragmatics*, Habermas has emphasized "the rational foundation of the illocutionary force" (—the title on an important section in the essay).[93] We have seen that the illocutionary component, although constituting only one out of three essential components in speech-acts (the locutionary, the illocutionary, and the expressive), over-determines its two neighbors, and is regarded the most important: The illocutionary role, Habermas stated, "determines the aspect of validity under which the speaker wants his utterance to be understood *first and foremost*."[94]

The illocutionary force represented the speech-act in its embryonic first stage, the stage where the speaker addresses someone with a certain performative attitude (or 'illocutionary force'), 'I doubt . . .', 'I promise . . .', 'I assert . . .', etc. This embryonic instance already inscribed a rational foundation for speech acts; it activated the universal communicative *a priori*. It was qua the illocutionary force that interlocutors 'bind and bond,' that is, mutually accept each other as competent and rational speakers.

If we now follow up on contemporary linguistics (notably Benveniste's[95]), we can designate this instance, *the instance of enunciation*. It indicates an act, in which an 'I' addresses a 'you' 'here and now.' According to Habermas, rationality is already inscribed in this instance. He can argue this, because he believes that in the instance of enunciation the speaker makes a so-called 'speech-offer,' which the hearer can in principle accept or reject. The hearer may take a so-called 'yes' or 'no' position to the utterance on offer. In order not to risk the 'no,' in order to make the hearer accept the speech-offer, the speaker must fulfill the three validity claims. Otherwise, the interlocutors do not seriously intend to enter a dialogue. Speakers intend to fulfill validity-claims, and hearers expect them being fulfilled.

Already in its most embryonic state, the speech-offer is directed toward redeemable validity-claims. That is, rationality is in effect at the very moment a speaker in her performative attitude refers back to herself as 'I' in her address to the other as 'you.' In the instance when a speaker says 'I,' she engages in a process directed toward fulfillment of rational expectations in the hearer. In this embryonic instance of enunciation, the speaker promises to fulfill rational expectations and, accordingly, she executes rational standards.

Under that interpretation, it is now clear why it is impossible for Derrida to state, 'I doubt the existence of rational dialogue.'[96] Derrida speaks, and insofar as he speaks, he addresses someone, and insofar as he addresses someone, he expects to be 'accepted' as a competent (~ 'rational') speaker. The embryonic instance of enunciation, the situation of 'I' opposed to 'you,' is what actualizes the 'binding and bonding' in rational dialogue. We see that in the strategic concept, *performative contradiction*, Habermas undermines any attempt to criticize the ideal of rational communication—criticism is self-contradictory, self-destroying, and self-eliminating. Insofar as I speak, I situate myself as an 'I' opposed to a 'you,' I enter a dialogue. Now, a certain immanent communicative imperative dictates me to fulfill an obligation; unwittingly, I enter a pact; I have to do something, but what exactly? — To do what I already do, to enter a dialogue! —And how could I possibly (in all sanity) refuse to do what I already do?

The assumption behind the 'performative contradiction' as employed in Habermas, is thus *exemplary* metaphysical, and, in general, the theory of communicative action is securely placed within the tradition of Western Thought that Derrida labels phono-logocentric. It is indeed difficult to recall a philosophy that is purer in its phono-logocentric assumptions. Rarely have we seen a so insistent defense of subjective rationality immanent in the self-presence of the speech-act; rarely has it been so emphatically accentuated how reason (*Logos*) permeates the spoken word (*Phoné*).

4) CONCLUSION

Self-protective devices are not merely rhetorical; they are not only stylistic smoke-screens that philosophers disperse around themselves in order to dodge evaluation and judgment. If self-protection is a smoke-screen, it is so at the core; it covers up a void, an emptiness, residing at the core of any philosophy. As well as we today accept that there is a breakdown of the laws of physics in the singularity of a black hole (or at the big bang explosion), we are pressed to accept in metaphysics an analogous situation: a breakdown of the laws of logic in the singularity of founding axioms.

This situation—this emptiness residing at the core of philosophy—has traditionally fueled the objections of so-called 'skeptics' against foundationalist philosophers. And it is in this situation that foundational philosophers have sought to preempt predictable skeptical objections by constructing a series of protective devices in order to *obscure* the emptiness, the breakdown of law, at the core. They have developed 'refutations' meant, once and for all, to mute the skeptics, and in this century, these 'refutations' take the form of 'performative contradiction.'[97]

Generally, anti-foundationalists doubt the power and objectivity of the theoretical explanation, and foundationalist cannot imagine that we could do without is. Foundationalists believe in *Philosophy* (capitalized-emphatic-anasemic) as a necessary remedy against chaos, and the immunizing strategies we find at the core of their thinking are defenses of this anasemic and inflated notion of philosophy. Immunizing strategies thus appear to be immanent, often unconscious, self-defenses against an incredulous world that never did believe that philosophy truly has an explanation potential that supersedes commonsense. By means of immunizing strategies, the philosopher suspends the disbelief of the world—at least as long as his immunization tactics remain effective, that is, *concealed*.

Because of the existence of these defense mechanisms, philosophy is able to deafen itself to objections, and one is inclined to conclude that it is essentially 'monadological.' It is 'windowless,' and reluctant to, perhaps incapable of, stepping outside its own immanent realm. Contrary to what Habermas believes, or rather, thinks he believes, philosophy is thus never open for, and it never benefits from, discussion. It has been my purpose to demonstrate that Habermas somehow 'knows' this, although he is fond of saying the opposite. Habermas *states* that he believes in dialogue, but he *performs*, qua a set of excellent and intelligent defense mechanisms, an insight into its ultimate futility. This, of course, is also a so-called 'performative contradiction.'

THE USES AND ABUSES OF PLEASURE

THE MANY INCOMPATIBLE VOICES IN JOHN STUART MILL'S *UTILITARIANISM*

> *Student*: But words must have some sense, it seems to me.
> *Mephistopheles*: Yes, yes, but don't be bothered overmuch by that.
> It's just when sense is missing that a word comes pat, and serves one's purpose most conveniently.
> . . . .
> *Mephistopheles*: Let error, not the truth be told—
> Make one of three and three of one;
> That's how it always has been done.
> Men hear mere words, yet commonly surmise words must have intellectual content too.
>
> — Goethe: *Faust*.[1]

1) INTRODUCTORY REMARKS
(i) How to Interpret Mill's Inconsistencies. (ii) The 'Naturalistic Fallacy' and the 'Anasemic Fallacy'. (iii) Three Distinctions Between Logical Analysis and Deconstructive Analysis. (iv) Elements of a Logic of Illogicality or an Oneiric Logic.

(i) How to Interpret Mill's Inconsistencies. When we read commentaries on John Stuart Mill's essay *Utilitarianism*, typically, commentators are aware of the many inconsistencies and self-contradictions of the work. It is understood that Mill's brand of utilitarianism is incompatible with Bentham's, that he stretches the meaning of the term 'pleasure,' that it is undecided whether happiness applies to the individual or to society only, or, insofar as it applies to both, unexplained how individual happiness conforms to the duty to maximize happiness for the highest number. Furthermore, if pursuit of happiness is inherent in human nature, it seems redundant to dictate the individual to pursue as a duty a thing that is already existent in its constitutional make-up. We cannot ask a red

thing to turn red, G. E. Moore objects; we cannot ask a tree to grow. Or, we cannot derive an 'ought' from an 'is,' as Hume would famously state this sort of objection. (Mill is himself aware of this type of fallacy in his *A System of Logic*, which does not imply, as we notice, that he is incapable of committing it in his *Utilitarianism*.)

When certain commentators (like Fred R. Berger, Roger Crisp, Alan Ryan, or John Skorupsky[2]) set out to defend Mill against critical commentators (like F. H. Bradley, Henry Sidgwick, G. E. Moore, or Bertrand Russell[3]), also the apologetic commentators are aware of these inconsistencies. They just surmise that there is a consistent intention behind apparent inconsistencies, and they embark on reconstructing this consistent intention. To use a language from the preceding essay on Grice's conversational logic, they 'cooperate'; they assume that a writer's writing is meaningful, and that if a paragraph, *p*, does not make sense then it is or should be possible to reconstruct a content, *q*, that reinstates it as meaningful. In this project, it is less important to *perceive* what Mill *writes* than to *reconstruct* what he *means*. We even encounter defenses that unblinkingly explain that Mill doesn't mean what he writes in a particular instance, because that wouldn't be logical (or another variation: Mill doesn't mean what he writes in a particular instance, because elsewhere in his considerable opus he has written the opposite). Supposedly, we cannot take for granted that sentences and statements mean what they appear to mean.[4]

A Deconstructive Analytic will naturally regard the textual surface as the only evidence we have of Mill's *meaning* (or rather, *meanings*, since, as we shall see, there are several). An analysis that fails to read the text for what it is—an analysis that believes that there is more in the text than what it *presents*—is regarded as biased and ideological. In that sense there 'is nothing outside the text' as Derrida poignantly has asserted in a notorious formulation which some of his critics never gets tired of deriding.[5]

Of course, any philosophical author is entitled to take upon himself the improvement of Mill's Utilitarianism, and to introduce new distinctions that can help solve logical problems in Mill's rendition (like Sidgwick's egoistic versus universalistic utilitarianism or Urmson's act- versus rule-utilitarianism). The problems begin when there are attempts to improve Mill against himself. Likewise, we no longer expect a theater director to rewrite plays of Shakespeare, improving on his plots, his verses, or the morality of his characters. Surprisingly, the 'cooperative' reading of Mill is adopted as a 'modern' trend in Mill-scholarship. At the end of the 19th and beginning of the 20th centuries, there is no shortage of critics of Mill, and after having read several cooperative commentators ('modern' scholarship that has devoted itself to 'reassessment' of Mill, and believes that it is correcting mistakes of the past), it is refreshing to return to Moore's (to some extent Sidgwick and Russell's) logical analyses.

(ii) The 'Naturalistic Fallacy' and the 'Anasemic Fallacy'. According to Moore, Mill is guilty of the so-called 'naturalistic fallacy.' Mill defines 'good' naturalistically as 'pleasure.' However, according to Moore, 'good' is indefinable in the absolute sense to which ethics aspires. To use Kantian terms, 'good' can be defined synthetically, that means, the predicate that lays itself to 'good' is outside of and not contained in the subject. As such, the 'good' is not defined as some one thing, but as several, such as health, justice, friendship, or eating well. It makes no sense to assert general statements defining the *only* good ('good is *nothing but*. . .'), since thus a synthetic statement has been turned into an analytic statement. When the synthetic statement is turned into an analytic, the statement is tautological, and therefore absurd—if the only good *is* pleasure, then pleasure is already the good, and the statement says nothing but that the good is equal to itself. When moral philosophers nonetheless define the only good as now this now that, they are guilty of Moore's 'naturalistic fallacy.' And when Mill defines the good as pleasure or happiness, he has committed this fallacy: "Mill has made as naïve and artless a use of the naturalistic fallacy as anybody could desire."[6] To Moore the core problem in Mill is thus that he defines the good as pleasure, whereas Moore contends that hedonism cannot be defined.

I acknowledge this criticism and take for granted that Moore is right in holding hedonism indefinable. Therefore, it is not essentially a contradiction of Moore's analysis when I displace the core problem in Mill to be the definition of 'pleasure,' not the definition of 'good'— shifting now the emphasis from good to pleasure in the equation. It is rather a continuation of analysis on a deeper level. However, in my preferred understanding, exercising analysis on this 'deeper' level turns Logical Analysis into Deconstructive Analysis.

Pleasure—or its synonym, happiness—is the most frequently occurring notion in Mill's essay, but paradoxically Mill has no clue as to what 'pleasure' is, what it means, or what it includes or entails. This fundamental ignorance, on the other hand, completely escapes him, and he continues to use the notion as if it was an established fact in need of no further explanation. He ends up with five pleasures that approximately all have the remarkable quality that they are as painful as they are pleasurable.

'Pleasure' becomes a 'dummy' (like 'intention' in the preceding essay on Grice); it becomes a blank, a hollow or empty word that represents something supposedly well-known. It displays an appearance by duplicating a supposedly well-known thing, pleasure—like a human dummy duplicates a human being. But as little as we learn about human behavior by observing a dummy, as little do we learn about pleasure by observing Mill's notion of 'pleasure.' This impasse puts the theory in a strange perspective. If Mill's theory—somewhat roughly but not entirely off the mark—can be summed up in the imperative, 'pursue pleasure,' then, given that 'pleasure' is undetermined, nobody knows how to realize this dictum. The theory becomes empty on moral instruction. The discussions about *what we ought to do* are merely circling a non-entity, like a spider's intricate web around an empty center (—except for the important fact that a spider's web is not supported by its center, while Mill's utilitarian ethics is). Ultimately, Mill and commentators do not know what they are talking about. One the other hand, they remain blind to that fact, since the 'dummy' appears real.

If thus Moore in his acute and inspiring criticism draws attention to a 'naturalistic fallacy,' I will introduce a fallacy that is at least as typical in theoretical writing. I shall call it the 'anasemic fallacy,' indicating that the theorist or philosopher discusses a notion of fundamental importance in his theory as if the notion were transparent (—it may indeed appear commonplace and ordinary), but where the notion is in fact opaque and impenetrable. By being a seme that is beyond or against (*ana*) the existing class of semes, the *ana-seme* has no longer any distinct meaning, or it has in the progression of the theory been turned into a seme with several conflicting meanings, thus rendered meaningless.

The 'anasemic fallacy' consists now in discussing this anasemic 'x'—and the conditions for and the consequences of this 'x'—without knowing what 'x' *is*; without knowing, thus, what is being discussed, but oblivious to that particular ignorance.

(iii) Three Distinctions Between Logical Analysis and Deconstructive Analysis. I believe that the anasemic fallacy comes in a few variations in Mill's essay, but it is never clearer manifested than when it becomes apparent that 'pleasure' is no uniform concept, but can be invested with several mutually incompatible contents. Pleasure can be 'high' or 'low' or something in-between; it can be noble or virtuous or painful, but never lustful; it is and should be generally desired, but should also sometimes be avoided; at one point we read that it is a pleasure not to pursue pleasure. Mill's initial definition of utilitarianism: actions are right as they tend to promote happiness (by which we mean pleasure), wrong as they tend to produce the reverse of happiness,[7] is obviously worthless if the notion of pleasure glides in various directions according to the expediency of the polemic context. We furthermore notice that if

Mill can reject some obvious pleasures, and sanction others that imply frustration and pain for the agent, then his choices are motivated from 'another stage,' then he is driven by a stealthier 'moral passion' that is independent of and different from the official utilitarian doctrine he supposedly defends.

As a first distinction between Logical Analysis and Deconstructive Analysis, we may say that while Deconstruction is captivated by the emptiness of notions that linger at the foundation of the theory, Logical Analysis is obsessed with what can and cannot be argued. Another distinction is it that critics like Moore and Russell emphasize the understanding of logical consistency in a theory, while Deconstruction is more sensitive to the text itself, for example to rhetorical surface-structures of the text and brief ('personal') intersections that may have nothing apparently to do with the general argument, but which can explain certain of the theoretical choices of the writer. Finally, whereas it is not within Moore or Russell's program to *explain* self-contradictions in the text except in terms of logical fallacies (—and there is considerable critical potential in pointing out self-contradictions; they usually operate in disguise and are not in the habit of advertising themselves), a Deconstructive Analytic can add quasi-psychoanalytical explanations of the sometimes-rampant confusions reigning in Mill's essay, without loosing its hold on the understanding of the logical structure of the essay. One can adopt the hermeneutic practice that when logic and dialogue break down we are justified in reconstructing a psychoanalytical quasi-dialogue that can account for otherwise inexplicable textual lacunae.

(iv) Elements of a Logic of Illogicality or an Oneiric Logic. Implementing these guidelines, it is also my aim to understand by which means persuasion succeeds when rational argument is no longer present to direct a discourse. The interest becomes to reconstruct a *logic of illogicality*, an illogical logic that can be quasi-formalized and therefore more readily recognized when encountered elsewhere. Some of Mill's persuasive devices are astonishingly simple. They can consist in simple rejection of a position that is elsewhere consistently defended (p is the case, which does not mean that p is the case), or in introducing an opposition to a position consistently defended without noticing the contradiction in simultaneous defense of position and opposition (p is the case, which [add a rhetorical "of course"] does not imply that $\sim p$ is not the case). This simultaneous simplicity and negligence of illogicalities suggest that we are encountering a logic that has features similar to what Freud introduced in *The Interpretation of Dreams* under the concept *dream work*. That is, we deal with an *oneiric logic* whose

illogicalities are disguised under the veil of glib rhetoric. For example, one of the strongest motives in Mill's writing is his desire to preempt criticism of the utilitarian cause by accommodating his theory to the various objections of his critics. He often achieves this by simply appropriating the objections as true utilitarian principles; the critics supposedly confuse their *objections to the theory* and *the theory*. Therefore, since he has to fence off criticism from several quarters, Mill speaks with approximately as many voices as there are polemical contexts in the text. The attempt to determine these 'voices' is what we can call a 'quasi-psychoanalytical repair' of a dialogue that in itself offers little sense.

If there is such patent illogicality at stake in Mill's text, it is pertinent to ask the critical question, *how* is it possible, *why* is it not noticed? In anticipating the explanation—which I shall spend more time elaborating—I believe that the closest we get to an answer is that typically irrationality is disguised by means of *reasonableness*. The general rule is, the more irrational the discourse, the more *reasonable* the voice narrating it. It seems to be the case that *if/when* the narrating voice 'understands' itself as reasonable, it also easily 'forgets' that it under the cover of reason and goodwill is saying things that it cannot want to say or mean.

2) FORMALIZING NONSENSE
(i) Reinterpreting the Term 'Utility.' (ii) The Extreme Definitions of Utilitarianism and their Impossible Medium. (iii) A First Formula for 'Reasonableness.' (iv) The Pleasure-Principle of Utilitarianism—Simultaneous Defense and Rejection of a Principle.

(i) Reinterpreting the Term 'Utility.' Let us start at the beginning (disregarding, though, Mill's 'Introduction' where he demonstrates his misunderstanding of or, at least, 'abbreviated' understanding of Kant's ethics[8]). We shall start at the first chapter where Mill introduces the significant term, *utility*.

Already from the beginning, Mill is getting distracted. His has to spend time on a 'passing remark' before he can return to his task and retain focus. Somebody has misunderstood the term *utility*—paradoxically by understanding the word according to its ordinary meaning. Somebody supposes that the term means what in colloquial English it means (equating it with *use, useful, usefulness*). This 'ignorant blunder' spurs Mill, and it is the first mistake he has to set straight:

A passing remark is all that needs be given to the ignorant blunder of supposing that those who stand up for utility as the test of right and wrong, use the term in that restricted and merely colloquial sense in which utility is opposed to pleasure.[9]

Mill starts out doing something to a word. Utility customarily signifies that the practicality of an article or object prevails over its comfort, ornamentation, or beauty. In that sense, utility is traditionally opposed to *pleasure*. Thus, the word has a meaning we agree upon. Now, Mill starts out changing the meaning of the word, ironically by declaring that the word *utility* can neither have nor mean *use*—those who believed they could use it are mistaken, and if they believed they could use it to mean *use*, even more so. These erroneous assumptions seem to be the product of reactionary and conservative forces.

Mill is obviously not alone in the assignment of new meaning to the term utility. He inherits the definitions of Jeremy Bentham and his father, James Mill. However, he takes for granted what Bentham was sufficiently acute to perceive as a problem. At the beginning of his *Introduction to the Principles of Morals and Legislation*, Bentham admits the incongruence between the word and the neologistic meaning he is conferring to the word.

> The word 'utility' does not so clearly point to the ideas of *pleasure* and *pain* as the words 'happiness' and 'felicity' do. . . . This want of a sufficiently manifest connection between the ideas of *happiness* and *pleasure* on the one hand, and the idea of *utility* on the other, I have every now and then found operating, and with but too much efficiency, as a bar to the acceptance that might otherwise have been given to this principle.[10]

Traditionally, the term 'utility' were chosen in order to distinguish a 'practical' moral theory from *impractical* (interpreted as 'useless') moral theories. Moral theories advocating a contemplative state of mind as the utmost good, the *summon bonum* in Aristotle, or moral theories determining the moral worth according to the intention by which an act is carried out, the 'good will' in Kant, or intuitionistic moral theories contending that we inherently know right from wrong, all make the *consequences* of acts immaterial to their moral value.[11] A moral theory that is so-called 'useful' is in other words a moral theory that emphasizes the consequences of an action.

Still, a utilitarian or consequential moral theory emphasizing 'results' has nothing necessarily to do with pleasure, especially if by pleasure we mean the pleasure of the moral agent, and there is in the beginning of Mill's text no other meaning. So, we are back to the question, what has utility to do with pleasure, and why would the utilitarians choose the word 'utility' for a theory that emphasizes 'pleasure'? Why being spellbound by this word instead of by words customarily synonymous with 'pleasure,' such as, 'enjoyment,' 'satisfaction,' 'gratification,' or 'happiness'? If under a correct interpretation 'utilitarianism' is in fact a 'hedonism,' a 'pleasurism,' (Greek, *hedon* = pleasure), why unnecessarily confuse matters by terming it utilitarianism?

The term 'utility' and the label 'utilitarianism' are from the beginning awkward, but Mill does not recognize this as a legitimate objection. He instead reacts to the voices of criticism, the voices of those who believe that utility and pleasure are opposites. Against the authority of Bentham and his father, this criticism appears to him to be extraordinary primitive.

> An apology is due to the philosophical opponents of utilitarianism, for even the momentary appearance of confounding them with anyone capable of so absurd a misconception; which is the more extraordinary, inasmuch as the contrary accusation, of referring everything to pleasure, and that too in its grossest form, is another of the common charges against utilitarianism.[12]

(ii) The Extreme Definitions of Utilitarianism and their Impossible Medium. The quotation introduces yet another group of opponents. First, we have (more or less sophisticated) opponents asserting that utility has nothing to do with pleasure; secondly, we have an equally absurd group of opponents asserting that utilitarianism refers everything to pleasure. Each group becomes doubly absurd, because of the existence of its respective opposite. It appears as if opponents cannot make up their mind as of how to attack utilitarianism. They both interpret utilitarianism wrongly. One group denounces the theory because it is "impracticably dry when the word utility precedes the word pleasure," the other group because it is "too practicably voluptuous when the word pleasure precedes the word utility."[13]

These adversaries constitute two extremes, two borders of the theory within which the theory can (supposedly) be correctly defined. As extreme interpretations of the theory, they are equally wrong. One emphasizes utility and brackets pleasure, another emphasizes pleasure and brackets utility. The following formula emerges: UTILITY(pleasure) vs. PLEASURE(utility).

The theory, or rather, the fundamental axiom of utilitarianism is situated between these two extremes: UTILITY(pleasure) & PLEASURE(utility). The axiom of utilitarianism would thus be the 'x' between utility and pleasure, the unknown and non-existent semantic entity that indefinitely needs further explanation and definition against an incredulous crowd of opponents, perpetually placing 'x' too close to one of its perilous borders. The formula for a compulsively repeated problem in Mill's thinking we can illustrate accordingly:

$$\text{UTILITY(pleasure)} \leftrightarrow \text{'x'} \leftrightarrow \text{PLEASURE(utility)}$$

We notice that the formula reminisces Aristotle's medium between two extremes from *Nicomachean Ethics*, but whereas in Aristotle, it is always linguistically possible to situate a medium between two excesses (for example, *courage* as situated between *foolhardiness* and *cowardliness*; *generosity* as situated between *frugality* and *prodigality*), it is not linguistically possible to situate anything between utility and pleasure. We can as an experiment think of something useful (on the one hand) and something pleasant (on the other), and then try to find the medium. For example, education is useful and drinking is pleasant, but we have no term for the medium between education and drinking. Or, a hammer is useful and sex is pleasant, but what is the medium between a hammer and sex? The problem is that if utility and pleasure constitute two extremes, they don't do so on the same semantic axis; or in the language of Structural Semantics, they constitute two *sememes* in lack of a common *seme*. They are type-different; comparing them is like comparing a number to a letter and then ask for the midpoint. Consequently, it is precise to designate the utilitarian medium neutrally as 'x.' Mill sets up a linguistic trap for himself when attempting to define the indefinable 'x' between utility and pleasure as the major axiological principle of utilitarianism—a principle that he with increasing frustration will emphasize is "self-evident," the less self-evident it becomes. We shall again say that he tries to produce an *anaseme*: a *seme* that has no existence in any known dictionary, and therefore is *ana:* asserted *outside, beyond* or *against* the known universe of semes.

(iii) A First Formula for 'Reasonableness.' Mill engages himself in a perpetual balancing act; he is walking a tight-rope where he sways now to one side, now to another. The initial claim is that 'x' characterizes a moral action, where by 'x' we mean neither mere utility nor mere pleasure. By 'x' we mean *both* utility *and* pleasure and *neither* utility *nor* pleasure. Mill's logic is thus the following: *'both u and p' and 'neither u nor p,'* or:

$$\text{'x'} = (u \wedge p) \wedge (\sim u \vee \sim p)$$

It is an infinite challenge and task to explain 'x' within this nonsensical logic. Notice that this formula characterizes 'reasonableness'; a 'reasonable man' typically opts for a bit of this and a bit of that, but not too much of either. We shall return to this 'formula' for reasonableness, since it is precise to say that Mill is reasonableness incarnate. Irrationality and reasonableness are intimately intertwined companions in his arguments. The reasonableness of the author is supposed to supplant or suppress his lack of rational argument. It becomes exactly difficult to see the lack of rationality, because of the *reasonable appeal*, that is, the *appeal* to the reader's understanding acceptance of incoherence, the *appeal* not to take incoherence *seriously*. In Mill, we can apply the following rule of thump: his discourse is nonsensical in equal proportion to its reasonableness.

If we look at how the formula actually operates in the text, the first problem is that certain writers ("the herd") do not understand that there is pleasure in utility:

> Yet the common herd, including the herd of writers, not only in newspapers and periodicals, but in books of weight and pretension, are perpetually falling into this shallow mistake. Having caught up the word utilitarian, while knowing nothing whatever about it but its sound, they habitually express by it the rejection, or the neglect, of pleasure in some of its forms; of beauty, or ornament, or of amusement.[14]

So far, utility is a pleasure principle. If or when it is understood solely as a reality- or (better) practicality-principle, it is exposed to "utter degradation." The "degradation" consists in narrow-minded writers' incapacity to understand Mill's innovative new meaning of the word 'utility.'[15]

In the first passages of Mill's essay, we are thus firmly situated on the right side of Mill's formula: UTILITY(pleasure) ↔ 'x' ↔ PLEASURE(utility).

Pleasure is emphasized as governing the utilitarian moral act, and its government remains firmly in place as long as Mill 'hears' the voices of narrow-minded critics of himself, father James Mill, and father's friend Jeremy Bentham. However, as soon as these voices stifle, so do the emphasis on the pleasure-principle, and we slip back into the abyss of the unknown non-existent semantic entity 'x.' As we shall see shortly, the position of the *imaginary antagonist* determines entirely the direction of Mill's argument. For now the pleasure-principle governs, and a first famous definition of the utilitarian principle can be professed:

> The creed which accepts as the foundation of morals, Utility, or the Greatest Happiness Principle, holds that actions are right in proportion as

they tend to promote happiness, wrong as they tend to produce the reverse happiness. By happiness is intended pleasure, and the absence of pain; by unhappiness, pain, and the privation of pleasure.[16]

We summarize: a moral act is right insofar as it produces happiness by which we mean pleasure, wrong insofar as it produces unhappiness by which we mean pain or unpleasure. In a nutshell: pleasure is right, pain is wrong.

(iv) The Pleasure-Principle of Utilitarianism—Simultaneous Defense and Rejection of a Principle. The most sober conclusion on Mill's definition is thus that instantaneous and tangible bodily pleasures such as sex constitute the highest moral worth (or, at least, have high moral worth) in utilitarianism. Mill does not explicitly mention this immediate consequence of his formulation, but it is surely present in the following symptomatic redirection of his polemic. He senses immediately the danger of the above interpretation. He rightly feels that his definition could be construed as advocating 'sensuous pleasures,' that someone could be taking him to mean that such pleasures are morally right, and that he is arguing a case for sex, or—as he puts it—for pleasures in their 'grossest form.'

At this point, Mill has constructed a new antagonist, a new imaginary voice mocking and denouncing his theory. We have in general two sets of voices, conveniently situated at each of the extreme ends of Mill's theory. The first set constitutes the critics of the utilitarian for being too focused on practicality. These voices are now quieting down. To repel them, we have just been given a strong definition of 'x': *'x' is pleasure.* Now the danger is that pleasure by some could be understood to mean sex, and immediately we retreat from the definition and slip back into 'x' as the unknown semantic axiom of utilitarianism; the axiom I call Mill's *anaseme.* Reconstructed carefully, Mill's argument is approximately the following: I may say that 'x' is pleasure, but this does not necessarily mean that this is what I am saying (logic of illogicality: I may assert *that p,* but from this it does not follow that I am asserting *that p).*[17]

Our initial question was, Why is Mill using the term utility when he wants to talk about pleasure? Now we are facing the opposite problem. Why does he want to talk about pleasure when the promotion of pleasure has to be warded off with such energy? What, furthermore, *enables* him to assert that only pleasure is desirable as end, but *disables* his critics to repeat the same statement? Notice, for example, the following two passages found in the same paragraph:

> These supplementary explanations [of what is included in the ideas of pain and pleasure; PB] do not effect the theory of life on which this theory of morality is grounded—namely, that pleasure and freedom from pain are the only things desirable as ends. . . . Now, such a theory of life excites in many minds . . . inveterate dislike. To suppose that life has (as they express it) no higher end than pleasure—no better and nobler object of desire and pursuit—they designate as utterly mean and grovelling; as a doctrine worthy only of swine.[18]

Reading with a magnifying glass, we read again, emphasizing, "To suppose that life has (*as they express it*) no higher end than pleasure." Mill has forgotten that the hostile "they" express almost verbatim what Mill expresses a few lines above. What 'they express' is certainly a faithful rendition of Mill's statement.

Mill has just been asserting that *x is pleasure*, now the new set of antagonist voices repeat after him that *x is pleasure*, that utilitarianism is a pleasure principle, and what could they possibly be doing wrong. They repeat after Mill, *x is pleasure*, but apparently to Mill, they do it *maliciously*. They repeat, but not in good faith; rather, they take Mill to say that everything is about pleasure (what he has just said), as if they think that he thinks that only pleasure is desirable (what indeed one is led to conclude). These accusers of Utilitarianism suppose that humans are "capable of no pleasures except those of which swine are capable" (ibid.). Mill is caught in their accusation, and will automatically respond that utilitarianism do not promote 'gross' pleasures, but pleasures more refined—their refined nature to be determined in the remainder of the essay. This new set of voices is worse than the first set (those he had to correct by pointing out how pleasure is inherent in use), because they make him mean that utilitarianism is about 'ignoble' pleasures. Mill's next step is consequently to argue—less through argument than through a rhetoric of indignation—that by pleasure he does not mean pleasure, or at least, that there are many pleasures, and some of them ought not to be taken into consideration. We notice here the beginning of a consistent trend in the present essay, it is always the more obvious pleasures that should *not* be considered pleasures, and it is always the less obvious that should.[19]

3.1) DEFINITIONS AND REDEFINITIONS OF PLEASURE
(i) Higher and Lower Pleasures. (ii) Replacing Quantity with Quality.

(i) Higher and Lower Pleasures. Mill is engaged in answering critics portraying utilitarianism as a pleasure-theory. From this point onwards, he starts a redefinition of pleasure. "Human beings have faculties more

elevated then the animal faculties, and when once made conscious of them, do not regard anything as happiness which does not include their gratification."[20]

We are introduced to a distinction between 'higher' and 'lower' pleasures. Higher pleasures are obviously pleasures not intrinsic in human nature, since we have to be made conscious of them before we can have them. They are also 'pleasures' that replace the 'lower' pleasures once we are conscious of them. After that point, they are the only pleasures we prefer.

> There is no known Epicurean theory of life which does not assign to the pleasures of the intellect, of the feelings and imagination, and of the moral sentiments, a much higher value as pleasures than to those of mere sensation.[21]

Whereas Bentham has only quantitative distinctions between pleasures, Mill introduces a qualitative distinction; certain *kinds* of pleasures are more valuable than other kinds.

> It is quite compatible with the principle of utility to recognize the fact, that some *kinds* of pleasure are more desirable and more valuable than others. It would be absurd that while, in estimating all other things, quality is considered as well as quantity, the estimation of pleasures should be supposed to depend on quantity alone.[22]

(ii) Replacing Quantity with Quality. We will here have to enter a classical discussion of Mill's distinction between quality and quantity.

First, it is apparent that Mill is here modifying Bentham's hedonistic utilitarianism. To Bentham, pleasure and pain are quantifiable entities according to seven 'circumstances,' for example in respect to intensity, duration, certainty/uncertainty, or fecundity (the chance a sensation has to be followed by more of the same kind; more pleasure following pleasure). In these seven respects, pleasures and pains can be quantified; a 'felicific' or 'hedonic' calculus—supposed to measure amounts of pleasures and pains in various situations—can be devised. The legislator is in this 'felicific calculus' supposed to have a tool for the appraisal of various legislative alternatives according to their final pleasure-value. The principle is purely quantitative, and is by Bentham neatly summed up in the phrase, "Quantity of pleasure being equal, pushpin is as good as poetry."

Mill is now retreating from this purely quantitative principle; he wants to be able to argue that poetry is at any time better than pushpin. His strategy is to introduce different *kinds* of pleasures, that is, to introduce qualitative differences, enabling him to argue that certain kinds of pleasure are more valuable than other kinds. He does not seem to see that he in the proceeding argument controverts the framework of Bentham's utilitarianism, which indeed he thinks that he is promoting.[23]

Moreover, there are inherent logical problems in introducing a notion of qualitative differences between pleasures. *If and insofar as* we wish to distinguish between pleasures *per se*, the principle of discrimination can only be quantitative. If we want to calibrate the pleasantness of different pleasurable experiences, the distinguishing principle can be nothing but pleasure itself.

We are bound to arrive to this conclusion through the following argument. What we mean by saying that some experiences are pleasant is that they contain some one quality common to all pleasant experiences. If now one experience is more pleasant than another experience, it is not because it contains a different pleasure-quality than the other—if this were the case, the two experiences could not be compared. We say that one experience is *more* pleasant, and mean that it contains *more pleasure* than the other does, that is, *more in quantity of the same quality*. This means that we can only quantify, measure degrees or judge between lower or higher intensities, more or lesser amounts, longer or shorter duration, etc. If, on the other hand, we want to qualify, we will have to introduce a standard other than pleasure itself.

In the last case, we are no longer talking about pleasure, but about the *pleasure-giving object or activity*, although we talk about the pleasure-giving object *as if* we talk about pleasure itself. If we talk about the pleasure-giving *object or activity*, it is relatively unproblematic that there are qualitative differences between pleasure-giving activities such as eating Häagen Dazs ice-cream and drinking vintage Port. However, it is not clear what the difference in the pleasure is, unless we measure pleasure by pleasure and return to quantification. We may for example 'feel' (or rather, think we feel) that Häagen Dazs gives the most intense pleasure, that is, it is so and so many degrees more pleasurable than drinking Port.

Therefore, if we want to qualify pleasures, we are, first, no longer talking about pleasure, but about pleasure-giving activities, confusing these activities with pleasure itself, and, second, we are introducing a standard other than pleasure to qualify pleasure-giving activities. If Mill wants to claim that some pleasures are higher than others, he effectively means that some pleasure-giving activities are superior to others, and he means this on the ground of a standard that he never makes clear; a standard that imposes itself subconsciously on his writing. Vintage Port, according to this standard, would probably be regarded as superior to Häagen Dazs, because, besides its taste of Port, it has the 'taste' of aristocracy and Old Europe, whereas Häagen Dazs 'tastes' too much of

Americana. The standard creating this distinction would obviously no longer be pleasure, but a conventional standard dependent on ethnic, cultural, and class identifications. On the background of these identifications, an *interpretation* of Vintage Port as a superior pleasure could be introduced and defended. We would now be able to rank Vintage Port above Häagen Dazs ice-cream; thus enabling ourselves to talk about 'superior pleasures' and 'inferior pleasures,' 'noble' and ignoble,' 'higher' and 'lower.'

A more valuable pleasure is therefore only a more valuable object selected according to a standard measuring value and not pleasure. (If poetry is better than pushpin and Beethoven better than The Beatles, it is not because the former gives higher pleasures, but because we think (or think we think) that the former represents activities more 'noble' or 'elevated' or 'dignified.') However, Mill does not understand that he is no longer talking about pleasures, but about a relatively anonymous standard, that is semi-private and subconscious. Especially, he does not understand that if this standard ever had anything to do with pleasure, it is only in the sense that it introduces the possibility of arguing *against pleasure*. It represents a pleasure that should never be underestimated, the pleasure of repressing pleasure.

3.2) DEFINITIONS AND REDEFINITIONS OF PLEASURE
(i) Voting on Pleasures—How to Rig the Vote Philosophy-Wise. (ii) Preferable Unbearable Pleasures. (iii) Pleasures For Pigs and Fools— Arguing One's Repressions.

(i) Voting on Pleasures—How to Rig the Vote Philosophy-Wise. Let us return to the text after this digression. Mill believes that he has established that we have different *kinds of* pleasures. The question is now, which ones are preferable, what makes one pleasure more valuable than another, assuming that the individual is able to determine preferable pleasures (an unwarranted and hazardous assumption, but let us for now ignore this). However, even if this assumption is granted, the problem is not solved universally; individuals have different tastes. Are we now thrown back into the relativism of individual tastes, or is there a formula for a solution to the problem?

Mill's solution to the problem is exemplary quantitative (in this, exemplary Benthamsk, whom, by introducing qualitative pleasures, he just modified). We simply take a vote. We ask people which pleasure out of two they prefer, assuming that they know both. We invite the relevant group of qualified individuals to declare their preferences, and select the pleasure favored by the majority.

Of two pleasures, if there be one to which all or almost all who have experience of both give a decided preference, irrespective of any feeling of moral obligation to prefer it, that is the more desirable pleasure. If one of the two is, by those who are competently acquainted with both, placed so far above the other that they prefer it, even though knowing it to be attended with a greater amount of discontent, and would not resign it for any quantity of the other pleasure which their nature is capable of, we are justified in ascribing to the preferred enjoyment a superiority in quality.[24]

On appearance, the method is uniquely democratic. Whenever sending these referenda to the electorate for approval or rejection, the legislator will have to enact the majority vote—disinterestedly and impartially.[25] However, because of obvious and unintended side effects of this magnanimous tolerance, the principle is rescinded and reformulated as soon as it is suggested. The electorate could approve of 'lower' pleasures, and this unwanted outcome has to be prevented. Out of two pleasures, an individual cannot *want* to vote for the 'lower,' but only for the 'higher.' If somebody still votes for the 'lower,' it merely proves that she is an unqualified voter; it can only be explained by the person being low herself.

The distinction between 'higher' and 'lower' pleasures is therefore refashioned into a new distinction between qualified and unqualified individuals. In order to secure the desired result, Mill has to declare certain persons incompetent to vote in the first place. Either they are inherently corrupt, or they are without knowledge of the 'higher' and sublime pleasures, and therefore incapable of making a choice. Supposedly, 'unqualified' voters do not know 'high' pleasures, and since they do not know all their options, higher and lower, their opinion is uninformed, and they cannot meaningfully decide on their preference. Strictly speaking, however, an objective 'choice' is never an option. A 'qualified' voter, familiar with 'high' as well as 'low' pleasures, would still forfeit her right to choose if she chooses poorly, and preserves it only if she chooses wisely; that is, in brief, *for* neurosis, *against* frivolity.

We thus end up with a theory not so much about valuable or non-valuable pleasures, but about valuable and non-valuable individuals. According to this theory, only people of intellectual acumen have a right to vote, since the votes of the intellectual unworthy are invalidated by their ignorance of intellectual pleasures—in effect, by their lacking capacity for sublimation and self-restraint. That we are in fact dealing with intellectual qualified persons is sufficiently explicit in the essay: "No *intelligent human being* would consent to be a fool, no *instructed person* would be an ignoramus; no *person of feeling and conscience* would be selfish and base. . . . A *being of higher faculties* requires more to make him happy . . . than one of an *inferior* type [my emphases]."[26]

The quantitative principle so grandiloquently introducing these considerations is therefore contravened by the two immediately following amendments: first, only higher pleasures can 'be wanted'; secondly, only intellectual qualified individuals (supposedly understanding both high and low pleasures) can vote. Mill does not seem to detect that his original Benthamisk principle turns into anti-Benthamism, that his democraticism turns into autocraticism, that, in brief, the theory becomes a blueprint for a society populated with images of himself, bent on repressing pleasure.

(ii) Preferable Unbearable Pleasures. After having done away with the uneducated and non-intellectual masses, Mill concentrates on the minority group he has left to his observation. Mill realizes that temptation threatens also this intellectually superior elite, but supposedly it is able to hold out against temptations—because of its 'sense of dignity.' If the educated minority prefer higher sublimated pleasures to lower sensual, it is because they posses 'dignity' to an exceptional degree. Some would say (some voices would object) that dignity rather opposes happiness, Mill suggests to himself, but these critical voices misunderstand and confuse happiness and contentment: "Whoever supposes that this preference takes place at a sacrifice of happiness—that the superior being, in anything like equal circumstances, is not happier than the inferior—confounds the two very different ideas, of happiness, and content."[27] It is here not clear what Mill means; is the superior being happy in his dignity, and the inferior only content, or is it the other way around? However, although here Mill's meaning is not clear, the passage is followed by one of the strangest arguments in the essay. Let us break the passage up in two:

> It is indisputable that the being whose capacities of enjoyment are low, has the greatest chance of having them fully satisfied; and a highly endowed being will feel that any happiness which he can look for, as the world is constituted, is imperfect. But he can learn to bear its imperfections, if they are at all bearable.[28]

We are again comparing the happiness of the superior and inferior human being. The pleasures of the inferior being are easy to satisfy, but the superior being, opting for the higher, sublimated pleasures, finds these pleasures difficult to satisfy. There is always *imperfection* in their satisfaction. This, however, should not discourage her, she can learn to bear these imperfect pleasures, that is, *if they are at all bearable*. This is suddenly in doubt. Are higher pleasures bearable? Are there pleasures of a kind that are unbearable? Can one have pleasures that are nothing but suffering and pain? Finally we hear *Mill's voice*, not his father's, and not his friend and confidante, Mrs. Taylor's. For the first time, his voice is breaking through the inner turmoil, in all its insecure and feeble honesty. Finally, he suggests that the 'higher pleasures' (that everybody qualified would (and should) want to prefer) may be *unbearable*—and what happens if they are? What does now the person who has sought them as higher pleasures do? What happens when she detects that her pleasures are painful? Does she commit suicide?

(iii) Pleasures For Pigs and Fools—Arguing One's Repressions. The text is not quite as dramatic. We notice two things happening at the level of the text. We notice that Mill cannot help saying something he, in a more deliberate moment, cannot want to say. We also notice that he does not notice that this is what he is saying. Immediately he forgets this intersection. This moment of veracity is as brief as the sentence itself. However unbearable these higher pleasures may be, it is . . . (as he comforts himself in the following celebrated phrase) "better to be a human being dissatisfied than a pig satisfied; better to be Socrates dissatisfied than a fool satisfied. And if the fool, or the pig, is of a different opinion, it is because they only know their own side of the question. The other party to the comparison knows both sides."[29] So, even if higher pleasures are unbearable, it is better to carry the burden of unhappy dignity than being a happy fool.

The passage constitutes one of the rhetorical highlights of the essay, and has entered language as a coin whose face is long worn down. Seeing this coin anew, we notice that it cannot make sense. More precisely, it makes sense only insofar as we again introduce another standard than pleasure itself for the value of being respectively a human being and a pig. If pleasure is the single standard, it is obviously more pleasant to be a satisfied pig than a dissatisfied human. As satisfied, the pig *necessarily* experiences more degrees of pleasure that the dissatisfied human. If the one and only desirable end for my actions is pleasure, it does not matter how I realize this end, whether as a lower or a higher pleasure. Pleasure being the only desirable end, it is indeed absurd to talk about 'lower' and 'higher' pleasures, since a 'lower' pleasure is as much a pleasure as is a 'higher.' (An example—in part borrowed from Moore[30]: if the end of all action is 'color,' it does not matter whether I achieve 'color' as red or as blue; red is as much a color as is blue. It is absurd to claim that red is a 'higher' color and blue is a 'lower' one, and that it is incumbent on us to prefer red to achieve 'color.')

Therefore, if we can not prefer to be satisfied pigs, we are explicitly no longer talking about pleasure as the supreme value. The passage, in fact, *attacks* pleasure as supreme value. It makes it abundantly clear that pleasure/satisfaction is an inferior value, best suited to fools and pigs, that is, inferior and unqualified creatures.

We therefore have to look for another standard making it 'better' to be a dissatisfied human, a standard so far superior to pleasure that it makes pleasure an immaterial quality; so far superior that dissatisfaction becomes preferable to satisfaction, pain preferable to pleasure; a standard, finally, that completely erases pleasure as "the only desirable end." —What is this standard? First, this will never become explicit, since the question is never posed or attempted answered by Mill. Despite making assertions to the contrary, Mill unfalteringly believes he is defending pleasure as the ultimate end of moral actions. Mill is somehow able, despite his writing (despite a thousand blinking warning lights), to maintain that 'pleasure' is the only good. Secondly, if we look into the paragraph in order to construe or reconstruct a standard that might have left a trace of itself, a shadow in the text, we only find a tautology of the simplest kind. If we want to be humans and not pigs it is because we want to be humans; if it is better to be humans it is because it is better. The reason why this is asserted with such vehemence may be that the textual 'we' (alleged connoisseur of both higher and lower pleasures) exactly *does not know both*; that the textual 'we' could not know what it opted for if it were to choose a pig's existence; that the textual 'we' have never tried to live a pig's existence—undoubtedly because of its exceptional 'sense of dignity.'

If there is an autobiographical connection between the textual 'we' and Mill (as it is difficult not to assume that there is), we can infer that Mill almost certainly does not know the mode of existence of a pig; — whatever metaphorically this is supposed to represent. He must know (approximately) that it involves to dirt oneself, to wallow in the mud (whatever we want to think that means), and he looks upon this satisfied but 'dirty' existence with abhorrence, flees in panic, stammering that it is better to be Me . . . Mi . . . Mill because it is better.

3.3) DEFINITIONS AND REDEFINITIONS OF PLEASURE

(i) The Standard and the Exception—A Fragile Hierarchy. (ii) The Pleasure of Promoting Pleasure. (iii) Condensation as a Means to Erase Discrepancy. (iv) The Value of Self-sacrifice—The Pleasure of Promoting Pleasure Continued. (v) Happiness as a Coin—The Pseudo-Logic of Economy. (vi) A Fourth Paradoxical 'Pleasure': Renunciation of Pleasure. (vii) Five Self-Contradictory Pleasures—The 'Moral Passion' Behind the Moral Theory.

(i) The Standard and the Exception—A Fragile Hierarchy. In Mill, we notice in the progression of an argument a typical reversal: *the exception to the case becomes the standard.* Mill introduces with appreciation a certain dominant state of affairs; in this state of affairs exceptions unfortunately, and occasionally, occur (for example, due to the weakness of human nature). Still, this does not disturb the appreciated state that continues to reign supreme; a slight aberration from the standard is no threat. However, as the argument progresses the aberrations become still more overpowering, frequent, and threatening, and soon they constitute the standard to which the appreciative state of affairs is merely the exception. We see how this reason unfolds when talking about the higher and lower pleasures. First, the 'higher' pleasure is the standard.

> It may be objected that many who are capable of the higher pleasures, occasionally, under the influence of temptation, postpone them to the lower. But this is quite compatible with a full appreciation of the intrinsic superiority of the higher.[31]

Now, it is not clear how the choice of lower pleasures can indicate a "full appreciation" of the superiority of higher pleasures. The idea must be that the noble pleasures are superior and generally chosen, and the cases where they are replaced with lower pleasures are few, and merely aberrations from the normal course. There is thus a certain substantiality intrinsic in higher pleasures, while lower pleasures are transitory. This, at least, is what Mill wants to believe (and wants us to believe), but we have already seen how fragile this conviction is, and how easily it breaks down under the pressure of another voice expressing all the remembered suffering related to the pursuit of 'noble' pleasures. Once again, in the course of argument, this stoically defended conviction symptomatically breaks down. Now, the 'noble feeling' is like a 'tender plant' one has to carefully nurture in order for it to flourish and even survive. The standard has become exceptional.

Capacity for the nobler feelings is in most natures a very tender plant, easily killed, not only by hostile influences, but by mere want of sustenance; and in the majority of young people it speedily dies away if the occupations to which their position in life have devoted them. . . . are not favorable to keeping that higher capacity in exercise.[32]

A noble pleasure is difficult to cultivate, and in the process toward cultivation it begins immediately to deviate from its noble course, if not carefully nursed. It is in itself paradoxical that pleasures need care, especially if they are the 'only desired end.' Furthermore, if a noble pleasure is a tender plant that withers and dies without care, then the labor we take upon ourselves to keep it alive indicates that the noble pleasure is not an end in itself, but the means to another end. There must be a reason why we take upon ourselves the labor.

(ii) The Pleasure of Promoting Pleasure. Even Mill is not entirely immune to the thousand blinking warning lights that tell him that noble pleasures are not pleasures after all. However, since he also cannot give up his defense of noble pleasures, he introduces a compromise-solution; noble pleasures become means to another end. First they were supposed to be ends in themselves; but at this point, the text has broken this initial optimism and shown Mill that there are too many problems associated with higher pleasures. Mill's response is the compromise that if they cannot be ends in themselves, they can at least be means to another end (—eventually, they can be both at the same time). The end of which they are means is a pleasure too, but type-different from the above mentioned lower and higher pleasures; this pleasure will no longer apply to the agent herself.

That standard [the utilitarian standard] is not the agent's own greatest happiness, but the greatest amount of happiness altogether; and if it may possibly be doubted whether a noble character is always the happier for its nobleness, there can be no doubt that it makes other people happier, and that the world in general is immensely a gainer by it.[33]

If a noble pleasure does not necessary produce happiness in the individual—and this is supposedly no longer the aim (although elsewhere it is reiterated often enough as the aim)—at least, it produces happiness generally. The noble individual "makes other people happier," and this is the true end, "not the agent's own greatest happiness."

However, if we carry this thinking a step further than Mill does, it has as a consequence that the person, in whom the noble individual has produced happiness, ought to also sacrifice her happiness for the general good, and so on *ad infinitum*. If my happiness is no longer important, because of my obligation to make other people happy, then other people's happiness is also no longer important, because of their obligation to make me happy. Individual happiness is thus infinitely suspended; it remains unrealized in the individual, and has no existence except as an abstract idea of social happiness. The individual's happiness has evaporated into the thin air of general welfare. In that case, the end result of utilitarian thinking is general social if not *unhappiness*, then *non-happiness*, everybody being equally *non-happy* in the pursuit of the happiness of the other (I shall return to the question later).

(iii) Condensation as a Means to Erase Discrepancy. Mill has a problem at this point, because he is not ready to give up the idea of individual happiness as the ultimate end (what becomes of utilitarianism if it does not procure individual happiness?) On the other hand, he also believes that simple individual pursuit of happiness is a frivolous object, less desirable than "the greatest amount of happiness altogether." His text consequently vibrates between these two theses, between an egoistic and universalistic version of utilitarianism. However, since he is unable to explicitly differentiate these two versions, he does not *see* the difference. The distinction is first introduced by Sidgwick who makes it clear that the thesis that every man seeks his own happiness and the thesis that every man ought to seek general universal happiness are not mutually supportive. That every man seeks happiness is a *psychological* statement; that man ought to seek general happiness is an *ethical* statement, and ethical statements cannot be deduced from psychological ones. We cannot deduce an 'ought' from an 'is.' Sidgwick's criticism thus anticipates Moore's later criticism: the 'naturalistic fallacy' (in one of its formulations) is in Mill's case committed because an ethical concept, 'good,' is defined as a psychological state, 'pleasure.'

Without being able to see the discrepancy between the two theses, Mill can do no better than presenting them next to each other by *condensing* them *as if* they were stating the same thing. The Greatest Happiness Principle applies thus to both oneself and to other people at the same time.

> According to the Greatest Happiness Principle, . . . the ultimate end, with reference to and for the sake of which all other things are desirable (whether we are considering *our own good or that of other people*), is an existence exempt as far as possible from pain, and as rich as possible in enjoyments [my emphasis].[34]

An individual ought to pursue happiness for herself. But how does this prescription correspond to the directive that she ought also to pursue happiness for the whole? Individual pursuit of happiness does not effect the whole, or if it does, it is likely to clash with, rather than promote, the interest of the whole. *Condensation* helps erasing the problem of how one passes from self to whole, from one to other—happiness is pursued on both sides of the equation, and that suffices. By means of condensation, the problem of transition becomes blurred and is overlooked. Mill will throughout his essay continue to struggle with this transition-problem without solving it, except symptomatically, surrealistically, oneirically (about this later).

(iv) The Value of Self-sacrifice—The Pleasure of Promoting Pleasure Continued. Mill does perhaps not *see* a distinction, but it is fair to say that he *senses* a problem in the simultaneous pursuit of individual and universal happiness. This vaguer sense is symptomatically indicated in the questions he asks and the discussions in which he engages himself at this point in his essay. For example, is it desirable to sacrifice our own happiness for the sake of the multitude? How far should we go in our self-sacrifice? Can we do without happiness and should we?

We are back to the noble individual with his noble pleasures. If such noble pleasures were not an end in themselves, they were at least a means to the end, a better society. But Mill continues to think that the noble individual ought not sacrifice his own happiness, and Mill chides Carlyle for promoting self-sacrifice, *Entsagen*, as a higher quality: "They say, that man can do *without* [Mill emphasizes in disbelief] happiness; that all noble human beings have felt this, and could not have become noble but by learning the lesson of Entsagen, or renunciation."[35] And Mill explains awkwardly: "if no happiness is to be had at all by human beings, the attainment of it cannot be the end of morality"—which is indisputably true; if the world contained no colors it would be futile to declare the perception of colors our duty.

Now we know that Mill always becomes distracted in polemic situations. In his eagerness to deprive his critics of objections to utilitarianism, he is able and ready to defend positions that are contradictory to the official utilitarian doctrines. This may be what is at stake in the above quotation. What he perhaps wants to say (and may think that he is saying) is that self-sacrifice has to result in *some sort of* happiness, if not for the agent then for the whole. It is, at least, along that track the discussion proceeds.

If the self-sacrificing individual renounces her own happiness for the sake of an increase in the general happiness, then the self-sacrifice is only acknowledged as justified, if general happiness is still pursued. If the self-sacrifice contributes nothing to the whole, it is worthless, and even perverse. In the latter case, the self-sacrificing individual has pursued neither her own happiness nor the happiness of society.

> All honour to those who can abnegate for themselves the personal enjoyment of life, when by such renunciation they contribute worthily to increase the amount of happiness in the world; but he who does it, or professes to do it, for any other purpose, is no more deserving of admiration than the ascetic mounted on his pillar. He may be an inspiriting proof of what men *can* do, but assuredly not an example of what they *should*. . . . The utilitarian morality does recognize in human beings the power of sacrificing their own greatest good for the good of others. It only refuses to admit that the sacrifice is itself a good. A sacrifice which does not increase, or tend to increase, the sum total of happiness, it considers as wasted.[36]

(v) Happiness as a Coin—The Pseudo-Logic of Economy. We notice that a certain economy supports Mill's thinking. 'Happiness' has become a 'general equivalent,' which the individual owns. One is justified in keeping this 'general equivalent' to oneself, but it is better to 'invest' it for the general good of the whole. Only to squander it is illegitimate and considered a 'waste.' 'Happiness' has become a *coin*, it can be spent on oneself or on somebody else; only, it cannot be thrown away. According to this economic logic, we have an owner-relationship to 'happiness.'

If 'happiness' is a coin (the metaphor is felicitous for another reason: a coin is neutral, it is an anonymous stand-in for any commodity, it does not discriminate, but, like Mill's *happiness*, it buys any item according to its owner's whims), one can in principle do three things with this coin (assuming that we are not allowed to throw it away). These three options correspond to three inherent versions of utilitarianism: one can (a) keep it, (b) give it away, and (c) invest it. Option (a) would correspond to the egoistic and hedonistic utilitarian who pursues his own happiness as first principle. Option (b) would correspond to the altruistic and universal utilitarian who sacrifices his own happiness for the happiness of the greatest number. Finally, option (c) would correspond to the pragmatic utilitarian who participates in promoting the general happiness in order to benefit her own happiness as a secondary goal. (Example: *A* does his best to avoid paying taxes, spending all his money on himself; *B* is not only happy to pay his taxes, but gives all his money to charity too; *C* is also happy to pay taxes, but because she knows that by supporting the infrastructures and institutions of society, she is in the end benefiting herself.)

The problem of the above is that all of our three candidates are utilitarians: the egoist, the saint, and the pragmatist. If therefore utilitarianism, as all moral theories, devises how humans ought to conduct themselves, the best instruction it can give is: either you ought to behave egoistically, virtuously, or pragmatically (take your pick). These three choices are the different recommendations Mill gives in various passages throughout his essay. On the other hand, they are also the different answers he in various passages *criticizes* throughout his essay. (This confusion of the text provides the *objective foundation* for the different interpretations of Mill that his cooperating commentators argue between themselves. When each commentator hopes to convince the scholarly community of the import of his favorite interpretation, he overlooks the fact that different interpretations find objective support in various paragraphs of Mill's polysemous text.)

The reason why this empty discourse has been canonized as serious moral philosophy may be that it is in fact *empty*—that is, able to passively accept any interpretation. However, it is also supported by a mode of reasoning that is immediately persuasive; not by logic (Moore and others have seen this clearly), but by an economic pseudo-logic that lies like a sub-structure behind Mill's reasoning. The idea that we can own something, give it away, or invest it is familiar to us all, and therefore so sufficiently persuasive that is it noticed neither as problematic nor is it offending ordinary thinking. The idea is easy to the mind. The essay's illusion of consistency is in part achieved by means of this economic pseudo-logic, this our owner-relationship to 'happiness.' This is also how Mill succeeds in *condensing* individual and general pursuit of happiness. Placing these two theses side by side is not seen as self-contradictory—the conflict of the theses is never detected—because in the transition from one to other, the coin of happiness is merely shifting hands. Now it is in my hand, now I give to my neighbor (—and there is no *contradiction* in giving a coin to one's neighbor).

(vi) A Fourth Paradoxical 'Pleasure': Renunciation of Pleasure. We can seek happiness egoistically, virtuously, or pragmatically—the only proviso being that we seek happiness. As if the theory was not already vague enough, the 'happiness' or 'pleasure' we are induced to seek can mean several different, ambivalent, and incompatible things. Mill's only stipulation is that 'happiness' or 'pleasure' must not degenerate to imply 'sensuous indulgences,' pleasures in their 'grossest form.' (Pleasures are always *non-sensuous*, *non-instantaneous*, and *non-tangible*; the various cravings of the body are not acknowledged, and are fended off furiously—significantly, Mill's only consistent position in the essay.) With this exception, pleasure can indicate everything related to the intellect, and to individual and social relationships. Listening to music, reading poetry, cultivating friendships, promoting justice could be examples of legitimate pleasures.

However, even this moderate version of pleasure-seeking Mill admits may be too ideal. Perhaps, he suggests to himself, humans do not always pursue happiness, but, as a minimum, they *do* pursue freedom from pain.

> Since utility includes not solely the pursuit of happiness, but the prevention or mitigation of unhappiness; and if the former aim be chimerical, there will be all the greater scope and more imperative need for the latter, so long at least as mankind think fit to live.[37]

Freedom-from-pain *and* pleasure, freedom-from-unhappiness *and* happiness are obviously two distinct issues. Pain and pleasure are positive sensations, whereas freedom-from-pain (or from unhappiness) must constitute a sensational neutral, a nothingness that consists simply in the negation of the positive sensation of feeling pain. Freedom from pain would constitute a not-feeling-pain, and since it is also distinct from pleasure it is in consequence a not-feeling-anything. Freedom-from-pain is something in the order of not-burning-my-hand; not-burning-my-hand is always preferred to burning-my-hand, like not-being-humiliated to being-humiliated, not-being-deserted to being-deserted, etc. If humans do not pursue pleasure, they at least pursue freedom-from-pain, a state where they have avoided pain, but do not experience pleasure. The principle is thus a principle of psychological self-preservation.[38] One protects oneself against the blows of life by avoiding engagement in circumstances that could strike such blows. The resulting state is one of withdrawal, of tranquility, and peace. It is a state where one has avoided pain, but also pleasure (for example, by not-falling-in-love one has avoided the pain of being-deserted by the lover, but one has also precluded the pleasures of love).

Although freedom-from-pain (or -from-unhappiness) is not a positive pleasure, there is no doubt that of the two general classes, pain and pleasure, it is organized under the class of pleasure. It is a pleasure, Mill later admits, that seems like a paradox, because it renounces the pursuit of happiness.

> I will add, that in this condition of the world, paradoxical as the assertion may be, the conscious ability to do without happiness gives the best prospect of realizing such happiness as is attainable. For nothing except that consciousness can raise a person above the chances of life, by making him fell that, let fate and fortune do their worst, they have not power to subdue him: which, once felt, frees him from excess of anxiety concerning the evils of life, and enables him . . . to cultivate in tranquillity the sources of satisfaction accessible to him, without concerning himself about the uncertainty of their duration, any more than about their inevitable end.[39]

Renunciation of happiness is also happiness; an outcome Mill admits seems paradoxical. The thinking behind the paradox could perhaps be illustrated the following way. According to Bentham's hedonic calculus, we could measure pleasure and pain in numbers; an individual exposed to an event experiences so and so many units of pleasure, so and so many units of pain. We add the units of pleasure, subtract the units of pain, and arrive to the individual's total number of happiness. If we apply this hedonic calculus to the *renunciation* of happiness-pursuit, the number could never come out negatively (on a lenient interpretation, it could only come out positively). The pursuit of happiness is in itself frustrating (desire reminds people of what they do not have; it inscribes a lack in the subject). By renouncing this pursuit, one avoids the frustration. That is, one avoids a unit of pain, and gains a unit of pleasure. At the same time, one does not run the risk of being rejected, which would add units of pain to one's account. The negative side of one's felicific account thus remains zero, while, on the positive side, the pleasures of avoiding frustrations are adding up. We have, as by magic, an individual that by *not* pursuing happiness is happier than an individual that pursues happiness. Mill is right in saying that this is 'paradoxical': by *not* following my utilitarian doctrine, you shall become a true utilitarian.

(vii) Five Self-Contradictory Pleasures—The 'Moral Passion' Behind the Moral Theory. I am of course using this example to illustrate my main thesis, that Mill does not know (and indeed, *we* do not know) what 'happiness' *is*. And if so, how do we pursue it? What do we pursue?

In itself, it would not be a problem to be ignorant about what 'happiness' *is* (and this is not my criticism of Mill), since, in any circumstance, it cannot be known. The problems start because Mill does not see or understand his lack of knowledge, because he ignores his ignorance. Because of this ignorance of ignorance, he believes that whenever he writes 'happiness,' his meaning is clear and transparent (he probably resorts to certain memories of 'warm' or 'comfortable' circumstances, and believes that this suffices). It is his secondary ignorance of his primary ignorance that makes him naïve, not his primary ignorance. We notice that the text tries to teach him of his ignorance, since it offers a multitude of different and conflicting suggestions as to what happiness is, which ought to have indicated to Mill the indetermination and indefinableness of the term. However, Mill ignores this teaching of his text. He cannot see what he writes. The picture of the text has dissolved into pixels, like to a person placed too close to a TV set.

Reading the teaching of Mill's text, we can isolate five distinct definitions of happiness/pleasure. In general, pleasures can refer to an agent's pleasure, or to society's pleasure (in which case we talk about social welfare). Among possible pleasures we have three referring to the agent, a hybrid between agent and society's pleasure, and finally the self-sacrifice of pleasure for the sake of society. Thus, the following five mutually contradictory pleasures are being discussed in the essay: low/sensuous pleasures, high/noble pleasures as end for the agent, the paradoxical renunciation of pleasure as pleasure, high/noble pleasures as means for the sake of the general good, and finally, self-sacrifice of pleasure for the sake of the general good. In a diagram:

Agent as end/ Individual pleasure				Society as end/ Social Welfare
Bestiality	Intellectuality	Stoicism	Pragmatism	Virtue
Low/sensuous pleasures	High/noble pleasures as end for the agent	Paradox: Renunciation of pleasure as pleasure	High/noble pleasures as means to the end: the general good	Self-sacrifice of pleasure for the sake of the general good

This classification results in five utilitarian attitudes: Bestiality, Intellectuality, Stoicism, Pragmatism, and Virtue. The only pleasure in the diagram not sanctioned by Mill is, as mentioned, the low sensuous pleasure. 'Bestiality' is consistently rejected. Otherwise, Mill sanctions four 'pleasures,' where we notice that one of them, the high/noble pleasure, is ambivalent because it can entail pain, it can be 'unbearable.' Furthermore, another two 'pleasures,' renunciation and self-sacrifice of pleasure, are non-pleasurable (albeit, not necessarily *painful*) to the agent, not preventing them from being inherently utilitarian.

However, if certain obvious pleasures (sensuous, carnal) are not sanctioned in utilitarianism, and certain obvious non-pleasures, on the contrary, are, then there must be another morality dictating these judgments, another 'pre-moral' code anterior to Mill's discourse of morality. This code is not thematized by or in the theory, but nonetheless, it decides Mill's choice of what is good or bad. This pre-moral code can for example dictate that factual pleasures are bad, and renunciation of pleasure is good, but it does so stealthily and unconsciously. In that case, Mill's representation of the official utilitarian doctrine is not really his deepest moral conviction, it is merely a surface, an outer layer for an independent and different 'moral passion' that antedates his moral theory and shapes it into the confused mess that it is. As a 'passion,' such a stealthy morality has of course no sense of logic; as a 'passion,' it wants instant gratification of its dark, hostile desire, and logic never offered instant gratification.

We can give this different moral passion a label (labels are easy)—I have tried 'Victorian' (see below)—but we can never fully determine it. It is the nether limit of Mill's text, a stealthy desire, that controls him and his writing, and only shows itself in his decisions of what is good and evil (—and this is almost identical to the text itself). This stealthy desire is *only* represented, and we cannot see through its representation. But although we cannot know it, we can say that it is a moral passion, which is completely different from the utilitarian doctrines. It is, if I fine-tune my ears to hear its undertones, darker and more self-destructive. To use Freudian vocabulary: it does not work in the service of life, but rather in the service of death; this being of course utterly un-utilitarian.

4) THE NATURAL AND THE ACQUIRED
(i) The Supplemental Fallacy. (ii) Cultivating What Comes Naturally. (iii) Subjective and Social Feelings as Natural Supplements.

(i) The Supplemental Fallacy. In early writings (especially in the essay on Rousseau[40]), Derrida extracted from the texts he read a 'logic,' which he gave the name, 'the supplement.' In the case of Rousseau, the supplement is introduced as 'dangerous,' and Derrida draws the conclusion that 'supplementation' is in principle dangerous. In extracting and naming this concept, Derrida has widened our understanding of the inherent illogicality of the metaphysical text.

First, what does Derrida understand by 'supplement'? Supplementation indicates a relationship between two terms, a primary and a secondary, the supplemental term being secondary but filling in a lack characterizing the primary term; one 'adds' or 'supplies' something to a deficient situation, thus, complementing the deficiency. As such, the 'supplement' has advantages over the disadvantages of the primary term. Yet, the supplement—being secondary—is an addition to something that was already there from the beginning, something primordial and original. The supplement is meant to be something temporary, an *ad hoc* addition, and not the 'real' state of affairs. Consequently, the supplement represents a concept that the metaphysical text at once summons forth and tries to stamp out and suppress.

The best example of supplementation in Rousseau is 'writing,' Derrida argues. Writing is in Rousseau understood as a temporary, 'dangerous' supplement to a life lived in presence. Writing represents a necessary absenting oneself from wholesome social activities. That is, writing is at once necessary and regrettable, essential and secondary—it *is* necessary, yet *ought-to-not-have-been* necessary. The reason for the need to repress this necessary 'danger' is to Rousseau (and generally to metaphysics) that the supplement claims to *be* what it only *represents*. One might confuse it with the actual and real object, Rousseau believes; one might not realize that the supplement is merely a poor imitation of the authentic object. This happens, for example, if one assumes that 'writing,' and not speech, constitutes an original object. The supplement is 'dangerous' because it reverses the relationship between inauthentic and authentic, false and true, etc.

Although Derrida super-generalizes the term 'supplement' as a label for 'writing' always marked by repressive desire in Western Metaphysics, his reading (which applies to Rousseau and typically to Enlightenment Philosophy) seems narrow and one-sided in its negative emphasis on the 'danger' of supplementation. On one hand, I believe that it is important that Derrida has identified 'supplementation' as a typical 'logic' (a logic of illogicality) in philosophical texts. It must also be true that it exists in a two-term relationship as an *ad hoc* construction, as an auxiliary device to 'help' a term that was supposed to stand alone. On the other hand, I do not see that this device is *necessarily* marked by repressive desire. Often, it operates as an illogical helping-device, meant to *rescue, not repress*, the *metaphysical* positions of the text. Sometimes we notice a hierarchy where the distribution of value is not arranged according to positive vs. negative, but, for example, according to positive vs. positive—that is, we find only minute gradations in valuation between one positive term and another positive term. (In Derrida's own reading of Rousseau, 'writing' is marked by ambiguity, since it can be seen as a *help*, a prosthesis supplementing a self that is overly sensitive to social intercourse.)

Furthermore, reading Enlightenment Philosophy, predominantly it may be the case that the supplement either represents writing literally or represents generically something 'mechanical,' and is thus bound up with 'writing' in Derrida's anasemic sense. However, this definition does not hold in Mill. In Mill, 'writing' is no longer the issue, unless we stretch the meaning of 'writing' to include everything non-natural in the text; unless the term 'writing' is meaninglessly inflated.

Thus, the *supplement*, as extracted from *Mill's text*, has some of the qualities Derrida points out, but lacks others. It is a *good* that completes something that is *better*. It complements something original that cannot stand alone. It is an *ad hoc* construction—and an illogical and fallacious one, since it helps something that according to the text should not be in need of help. It *cultivates what comes naturally* and *realizes what is already there*. It is illogically inserted as an explanation of how the already existent comes into being; it helps the already present to become present. However, since presence does not need help to manifest itself (as little as God would need help to come into being), the supplement is not only superfluous, but also an involuntary admission of a failure in the primary term. We will therefore add the device to our list of fallacies as 'The Supplemental Fallacy.'

(ii) Cultivating What Comes Naturally. In Mill, we see this fallacy operating in a few variations. Mill starts defending the utilitarian standards because they correspond to human nature. It is our inclination to seek happiness, and utilitarian ethics is thus in harmony with human nature when it pronounces happiness as being the end for individuals as well as society. However, pursuit of happiness is an inclination that does not find realization without education. Young people need to be informed about their desire, and trained to pursue it. *Nature needs help.*

In one instance, the problem is (again) the transition from individual pursuit of happiness and pursuit of happiness for the greatest number. Since Mill refuses to separate these two pursuits, his question is, how does an individual pursue both her own happiness and the happiness for society? This is at least what he means to ask. The question he answers, however, is rather, how does an individual sacrifice her own happiness for the sake of society? According to the diagram above, we are dealing with the utilitarian attitude we called 'Virtue.' Mill best example of utilitarian virtue is "Jesus of Nazareth" as the "complete spirit of the ethics of utility."[41]

To love one's neighbor as oneself is now the ideal that has to be cultivated; the educational institutions of society become the means to achieve the ideal.

> As the means of making the nearest approach to this ideal, utility would enjoin, first, that laws and social arrangements should place the happiness, or the interest, of every individual, as nearly as possible in harmony with the interest of the whole; and secondary, that education and opinion, which have so vast a power over human character, should so use that power as to establish in the mind of every individual an indissoluble association between his own happiness and the good of the whole . . . so that not only he may be unable to conceive the possibility of happiness to himself, consistently with conduct opposed to the general good, but also that a direct impulse to promote the general good may be in every individual one of the habitual motives of action.[42]

At the basis of the argument, we have a well-known distinction, nature vs. culture, or, natural vs. acquired. Throughout his essay, Mill wants to assert the utilitarian doctrine as natural (we *do* pursue pleasure), but almost as soon as this is proposed, the assertion starts to self-deconstruct. We have already seen that it self-deconstructs regarding the high/noble pleasures; but especially, it is unsustainable in regard to self-sacrifice and virtue. These are utilitarian attitudes that are non-natural and have to be acquired.

If we call Mill's wish to maintain the *naturalness of utilitarianism* his *desideratum*,[43] throughout his text, he defends this *desideratum*, also when it starts to self-deconstruct. Therefore, when it becomes impossible to understand self-sacrifice as an individual inclination, Mill needs a series of *ad hoc* constructions, such as upbringing and education, which are supposed to gradually guide the individual into adopting a virtuous attitude.

If it can be argued that people are 'naturally' self-sacrificial or 'virtuous' it solves certain problems in Mill's utilitarianism (to which I come back shortly), and he therefore discuss how we 'naturally acquire' this 'will-to-be-virtuous' (we 'acquire' a 'will' we already have). Towards the end of the essay, this question is brought up again: "How can the will to be virtuous be implanted or awakened?"[44] Mill asks. How do we implant such a will? The answer of Mill begs the question: "only by making the person desire virtue—by making him think of it in a pleasurable light, or of its absence in a painful one."[45] But again, how do we make a person desire virtue? And again, how do we make him think of it in a pleasurable light?

This 'will-to-be-virtuous' must be seen as an *acquired* will, since it has to be *implanted*. However, even if this is indisputable, Mill does his best to argue that the 'implantation' is *natural*—he defends his desideratum *in its opposite*. Cultivation and education may contradict his general desideratum (culture was never identical to nature), but in his desire to overlook a potential logical conflict, Mill argues that *cultivation is natural* activity—there is nothing unnatural about cultivation. His logic of illogicality follows this fallacious syllogism: *nature* is the desideratum; if *culture* is necessary in order to educate people's *nature*, then *culture* is also *nature*. Again, Mill's desire directs his 'rationality.'

(iii) Subjective and Social Feelings as Natural Supplements. In the question of the sanction of utilitarianism, the dichotomy between naturalness and acquisition is brought up again. First, 'sanction' has a particular meaning in utilitarianism. 'Sanction,' Bentham would explain, signifies the obligation to follow a moral code of conduct:

> Sanction, in Latin, was used to signify the *act of binding*, and, by a common grammatical transition, *anything which serves to bind a man*— to wit, to the observance of such and such a mode of conduct. . . . A

sanction, then, is a source of obligatory powers or *motives*: that is, of *pains* and *pleasures*; which, according as they are connected with such and such modes of conduct, operate, and are indeed the only things which can operate, as *motives*.[46]

Mill follows up on this definition, posing the question: What is the ultimate sanction of the principle of utility? Why ultimately do we feel obligated to follow this principle? What binds us? If we talk about egoistic utilitarianism, the question is futile, since in that case, we redundantly ask why humans desire pleasure and are averse to pain. Less redundantly, Mill instead asks why we want *general* happiness, happiness for the greatest number. "Why am I bound to promote the general happiness? If my own happiness lies in something else, why may I not give that the preference?"[47]

We are again discussing the utilitarian attitude, virtue. What makes us promote general happiness? The following passage contains the answer: "the ultimate sanction, therefore, of all morality (external motives apart) being a subjective feeling in our own minds."[48] Besides the awkwardness of the formulation (have anybody ever heard about feelings that were not subjective or feelings outside our minds?), the answer situates the non-natural and acquired attitude, virtue, as *natural*. We have certain innate feelings that account for our readiness to self-sacrifice. These feelings are also described as (not less awkwardly), "the conscientious feelings of mankind."[49] It is these 'conscientious feelings' in 'our own minds' that drives us to pursue happiness for the whole. These natural and innate feelings make us feel obligated to act and perform according to duty.[50] We have an inclination to duty, Mill declares contrary to Kant (contrary to common sense), for whom inclination and duty are antithetical. We have a natural desire to fulfill obligations. We have a natural desire to pose restrictions on our desire.

I am aware that Mill-scholars might object that this is a distorted account of Mill, because Mill *explicitly* states that he does not regard moral or conscientious feelings as innate. And it is indeed correct that he *also* says that. We can for example try to understand the following paragraph: "If, as is my own belief, the moral feelings are not innate, but acquired, they are not for that reason less natural."[51] So, are they natural or acquired? The illuminating answer: "Like the other acquired capacities . . . the moral faculty, if not a part of our nature, is a *natural outgrowth* from it; capable . . . of *springing up spontaneously* [my emphases]."[52] They are acquired capacities that *grow out naturally*, they are faculties that *spring up spontaneously*. So, are they natural or acquired? Mill wants to have it both ways, so they are *naturally acquired*. They are "not a part of our nature," but they are a "natural outgrowth" from our nature.

There is yet another principle that needs to help this natural acquired agency in 'growing out naturally'; 'springing up spontaneously.' We need an auxiliary to the auxiliary, a supplement to the supplement. Not only do we have the agency of conscience to help us perform a duty that needn't be a duty, we furthermore have a new agency helping this agency in developing at all (—however 'spontaneous' this development was supposed to be). We have to add to the 'subjective' or 'conscientious' feeling a 'social' feeling. The basis of the naturally acquired sense of duty "is that of the social feelings of mankind; the desire to be in unity with our fellow creatures, which is already a powerful principle in human nature, and happily one of those which tend to become stronger . . . from the influences of advancing society."[53]

We notice that it is important to Mill at every turn, at each addition to emphasize that the supplement is 'natural.' Conscientious as well as social 'feelings' are natural. Conscientious feelings are acquired, but "are not for that reason less natural," and social principles constitute "powerful principles in human nature." The reason for the importance of this rhetoric is that the duties that regulate human behavior must never contradict human nature; utilitarianism must be in accordance with human nature. Applying an *ought* is seen as artificial and dogmatic unless it represents a desire that already *is*.

Mill derives an ought from an is, not *only* because of a logical confusion (as the Analytic Philosophers correctly points out), but *also* because he is in the grip of and controlled by his general *desideratum*. To obey a 'conscientious feeling' would be an artificial obligation if it were not already naturally present in the subject. In Mill, a subject already desires what it ought to do.

The ultimate sanction of utilitarianism, Mill-style, can therefore be nothing but the empty, 'a subjective feeling in our minds,' or simply, *human nature*. And if we need to add to these subjective feeling certain social feelings (as a last attempt to fill the hollow phrase with some sort of content), these social feelings are as much a part of human nature as are the subjective feelings. They can never merely be added from the outside. If Mill must admit that it is society (that is, an agent from the *outside*) that cultivates the social feelings in the human being, he does his very best to contain the damage by declaring that this necessary cultivation is 'instinctive'—again *natural*. The human being becomes *social-of-course*: "He comes, as though *instinctively*, to be conscious of himself as a being who *of course* pays regard to others. The good of others becomes to him a thing *naturally and necessarily* be attended to [my emphases]."[54]

5) VIRTUE AS 'PROOF' OF UTILITARIANISM
(i) Desired and Desirable. (ii) Explaining Self-Contradiction. (iii) Condensing Means and Ends. (iv) 'Virtue' as Pseudo-Solution to the Transition-Problem.

(i) Desired and Desirable. Mill starts his fourth chapter ("Of What Sort of Proof the Principle of Utility is Susceptible") with the following observation:

> It has already been remarked, that questions of ultimate ends do not admit of proof. . . . To be incapable of proof by reasoning is common to all first principles; to the first premises of our knowledge, as well as to those of our conduct.[55]

This remark is very much in agreement with the general approach of the present work. First or foundational principles cannot be proved; attempts must necessarily be seen as abortive. Foundational principles only duplicate decisions already taken in the theory. From this perspective, Mill's passage is a promising start of the chapter. However, Mill's chapter soon digresses into a speculation about *how to prove* utilitarianism; this speculation, in turn, digresses into a defense of 'virtue' as the pivotal utilitarian concept. These digressions occur almost immediately. In the following passage, we learn that:

> The only proof capable of being given that an object is visible is that people actually see it. The only proof that a sound is audible, is that people hear it; . . . in the like manner, I apprehend, the sole evidence it is possible to produce that anything is desirable, is that people do actually desire it.[56]

G. E. Moore has commented extensively on this paragraph. He objects that there are no semantic parallels between visible/audible and desirable, as Mill assumes. A visible object is an object that *is* or *can* be seen, while a desirable object is an object that *ought* to be desired, therefore an object that not necessarily *is* desired, but an object that is good to or worthy of desire. If 'desirable' means what ought to or deserves to be desired, 'good to desire' and 'actually desired' are not correlative statements; is not 'proved' that something is 'desirable' by observing that is actually desired. Reversibly, it cannot be inferred that if people actually desire an object then the object is desirable. According to Moore (and Russell repeating Moore's objection[57]), Mill does not notice this double hiatus, (1) what is good to desire is not necessarily actually desired, and (2) what is actually desired is not necessarily worthy of desire. (For example, if in some social or religious contexts, premarital sexual abstinence is desirable, this does not imply that abstinence is *actually* desired. Or, to repeat the same thought in the reverse, it is well known that individuals desire things that are deemed unworthy of desire, for example, premarital sex. For centuries, religions have taught the dangers of 'bad' desires.)

Therefore, if Moore and Russell are right in saying that 'desirable' means 'worthy of desire,' Mill cannot infer from the good being 'desirable' that it is 'desired.' The following equation is under that assumption fallacious: good = (desirable/good to desire) = desired. However, Moore and Russell's now classical objection hinges on the assumption that 'desirable' means 'worthy of desire'; and this is not completely obvious. We also say about an object that *arouses* desire that it is 'desirable.' A 'desirable' woman is not a woman that is 'worthy' of desire, but a woman that arouses desire, therefore *is* desired. We can talk about a 'desirable outcome' of negotiations, and mean then that this outcome *is* desired, not that it is advisable or recommended to desire it. Mill could therefore be right in asserting that happiness *arouses* desire, and therefore *is* desired. His parallel between visible and desirable is not necessarily fallacious. Moore and Russell's criticism of Mill's 'proof' is therefore not completely effective; the problem with Mill's 'proof' lies elsewhere.

As Mill rightly concedes, we may not be able to carry out a rational and deductively valid proof of happiness as "the only thing desirable, as an end; all other things being only means to that end."[58] In Mill's language, the case does not "admit of proof, in the ordinary acceptation of the term."[59] But by appealing to experience, we can evidence our case. The 'proof' of happiness as the ultimate end of human action is that one may observe that people actually *do* desire happiness.

I shall suggest that the reason why the statement, 'Happiness is desirable' does not 'admit of proof' is that the notion of happiness already includes 'desirability' as one component of its semantic content. 'Happiness' is indicative of pleasure; it connotes an active or passive sense of pleasure. The analytic content of the statement, *happiness is desired*, is an integral part of the definition of happiness; the predicate is part of the definition of the subject. If we form the statement as a question 'Why is happiness desirable?' we tautologically ask why happiness makes happy, why people in general are more happy being happy, than being unhappy? It is therefore meaningless to try to *establish* the desirability of happiness. Questions like, why is happiness desired are equivalent to questions like why is a circle round, or why is a bachelor an unmarried man. If the circle weren't round, it wouldn't be a circle, if the bachelor weren't unmarried, he wouldn't be a bachelor, and, finally, if happiness weren't desirable, it wouldn't be happiness.

Furthermore, if the circle were not round, we could not ask the question, why is it round? We can only ask the question because it is already presumed knowledge that it is round. The same applies to happiness being desirable: Why is happiness desirable? —Because it is already presumed desirable.

Therefore, as Mill rightly concedes, happiness does not "admit of proof by reasoning." However, Mill still feels compelled to deliver a 'proof' of the official doctrine of utilitarianism. In some qualified sense, he must establish that happiness and only happiness is desirable as an end. A problem with this 'weak' 'proof' Mill nevertheless feels he must deliver, lies in the absentmindedness of his presentation, in the obvious inconsistency and indecisiveness of his text.

(ii) Explaining Self-Contradiction. The quotation above (repeated several times in slightly different variations) clearly establishes that happiness and only happiness is desirable as an end, other things being means to that end. Happiness is the *only ultimate end*. This does not prevent Mill from stating, half a page further on, that "now it is palpable that they [people] do desire things which . . . are decidedly distinguished from happiness. They desire, for example, virtue, and the absence of vice, no less really than pleasure and the absence of pain."[60]

These two statements are, of course, in naked self-contradiction: pleasure is the only end and the ultimate thing desired, but besides this one and only desire, virtue is as real a desire. If virtue is as real a desire as is pleasure, utilitarianism has been significantly revised. According to this revised version, people now pursue two ends, pleasure (according to the official doctrine) and virtue (according to Mill's remedial version). Within the space of a page, Mill contradicts himself no less than three times. Mill toggles between positing pleasure as an end in itself, then virtue as an end in itself, then virtue as a means to pleasure as an end, and finally, back to virtue as an end in itself. At no point does he make up his mind about whether to assert virtue as an end or as a means. We may wonder how he fails to see these apparent inconsistencies in his mode of writing. To spell out his operations, he starts by stating his official position.

> *Position*: "The utilitarian doctrine is that happiness is desirable, and the only thing desirable, as an end." Thereupon we read the following negation.
> *Negation of position*: "It [utilitarianism] maintains not only that virtue is to be desired, but that it is to be desired disinterestedly, for itself." Thereupon we read a negation of the negation.

Negation of negation of position: "However, they [utilitarians] may believe (as they do) that actions and dispositions are only virtuous because they promote another end than virtue." Finally follows a return to the first negation.

Negation of negation of negation of position: "Yet this being granted . . . they [utilitarians] do not only place virtue at the very head of things which are good as means to the ultimate end, but they also recognize as a psychological fact the possibility of its being, to the individual, a good in itself, without looking to any end beyond."[61]

Analytic philosophers do not fail to see such basic self-contradictions in Mill's text, but they do not attempt to *explain* them, because, within their vista, how does one *explain* a self-contradiction? As indicated in the introductory remarks, I suggest that a deconstructive analytic can explain something like self-contradictions 'quasi-psychoanalytically.' I use the term with some caution, because it would be an analytical blunder to go back to orthodox psychoanalysis and explain a theory by the unconscious or infantile life of its author.[62] Still, we can demarcate deconstructive from logical analysis (the analysis of the truth-values of components and their composition) by the ability in the former to recognize features like *conflicting voices, desiderata, condensation, self-defense, obligation,* or *repression* in the text. Especially self-contradictions that are at the same time evident *and* ignored, manifest *and* overlooked, need explanation, because they indicate that the author is 'under pressure' (to be sufficiently vague). These self-contradictions can be seen as deriving from the pressure to conciliate various polemical objections. Granted that an author is never a self-identical entity, speaking throughout his life with only one uniform voice, but a 'label' for a sum of voices that speak in different political-polemical contexts presenting the author to different demands, forcing him into defending different interests, etc., self-contradictions emerge as the unsuccessful attempts to mediate these different interests. *Self-contradiction is the mediation of conflicting desires to satisfy conflicting interests.*

In the basic self-contradiction above, we noticed that Mill is defending two versions of utilitarianism, an official and a remedial version. But what is it that has to be remedied? It is obvious from the textual context that Mill reacts to certain objections. His reparations grow out of a certain criticism of utilitarianism. Opponents to utilitarianism have claimed that human action has other ends than happiness, for example, *virtue*. In other words, they take the moral high-ground, and consign utilitarianism to base egoism, materialism, and hedonism. This accusation provokes Mill, and incites him into a defense of utilitarianism as a morally responsible theory (in the heat, forgetting everything about the official utilitarian doctrines). The *Theoretical Mill* may know that according to utilitarian dogma, pleasure is the ultimate end; but more compellingly, the *Victorian Mill* knows 'subconsciously' that it is 'better' and 'nobler' to seek virtue than it is to seek pleasure. Subconsciously, he 'knows' (according to the contemporary social, religious, institutional (middle-class) moral code) that virtue is 'good' and pleasure is 'bad.' The self-contradiction comes about, in part, because the *Theoretical Mill* cannot contain his *Victorian* 'instincts.' Instead of defending utilitarianism against its critics, he makes a U-turn and claims that what the critics correctly perceive as lacking in utilitarianism, is on the contrary its must sacrosanct principle. In Mill, the critics always get it wrong because this readiness to claim that utilitarianism has included everything. He immunizes the theory against criticism by reiterating that either (1) utilitarianism never said what it says, or (2) utilitarianism has already said what it never said.

> But does the utilitarian doctrine deny that people desire virtue? The very reverse. It maintains not only that virtue is to be desired, but that it is to be desired *disinterestedly for itself* . . . they [utilitarians] not only place virtue at the very head of the things which are good as means to the ultimate end, but they also recognize as a psychological fact the possibility of its being, to the individual, *a good in itself, without looking to any end beyond it* [my emphases].[63]

(iii) Condensing Means and Ends. Mill has involved himself in a self-contradiction that could have been avoided had he made 'virtue' a *means* to the ultimate end 'pleasure' instead of an end in itself, but—as my emphases above underscore—this is clearly not the case: virtue is an end in itself.

Although one should never underestimate Mill's absentmindedness, one brief sentence indicates that he senses a problem in this new version of utilitarianism, and tries to solve it. He has previously said that virtue is a means, and now that it is an end in itself. The solution to this indecision is that there are things, such as virtue, that can be both means and end: "They are desired and desirable in and for themselves; besides being means, they are a part of the end."[64]

But this 'solution' only makes matters worse. It certainly needs to be explained how a thing can be both a means to an end and an end in itself. If the means to the end, *fame*, is writing a book, how can writing the book itself be fame? If the means to the end, *sex*, is flirtation, how is flirtation itself sex, etc.? How do means participate in the ends that they are conceived to produce? It seems that the celebrated author of *A System of Logic* has committed another logical blunder in order to escape from the first one, the second only resulting in suspending and rendering meaningless a distinction he otherwise relies heavily on.

Even if a thing can be both a means and an end relative to context, it cannot be both at the same time. Money, to take Mill's own example, is sometimes means and sometimes ends. If they are means, the end could be something like material comfort. If they are ends, the means to obtain this end could be something like hard work, or clever investment. Even if money is a tricky example—because, as financiers will testify, money is often a means to the end, to make more money—then there is still a distinction between the money invested and the money earned on an investment. (An easy example: "I love money!" Danny DeVito passionately proclaims in a recent movie, and continues, "there is only one thing I love more than money . . . other people's money!" Money is here the means to the end, 'other people's money,' but, as the joke stresses, *other people's money* is still distinct from *money* by being DeVito's true love.)

The distinction, means/end, collapses in Mill because he is condensing two equally desirable situations. Mill 'confuses' means and end, as the Analytic Philosophers correctly objects, but they do not see that the *means* to this confusion is the *condensation* of two desirable situations, one where virtue is a means to happiness, and another where virtue is an end in itself. The result of the condensation is that virtue becomes equal and identical to happiness. We can illustrate the condensation as an overlapping of two equations:

Virtue as means:	Virtuous actions → General Happiness
	+
Virtue as end:	Individual Actions → Virtue
	=
Condensation of means & end:	Individual Virtuous actions → Virtue = General Happiness

In this sense, virtue is both a means, and 'part of the end' which is still happiness. Because of condensation, the distinction between means and ends collapses. Virtue is both a means and an end.

The term 'condensation' is of course borrowed from Freud, who applied it, not to arguments, but to the dream-work. A dream 'condenses' two different dream-thoughts into one image. Thus condensed, the image will often appear unrecognizable to the dreamer because it appears as a confusion of components. The motive for condensation is a desire. In Freud, the desire is often to censor a compromising dream-thought.

Applied to arguments, the result of condensation is also confusion. Condensation implies a break with the established rules of logic; it suspends logic, and makes it possible to arrange contradictory ideas side by side, without the author sensing a problem. That the two ideas in the contradictory statement negate each other is either not seen, or it is ignored. Usually, in order to make the condensed contradictory statement more acceptable, it is lubricated in reasonableness. This helps the author to deceive himself into believing that he is still a rational entity, whereas in fact, another order has taken over and is guiding his discourse, controlling it from sub-conscious parts of the psyche. In Mill's case, establishing virtue as both means and end—within a theoretical framework where happiness is the only end—is motivated by desire rather than reason, I have said. We now notice that this desire is not sexual (as careful readers of psychoanalysis know that desires rarely are). If anything, it is the opposite; it is in Mill's case precise to talk about a desire for respectability and seemliness.

(iv) 'Virtue' as Pseudo-Solution to the Transition-Problem. Why this 'will' to virtue? If Mill can argue that virtue is the true candidate for happiness—instead of more obvious candidates like sex, money, fame, power, honor, etc.—it has several advantages. First, as already mentioned, there is the obvious polemical advantage since utilitarianism can reclaim the moral high-ground from its critics by declaring 'virtue' the ultimate end—as such, reinventing itself as a most (indeed, *the* most) respectable and 'virtuous' ethical theory. Mill mutes critics representing utilitarianism as hedonism. Secondly, asserting virtue as the ultimate end mediates the conflicting demands in requiring both happiness in the individual and happiness for the greatest number. At least, this mediation becomes considerably easier, because a person acting virtuously does not clash with the interest of others, as for example a money- or power-hungry person inevitably does. On the contrary, a virtuous individual promotes the interests of others.

> With this difference between it [virtue] and the love of money, of power, or of fame, that all of these may, and often do, render the individual noxious to the other members of the society to which he belongs, whereas there is nothing which makes him so much a blessing to them as the cultivation of the disinterested love of virtue.[65]

There are thus strong reasons for Mill to discuss 'virtue,' and apparently, they are so strong that he forgets what he originally set out to discuss, the proof of utilitarianism. The title of the chapter is therefore deceptive, not only because Mill does not give us any proof—what he from the outset (sorts of) admits—but because a proof is never addressed except in a few sentences. The chapter is consumed by a desire to promote 'virtue' as the pivotal concept of utilitarianism.

However, in one passage, Mill briefly returns to the discussion of the proof that introduced the chapter. After extensively having discussed virtue, Mill returns to his initial project in a passage that is meant to conclude the discussions we have been through: "We have now an answer to the question, of what sort of proof the principle of utility is susceptible," and he then repeats, almost verbatim, the idea from the first page.

> If human nature is so constituted as to desire nothing which is not either a part of happiness of a mean of happiness, we can have no other proof, and we require no other, that these are the only things desirable. If so, happiness is the sole end of human action.[66]

In an essay that is not scant on surprising twists and turns, this is not the least baffling intersection. Not only has Mill *not* spent any time on his so-called proof of the utilitarian doctrine, but he has gone further than any utilitarian in qualifying, if not refuting, the same doctrine. Not only is the passage unmotivated (he could for that sake just as well have started discussing the mating behavior of peacocks, or, if too frivolous, the noxious side-effects of excessive coffee drinking), but it also neglects his discussion of virtue as the ultimate end. As if nothing had been said about virtue as an end in itself, we suddenly read, "happiness is the sole end of human action." Now, with oblivious confidence, Mill believes he is in a position to conclude discussions that have been entirely absent, the 'conclusion' being a repetition of the problem initially stated, besides—for good measure—contradicting the discussions that it is meant to conclude.[67]

In his 'conclusion' on the proof of utilitarianism, Mill returns to the previous problem of how to mediate between individual happiness and happiness for the greatest number. As we have seen, in prior formulations, Mill condenses these two dicta; he skates over the dichotomy and leaves it unsolved. Now, he seems to sense an incompatibility between the two pursuits. He feels he needs to bridge them and offers the following argument:

> No reason can be given why the general happiness is desirable, except that each person, so far as he believes it to be attainable, desires his own happiness. This, however, being a fact, we have not only all the proof which the case admits of, but all which it is possible to require, that happiness is a good: that each person's happiness is a good to that

person, and the general happiness, therefore, a good to the aggregate of all persons.[68]

The argument is that since happiness is good for one person, 'general happiness' is good for the 'aggregate of all persons.' It has been argued that one cannot conclude that from members having a quality it follows that the set of the members has the same quality. Mill is committing what has been called the fallacy of composition. If power is a good for each member, it does not follow that power is good for the set of all members. Self-preservation is a good for the individual, but it is not typically regarded as good for the whole. To own a car is good for the individual, but it is not necessarily good for society as a whole.

Mill's thinking is that if happiness is good for person A, for person B, for person C, etc., then general happiness is good for the sum of all. He explains in a letter: "I merely meant by this particular sentence to argue that since A's happiness is a good, B's a good, C's a good, etc., the sum of all these goods must be a good."[69] By adding up individual pleasures one by one, Mill believes that he has solved the transition-problem in coming from one to the whole.

However, we notice that in this case, the sum of the parts is not equal to the whole. When individuals pursue happiness, they concretely pursue certain objects. Let us say that *subject A* and *subject B* both pursue objects q, r, and s. I will now suggest that *as individuals*, A and B pursue the objects of happiness q, r, and s, *in agreement*, but *as a whole*, A and B pursue the same objects, q, r, and s, *in disagreement*. That is, they compete over the same objects. This suggestion rests of the deeper assumption that when we are talking about happiness-pursuit we must necessarily presuppose *scarcity* of objects (such as money, fame, power, success in career, or attractive women/men). We must presuppose this scarcity, because we can only meaningfully talk about pursuing something we do not have, not something we already have. If objects are abundant, we already have them, and we do not pursue them. *Subject A* and *subject B* may therefore as individuals agree upon that q is good, and exactly because of this agreement, they pursue in disagreement q.

Only under one condition does Mill's argument seem to hold (and symptomatically and unconsciously he 'realizes' this), namely in the paradoxical case where the individuals give up their pursuits of the objects q, r, and s, and replace their pursuit of objects with the pursuit of *the happiness of the other*. In this case, individual and general pursuit of happiness converges, because individual happiness is identical to pursuit of happiness of the other. The desire for own happiness has become desire for the other's happiness. The notion, 'virtue,' is an appropriate label for this attitude.

In Mill's *oneiric logic* it is thus strangely appropriate to discuss 'virtue' under the title 'proof'—'virtue' does not exactly 'prove' utilitarianism, but it offers a 'quasi-solution' to its main inherent problem. Virtue implies that the individual no longer desires his/her own happiness but the happiness of the other.

Virtue = df. "The individual's desire for the pleasure of the other."

It is still important that the individual *desires* the pleasure of the other, because if there is no desire for this pleasure, the utilitarian doctrine is refuted and utilitarianism is no longer a hedonism (and in his dream-language, Mill never stops believing that he is defending utilitarianism as a hedonism (—while he is attacking the interpretations of utilitarianism as a hedonism)). If the individual *truly desires* the pleasure of the other, he has never given up his own pleasure, consequently, the utilitarian doctrine is intact and utilitarianism is still a hedonism. It has become a unique 'hedonism,' to be sure; a hedonism where the individual pursues his own pleasure only by pursuing the pleasure of the other; a hedonism where the objective of *A*'s pursuit of happiness is no longer desirable *q*, *r*, or *s*, but *B's* pursuit of *q*, *r*, or *s*. This implies that individual happiness-pursuit and general happiness-pursuit becomes the same thing. Individual happiness *is* pursuit of general happiness.

Evidently, the argument will have to presuppose a strange and counter-intuitive philosophical anthropology, since it presupposes that the primary desire of human beings is their neighbor's happiness; the most original desire of humans is the happiness of the other.

This is what is now meant by 'desire.' It is redefined into meaning 'virtue'—not to be confused with Aristotle's notion of virtue. Desire as virtue means that the individual finds pleasure in pursuing the pleasure of the other; it means that pleasure is the other's pleasure. This is what we will have to remember whenever we read Mill's famous definition, which in reformulation now reads: "Actions are right in proportion as they tend to promote happiness [of the other] . . . by happiness is intended pleasure [of the other]."

How we pursue the other's happiness is, of course, a no less complicated issue than how we pursue our own. Especially since happiness/pleasure cannot be determined within Mill's framework, the surprising new version of utilitarianism is as empty on moral instruction as were the conventional version. A new essay would have to be written about how we pursue the pleasure of the other, about what pleasures we ought to pursue and what pleasures we ought to avoid on behalf of the other. Particularly, the new essay would have to explain *why* it is a utilitarian goal to pursue the other's pleasure, when it ought not to be our own (since according to the new logic, we disclaim our own pleasures). We are, after all, necessarily somebody's other—and what do we do about that predicament? What do we do when the other starts pursuing our pleasures; do we sit back and enjoy or do we immediately mount a counter-attack? Maybe the new essay should start by explaining why we need to bother about pleasure in the first place.

The problems of this sequel to *Utilitarianism* are already beginning to pile up.

6) Conclusion

After reading Mill's *Utilitarianism*, we might ask why it is so difficult to determine what is pleasure. To put it squarely, is the problem in the signifier, in the signified, or is there a possibility in between? Is (1), the *conceptualization* difficult; implying that it is difficult to capture in words sensations with which we are all familiar? Or (2), is it more difficult to 'feel' and evaluate *sensations* than we think; implying that if sensations are poorly transmitted, it is no wonder that they cannot easily be conceptualized? Or (3), is conceptualization difficult because our language is too crude to classify a universe of minute differences in sensation, which somehow we have but has no adequate language to describe. Is an antithesis like 'pain' vs. 'pleasure' merely the crudest possible approximation? Is our language like a Procrustes bed on which we stretch, amputate, and shape sensations until they conform to our primitive concepts? According to this latter (Nietzschean) suggestion, we have sensations but we have only primitive knowledge about them, not because our 'body' is unaware of them, but because our language is deficient in classifying them, and because we cannot know what we cannot form into language. More precisely, *we do not know what it is to know them.*

For example, we cannot know whether it is a pleasure or a pain to read a book because several different sensations fuse in the reading-experience, sensations for which we have no name and no values. If we assert that reading a book is a pleasure (philosophers as well as laymen happily declare something like, 'there is nothing like after work to sit down and immerse oneself in a good book'), we are in other words merely *interpreting*. We are making a series of rash subconscious judgments that may and may not correspond to reality, and may or may not relate to 'reading' *per se*. According to this interpretation, we take for granted that it is a relief to *escape* from reality; reading is a *freedom* and a *relaxation,* while work is exhausting. We also grant that reading *educates* the mind, which we immediately translate as 'good.' But in reality (to the extent we can talk about a 'reality' beyond interpretation), reading is a *terra incognita*, a Dark Continent we populate with all sorts of bizarre and fanciful creatures. (Is reading a bad philosopher a pleasure or a pain, I might now with some justification ask myself. But what do I in all honesty answer? (—I tend to believe, to the extent I am able to gauge myself, perhaps a pleasure rather than a pain, but who knows?))

However, although complex sensations like reading may present us with certain difficulties, there may be other more primitive sensations that we have no difficulty in classifying into pain or pleasure. What characterizes such 'primitive' sensations is that our body seems to 'know' and 'recognize' them immediately as either one or the other. Our body reacts to them before we do. It is not necessary to consult our consciousness for their classification. It is for example impossible not to admit that a sensation like burning one's hand is recognized as a pain qua the immediate flight-reaction of the body. We can probably also accept that sleep when exhausted, food when starved, and drink when thirsty are recognized by the body as pleasures, and the same regarding the sexual climax.

However, although sexuality is typically regarded as the universal symbolization of pleasure, already regarding sexuality, pleasure becomes ambiguous, not only because, physiologically, sexual sensation is tingled with pain, but because, regarding the total sexual situation, our body is no longer the sole judge. The subject intervenes. Human sexuality is characterized by not being purely instinctive. Humans interfere in their instincts by evaluating the 'quality' of the sexual object before giving in to the drive. We negotiate with ourselves as to whether or not pursuing this instinctual reward, and we do so to such an extent that we can easily decide to forestall pursuit.

Our *desire* in other words replaces our *drive*; and desire does not want sex, but recognition. Undiluted instinctual gratification is no longer sought from the desired object, the desired object is never a mere pleasure object. It is instead pursued because something is added to its sexual magnetism. An aura or corona that is coexistent with the object, bathing it in a particularly favorable light. With this complication, sexuality becomes at best a very ambivalent pleasure; as the romantic writers tirelessly tell us, desire is more painful than pleasurable.

If we return to Mill's distinction between lower and higher pleasures, but reapply and refashion it into our new theoretical context, a 'low pleasure' represents now rudimentary bodily pleasures such as sleep when exhausted, food when starved, drink when thirsty, and the sexual climax as the primitive instinctual reward for propagating the species. Whereas pursuit of sexuality already belongs to the 'higher pleasures.' Thus, lower pleasures are much lower than Mill thinks, and higher pleasures start much sooner than he believes. Furthermore, since I argue that everything that in Mill falls under the label 'high pleasure' is stamped with ambiguity, a 'high pleasure' is no longer identifiable as a pleasure. On the other hand, this will not imply that it is a pain (*non-pleasure* is not necessarily *pain*). At best, we can say that it is an ambiguous *pleasure-pain* (or a *sensational neutral*), which it is left to the interpretive creative subject to specify. Thus, sexual pursuits are pleasure-pains, as is lying in the sun, taking a swim, reading a book, and listening to music. We know with some certainty that *work* is a pleasure-pain that is typically interpreted as a pain, *because* also *being-out-of-work* is a pleasure-pain that is typically interpreted as a pain. We notice the following tendency in the interpretation of pleasure-pains. As a rule of thump, they are interpreted as pleasures whenever one has been barred from achieving them over a period of time—and reversibly, as pains, whenever one has had them in abundance over a period. That is the reason why work is a pain for he who is in work and a pleasure for he who has been out-of-work. The same logic applies to sexuality and generally—we appreciate scarcity, and depreciate abundance.

Usually society assists the individual in interpreting pleasure-pains. The individual is rarely on her own in these evaluations. For example, there are elaborate social codes to determine how we eat and drink well. These codes change radically from society to society, and even between classes within the same society. Without this interpretive support network, the individual would be at a loss and thrown back into her own indecisive pleasure-pains, forced to do all the evaluative work herself. This can be done, and when it is, we usually regard such individuals as 'eccentric'; they deviate from our recognized center; they defend curious opinions like, gore and slash movies are great art, rats make wonderful pets, or, Budweiser is the world's best beer.

It is now fair to conclude that if all the 'pleasures' that Mill wants to defend in his utilitarian utopia are higher pleasures, and if higher pleasures are *pleasure-pains* or *sensational neutrals*, they cannot be determined in a metaphysical language. There *is* no good. By necessity, there could never *a priori* be a high pleasure. Such pleasures can only be determined in acts of evaluation which are, *mutatis mutandis*, always social, and internalized as subconscious social constructions in the individual.

When therefore Mill and commentators ask, what *is* good, they pose a question that cannot, in principle, be answered. We cannot devise a metaphysical theory of what is good; a theory, for example, that wants to elucidate 'human nature' in order to determine what 'human nature' *needs*. We can at best set up a political program based on pooling and political instinct of what seems to be *interpreted* as being needed within a certain segment of a population. This is a job handled better by politicians than by philosophers. We find this pragmatic component in the theory of Mill when he introduces his principle of voting on pleasures according to educated preference. However, it is immediately rescinded in the ensuing attempt to determine what *ought* to be chosen as good, because it *is* good.

NOTES

LIST OF LITERATURE

INDEX

NOTES

NOTES TO "INTRODUCTION"

1.   Nietzsche, Frederich: *The Will to Power*. Translated by Holllingdale & Kaufmann (New York: Random House, 1967), p. 267.
2.   Wittgenstein, Ludwig: *On Certainty* (New York: Harper Torchbooks, 1969), p. 33e.
3.   Deleuze, G. & Guattari, F.: *What is Philosophy?* Translated by H. Tomlinson & G. Burchell. (New York: Columbia University Press, 1994), p. 15.
4.   Nietzsche, Friedrich: *Beyond Good and Evil*. Translated by J. Norman (Cambridge: Cambridge University Press, 2002), p. 41. *Jenseits von Gut und Böse*. In *Sämtliche Werke* bd. 5. (Berlin: De Gruyter, 1980), p. 24.
5.   I am far from alone in this desire to establish a cogent deconstruction in distinction to playful practices of deconstruction. This is a project one may find is the works of Rodolphe Gasché, Christopher Norris, and Samuel C. Wheeler, to mention just a few.
6.   See Hartman, Geoffrey: *Criticism in the Wilderness* (New Haven-London: Yale University Press, 1980) & *Saving the Text* (Baltimore: The Johns Hopkins University Press, 1981).
7.   See Fish, Stanley: *Is There a Text in this Class* (Cambridge: Harvard University Press, 1980) & *Doing what Comes Naturally* (Durham: Duke University Press, 1989)
8.   See Gadamer, Hans-Georg: *Truth and Method* (New York: Seabury Press, 1975); Ricoeur, Paul: *Hermeneutics and the Social Sciences* (Cambridge: Cambridge University Press, 1981) & *Interpretation Theory* (Texas Christian University Press, 1976); Iser, Wolfgang: *The Implied Reader* (Baltimore-London: The Johns Hopkins University Press, 1974) & *The Act of Reading* (London-Henley: Routledge, 1978). There is no doubt to Gadamer, Ricoeur, and Iser's mind that there is a textual object to be 'appropriated'; and therefore, distancing my reading-strategy from the Hermeneutical school is perhaps not fully justified since I am so far saying approximately the same. I do, however, detect the following problem in hermeneutics from Gadamer over Ricoeur to Iser. Although they make earnest attempts to prevent 'relativization' of textural analysis, it is hard to see how it is effectively avoided when the meaning of a text is 'actualized' *in* the reader, and consequently actualized differently in different readers. The hermeneutical tradition is typically interested in aesthetic response, in how a text is actualized or appropriated by a reader. It is typically interested in how meaning emerges in the dialectics between text and reader. This approach necessarily poses the question of what textual meaning would be in-itself, or whether such a construction is even possible. It is therefore doubtful whether the solution to this quandary of a less-radical hermeneutics is significantly different from the radical solution Fish suggests. In his essay on Wolfgang Iser, "Who is

Afraid of Wolfgang Iser," Fish of course sees a radical distinction between himself and Hermeneutics; and he offers of this hermeneutic double-bind a criticism, which is in itself clever and acute. (See *Doing What Comes Naturally*, loc. cit.)

9.   'Infinite' is an impossible high number. As absolute minimum, infinite interpretability presupposes that the human species has an infinite future, that we will never become extinct. Throughout this infinite future, we will also have to sustain our interest in the same pieces of literature. Each work of literature would end up with its own 'Library of Babel' (cf. the wellknown short-story by J. L. Borges). It would have a library containing an infinity of interpretations, rendering, of course, any communication about the actual work impossible. Any of these assumptions are equally absurd. (—But I must be exaggerating! Let us grant that the term 'infinite' is being used merely as a poetic flourish, that it actually means 'multiple.')

10.   Wittgenstein, Ludwig: *Philosophical Investigations* (Oxford: Blackwell, 1997. Re-issued 2nd ed.), p. 193.

11.   See Ingarden, Roman: *Vom Erkennen des literarischen Kunstwerks* (Tübingen, Niemeyer, 1968) & Ricoeur, Paul: *Hermenutics and Social Sciences*, loc. cit.

12.   See Greimas, A. J.: *Structural Semantics. An Attempt at a Method* (Lincoln-London: University of Nebraska Press, 1983) & *On Meaning. Selected Writing in Semiotic Theory* (Minneapolis: University of Minnesota Press, 1994).

13.   It is an inconsistency that remains unresolved even in Jacques Derrida. Whereas I believe that Derrida in general emphasizes 'structural instability'—at least so in early essays—he has made a famous case for interpretational instability in his debates with John Searle (See Derrida: *Limited Inc.* (Evanston: Northwestern University Press, 1977)). Thus, it seems that also Derrida lumps together structural and interpretational instability.

14.   The assertion that texts and systems are 'interpretable' has no particular consequences regarding the understanding of foundations of texts or systems. The question is hardly being addressed. Whether a system, a theory, or a text, seen as relativized by interpretations, has a foundation or not, is not ascertainable. Since the supposed foundation would be part of the immanent logic of the theory, and the value of the theory is relative to the interpretive community, its supposed foundation would be relative as well; or it would not be an object of investigation. Ultimately, proponents of interpretive instability have nothing better to offer than the cognitive non-starter that some textual feature would be something in one context and something else in another. The thesis of interpretational instability results in relativism that closes off all further investigations of theories, including investigations into their lack of foundation.

15.   Stanley Fish especially in the works, *There is No such Thing as Free Speech and It Is a Good Thing Too* (Oxford: Oxford University Press, 1994) and *The Trouble with Principle* (Cambridge, Mass.: Harvard University Press, 1999).

16.   Now, if an imaginary opponent objects that there are other 'societies' than 'the Bond-society,' and these impute their critical standards on this newly formed society, the problem that here I find unnecessary to represents on more

than one level is merely repeated on a new and deeper nested level: how do these 'other societies' in the beginning of their critical activity know their critical standards. This point can be repeated at any level *ad infinitum*.

17.   The 'logician' I have in mind at this point, is the—to the Anglo-Saxon world—little-known Paul Lorenzen, who in his *Constructive Philosophy* (Cambridge, Mass.: MIT Press, 1987) has suggested new ways of grounding philosophy.

18.   The Platonist logician has accumulated several arguments in order to argue for this lack of right to dispute the self-present truth of the ground, for example, one of the all-time favorites, 'non-belief cannot refute belief'—because otherwise non-belief becomes a belief, and that is not allowed. In the desire to establish argumentative illegitimacy of the antagonists, it is ignored that one belief can still refute another belief, and Deconstructive logic, in my understanding, is not supposed to be more mysterious than that. It must be legitimate to replace one conception of origin with another conception. In the beginning of this century, it was also regarded as a matter of fact that the atom was indivisible; this was a fact until leading nuclear physicists proved that fission was possible, and demonstrated that the atom was composed of smaller particles. We encounter an analogous situation in metaphysics. The Platonist strongly hope that the 'origin' is indivisible, that there is *one* truth, that truth has only 'one component'—as Deleuze/Guattari might say. The deconstructionist logician, however (in the version I am here introducing), believes that the 'origin' is a rather crude illusion of unity of something that is composed of several parts. There can be no 'performative self-contradiction' in holding this view; it merely implies that a primitive concept of origin is being replaced with a complex notion.

19.   This is one of the insights of Derrida. Derrida often documents metaphysics in unguarded intersections and footnotes, in the so-called 'margins,' of a text; for example, when theoreticians chat about their grandchildren—as in the essay on Freud from *The Postcard*. See Derrida: *The Postcard: From Socrates to Freud and Beyond.* Translated by A. Bass. (Chicago: The University of Chicago Press, 1987).

20.   Wittgenstein: *On Certainty*, loc. cit., p. 33e.

21.   Descartes: *Discourse on the Method* in *The Philosophical Writings of Descartes* (Cambridge: Cambridge University Press, 1985), p. 113.

NOTES TO "THE SPIRAL AND THE PLANE"

1.   Franz Kafka: *The Castle*. Trans. Mark Harmon (New York: Schochen Books, 1998), p. 80-81.

2.   The most articulate exponent of this view is Richard Rorty. See for example the article, "Is Derrida a Transcendental Philosopher" (in: Wood (ed.) *Derrida—A Critical Reader*. Oxford: Balckwell, 1992). See also Rorty: "From Ironist Theory to Private Allusions: Derrida" in: *Contingency, Irony, and Solidarity* (Cambridge: Cambridge University Press, 1989).

3.   The two positions could be exemplified by two major names within the early so-called Yale School Criticism: Geoffrey Hartman and Paul de Man. Although a sympathetic approach, Rudolphe Gasché's recent book on Paul de Man (*The Wild Card of Reading*) amply demonstrates the insuperable problems in reading especially philosophical texts 'rhetorically.'

4.   I don't think we can know whether this was ever Derrida's intention when initiating a practice called Deconstruction, but I also think it is unimportant to try to second-guess Derrida's intentions. Deconstruction has already been applied in multiple ways, not all of which can have agreed with Derrida's 'intention.' It has attained a life of its own, it has been possible, and it is still possible, to develop Deconstruction in any desired direction, some of which are overlapping what was already achieved in New Criticism or in Rhetorical Analysis. It is perhaps a subtle complement, rather than a criticism, to dissociate a thinker's thinking and the thinker; one tacitly suggests that the thinking is larger than the thinker.

5.   See Grice, Paul: *Studies in the Way of Words* (Cambridge: Harvard University Press, 1989) & Schiffer, Stephen R.: *Meaning* (Oxford: The Clarendon Press, 1972).

6.   Gasché labels such deep structures 'infrastaructures'; see Gasché: *The Tain of the Mirror* (Cambridge: Harvard University Press, 1986), ch. 9.

7.   Incidentally, I think that the formula, empty-inner-mental-constitution-of-meaning, is one way of conceptualizing what Derrida could mean by 'self-presence.' However, there seems to me to be a slight change of focus. Derrida focuses on 'Presence,' I on 'Emptiness.' We would of course agree if 'Presence' can mean or imply 'Emptiness.'

8.   This criticism of Grice's 'infinite regress' can be found in, for example, Habermas, Jürgen: "Intention, Konvention und sprachliche Interaktion" & "Intentionalistische Semantik" from *Vorstudien und Ergänzungen zur Theorie des kommunikativen Handelns.* (Frankfurt: Suhrkamp Verlag, 1984); in Taylor, Kenneth: *Truth and Meaning* (Oxford: Blackwell, 1998); and in Davis, Wayne A.: *Implicature, Intention, Convention, and Principle in the failure of Gricean Theory* (Cambridge: Cambridge University Press, 1998). The criticism is therefore not original; however, there exist to my knowledge no 'deconstructive' analysis of Grice. In general, there are few deconstructive attempts to deal with Anglo-Saxon philosophy. Exceptionally, Christopher Norris has offered analyses of Quine and Davidson. See Norris: *Deconstruction and the Interest of Theory* (Norman: University of Oklahoma Press, 1989) & *Against Relativism* (Oxford: Blackwell, 1997). After this essay was written, I became aware of Samuel S. Wheeler's remarkably lucid work: *Deconstruction as Analytic Philosophy* (Stanford: Stanford University Press, 2000).

9.   In the above-mentioned articles, Habermas notices this as well.

10.   Here I am especially referring to four articles, all reprinted in *Studies in the Way of Words,* loc. cit.: "Meaning," "Logic and Conversation," "Utterer's Meaning and Intentions," and "Utterer's Meaning, Sentence-Meaning, and Word-meaning."

11.   Grice: *Studies in the Way of Words,* loc. cit., p. 117.

12.   Grice: *Studies in the Way of Words*, loc. cit., p. 121. To designate the remitter-end of conversational dialogue, Grice uses usually U (utterer), but sometimes S (speaker); Schiffer usually employs S; like also Searle and Habermas. For purposes of consistency, I have changed all Grice's U's into S's in the quotations cited, and in my comments.

13.   Grice: *Studies in the Way of Words*, loc. cit., p. 91.

14.   Grice: *Studies in the Way of Words*, loc. cit., p. 91.

15.   Grice: *Studies in the Way of Words*, loc. cit., p. 122.

16.   Grice: *Studies in the Way of Words*, loc. cit., p. 123.

17.   If, briefly, we recapitulate Brentano and Husserl's notions of intentionality, we notice that Grice's notion of intentionality hardly has any similarity to Brentano and Husserl's. Intentionality in Brentano is developed over discussions in late Scholastic thinking. Thoughts or experiences are intentional in the sense that they are directed toward objects or contents; in judgments we direct ourselves toward something judged, in perceptions toward something perceived, etc. The characteristic feature of the intentional object is that it is non-existent, a feature that defines it as psychological in contrast to real objects. Husserl, developing Brentano's notion, will later define this non-existing nature of the intentional content as noematic.

18.   Grice: *Studies in the Way of Words*, loc. cit., p. 26.

19.   Grice: *Studies in the Way of Words*, loc. cit., p. 26.

20.   Wayne Davis gives the following summary of the maxims: "*Maxim of Quality.* Make your contribution true; so do not convey what you believe is false or unjustified. *Maxim of Quantity.* Be as informative as required. *Maxim of relation.* Be relevant. *Maxim of Manner.* Be perspicuous; so avoid obscurity and ambiguity, and strive for brevity and order." (Davis: *Implicature*, loc. cit., p. 12).

21.   Grice: *Studies in the Way of Words*, loc. cit., p. 29.

22 .   There is a problem here, because on one hand, repeating a written text in speech is essentially identical to repeating it by reading it to oneself, but on the other hand, formal discourses seem to presuppose cooperation on the part of the audiences. This is a problem that I shall not attempt to address at this point.

23.   Grice: *Studies in the Way of Words*, loc. cit., p. 29.

24.   Grice: *Studies in the Way of Words*, loc. cit., p. 30.

25.   Deirdre Wilson & Dan Sperber give the following representations of this logic: "The basic rationale behind the notion of conversational implicature is that the hearer posits the existence of an implicature in order to preserve his assumption that the conversational maxims have been observed on the level of what is said." . . . "Grice defines a conversational implicature as a proposition which the hearer must take the speaker to believe, in order to preserve his assumption that the co-oprative Principle and macims have been obeyed." (Wilson/Sperber: "On Grice's Theory of Conversation." In Werth, Paul (ed.): *Conversation and Discourse* (London: Crom Helm, 1981)), p. 160 & 164).

26.   Grice: *Studies in the Way of Words*, loc. cit., p. 31.

27.   Temporary, if the auditor is able to reconstruct an implicature restoring the meaning of the conversation (as above); permanently, if such reconstruction is impossible

28. Grice: *Studies in the Way of Words*, loc. cit., p. 31.
29. Kafka, Franz: *The Castle*. Trans. Mark Harmon (New York: Schochen Books, 1998) p. 80-81.
30. Grice: *Studies in the Way of Words*, loc. cit., p. 31.
31. I would have liked to agree with Wilson & Sperber when they write: "The term 'theory of conversation,' though now standard, is really a misnomer. Grice's theory is in fact an account of how utterances are interpreted, and not a theory of conversation at all." (Wilson/Sperber: "On Grice's Theory of Conversation," in Werth, loc. cit., p. 175-76). However, although the theory is indeed a theory of interpretation, it seems too categorical to determine it as only that. In numerous passages it is evident that Grice has not made up his mind about whether he understands meaning from the perspective of the remitter or from that of the receiver—indeed, that he does not attempt any distinction as in the quote above.
32. See Searle, John: *Speech Acts* (Cambridge: Cambridge University Press, 1969).
33. My analysis of the minimalist dialogue, 'S: 'hello!' A: 'hello!', has obviously a focus different from Searle's (in *Speech Acts*, loc. cit., pp. 42-50). Searle primarily disputes that the speaker intends to produce an effect other than that of understanding in the hearer, that is, he disputes that the speaker intends to perform a perlocutionary act. Searle does not dispute the notion of inner-mental processes preceding and determining the understanding of utterances. Nor does he dispute that interlocutors have direct access to each other's intentional life; he takes the 'transparency thesis' for granted. Searle's revised analysis of Grice looks a lot like Grice when abbreviated to its two core phases: (1) S utters a sentence (U) and intends (i-1) to produce in H an illocutionary effect (IE) by means of (2) H's recognition of that intention (i-1). The upshot of the Grice/Searle debate is thus whether speakers intend to produce perlocutionary effects or merely intends illocutionary effects when addressing someone in a speech act. "The characteristic intended effect of meaning is understanding, but understanding is not . . . a perlocutionary effect." (Searle: *Speech Acts*, loc. cit., p. 47). Grice's analytical basis-assumptions are intact and taken for granted. This fundamental agreement about the intentional background for speech-acts is accentuated in Searle's later article: "Meaning, Communication, and Representation," in Grandy/Warner (eds.): *Philosophical Grounds of Rationality* (Oxford: Clarendon Paperbacks, 1986); and obviously in Searle's later work: *Intentionality* (Cambridge: Cambridge University Press, 1983).
34. Grice: *Studies in the Way of Words*, loc. cit., p. 31. In another article Grice sums up the same recognition (meant$_{NN}$ = meant non-naturally): "If A meant$_{NN}$ something by x, it is roughly equivalent to 'A uttered x with the intention of inducing a belief by means of the recognition of this intention.'"
35. Grice: *Studies in the Way of Words*, loc. cit., p. 124-25.
36. Here a potential problem arises. Does Grice imply that is it possible for an utterance-type to have *timeless* meaning for only one individual? Does something like *timeless private* meaning exist? The problem being, *if* timeless *private* meaning exists, timeless meaning can no longer be understood as

conventional meaning. Timeless meaning would have, for example, to include the private language of schizophrenics. This suggestion, however, inflates the notion of 'timeless meaning' beyond recognition. It renders the notion meaningless.

37.   Grice: *Studies in the Way of Words*, loc. cit., p. 125.

38.   Grice: *Studies in the Way of Words*, loc. cit., p. 125.

39.   Grice: *Studies in the Way of Words*, loc. cit., p. 126-27.

40.   Habermas has in a number of articles on Grice and Schiffer offered the same criticism, for example: "[A]n infinite regress is set in motion that could be prevented only if the participants were allowed to have recourse to shared knowledge, indeed in the final instance to the natural meaning of signals established through a causal chain. Yet this recourse functions only on the condition that both sides, speaker and hearer, already understand the natural meaning of such a signal in a way analogous to understanding language, that is, in the manner of an intersubjectively known, nonnatural meaning of a conventionally regulated sign." (Habermas: "Toward a Critique of the Theory of Meaning." In: *On the Pragmatics of Communication,* edited by M. Cooke (Cambridge: MIT Press, 1998), p. 285).

41.   Grice: *Studies in the Way of Words*, loc. cit., p. 31.

42.   Searle's example is: an American soldier is captured by Italian soldiers, and in an attempt to fool his captors to free him, he recites a German sentence in the hope that they will take him to be a German officer. Since he is ignorant of German (expecting that so are the Italian soldiers), he knows of no better than reciting a memorized verse-line, *Kennst du das Land, wo die Zitronen Blühen.* This sentence is now meant to mean, 'I am a German soldier,' but, Searle objects, this cannot possibly be one of its meanings.

43.   Grice: *Studies in the Way of Words*, loc. cit., p. 102-3.

44.   See Habermas: "Intentionalistische Semantik." In Habermas, Jürgen: *Vorstudien und Ergänzungen zur Theorie des kommunikativen Handelns* (Frankfurt: Suhrkamp Verlag, 1984/95); & Wayne Davis: *Implicature*, loc. cit.

45.   Searle: *Speech Acts*, loc. cit., p. 43-45.

46.   Searle objects to Grice's view in 1969 (*Speech Acts*), but appears in *Intentionality* (1976) to condone a intentionalist approach to meaning that is, if anything, more radical that Grice's.

47.   Searle: *Speech Acts*, loc. cit., p. 45.

48.   Grice: *Studies in the Way of Words*, loc. cit., p. 100-101.

49.   When the self-evidently true needs qualification, it is perhaps because the self-evidently true statement is regarded as a truism, and is therefore perceived as a boring and tedious distraction from the more exciting qualification.

50.   Grice: *Studies in the Way of Words*, loc. cit., p. 298.

51.   Schiffer: *Meaning*, loc. cit., p. 91.

52.   Grice: *Studies in the Way of Words*, loc. cit., p. 92.

53.   Grice expands his analysis in such a way that what becomes important is that S and A reach agreement about that the sentence (x) posses a 'crucial' feature f. This feature (f) is in a linguistic sense arbitrary relative to the sentence.

In order to reach this agreement they must also agree upon that this feature (f) is correlated (c) in a certain way to the sentence uttered. The expanded analysis now has this form:

$(\exists A) (\exists f) (\exists r) (\exists c)$:
S uttered c intending:
(1) A to think x possesses f
(2) A to think S intends (1)
(3) A to think of f as correlated in way c with
the type to which r belongs
(4) A to think S intends (3)
(5) A to think on the basis of the fulfillment of (1)
and (3) that S intends A to produce r
(6) A, on the basis of fulfillment of (5), to produce r
(7) A to think S intends (6).

If we read such a formula 'naturalistically,' I hold in mind, while uttering a simple sentence, no less of seven different intentions directed to A, all of them describing an expectation as of what A is supposed to think regarding my utterance. Ultimately, with my seven expectations to A, I intend her to produce a particular response. Because of the unquestioned law of symmetry in communicational exchanges, it is taken for granted that A understands all of my expectations, and responds adequately. The test of A's understanding of the meaning of my sentence is a certain response (r) which I intended. The meaning of an utterance is thus described in two ways: first, as the utterer's expectations imbedded in the utterance, and secondly, as the auditor's response equating the imbedded expectations.

54.   Schiffer: *Meaning*, loc. cit., p. 31.
55.   Interlocutors know that they see, and that they are being seen, because they are 'normal,' Schiffer asserts in a not very illuminating explanation: "If a 'normal person' . . . has his eyes open and his head facing an object of a certain size (etc.), then that person will see that an object of a certain sort is before him." (Schiffer: *Meaning*, loc. cit., p. 31). My guess is that also abnormal persons see; but the point is unimportant.
56.   Schiffer: *Meaning*, loc. cit., p. 32 & 36.
57.   Searle: *Speech Acts*, loc. cit., p. 44 & 47.
58.   Schiffer: *Meaning*, loc. cit., p. 49.
59.   Schiffer: *Meaning*, loc. cit., p. 11
60.   Grice: *Studies in the Way of Words*, loc. cit., p. 123.
61.   Ducrot & Todorov: *Encyclopedic Dictionary of the Sciences of Language* (Baltimore: The Johns Hopkins University Press, 1979).
62.   See Aarsleff, Hans: *From Locke to Saussure* (Minneapolis: University of Minnesota Press, 1982), especially the essays, "The Tradition of Condillac: The Problem of the Origin of Language" and "An Outline of Language-Origin Theory." See also Cassirer, Ernst: *The Philosophy of Symbolic Forms, vol. I: Language* (New Haven: Yale University Press, 1955).

63.   Rousseau and Herder's treatises on the origin of language are collected in: *On the Origin of Language*; translated by Moran & Gode (Chicago: The University of Chicago Press, 1966). Classical readings of Rousseau's language theory are: Starobinski, Jean: *Jean Jacques Rousseau* (Chicago: The University of Chicago Press, 1988) and Derrida, Jacques: *Of Grammatology* (Baltimore: The Johns Hopkins University Press, 1974). I offer an exposition of Rousseau and Herder in Bornedal, Peter: *The Interpretations of Art* (Lanham/New York: The University Press of America, 1996).

64.   Rousseau: *Essay on the Origin of Language*, loc. cit., p. 44.

65.   Herder: *Essay on the Origin of Language*, loc. cit., p. 116.

66.   Herder: *Essay on the Origin of Language*, loc. cit., p. 117.

67.   Herder: *Essay on the Origin of Language*, loc. cit., p. 117.

68.   Grice: *Studies in the Way of Words*, loc. cit., p. 292.

69.   Grice: *Studies in the Way of Words*, loc. cit., p. 292. Notice that Grice's distinction between *natural* and *nonnatural* meaning, is similar to Husserl's distinction between *indicative* and *expressive* signs, as introduced in the first logical investigation. See Husserl, Edmund: *Logical Investigations* (London: Routledge & Kegan Paul, 1970).

70.   Grice: *Studies in the Way of Words*, loc. cit., p. 293.

71.   Grice: *Studies in the Way of Words*, loc. cit., p. 293.

72.   Grice: *Studies in the Way of Words*, loc. cit., p. 294.

73.   Grice: *Studies in the Way of Words*, loc. cit., p. 294.

74.   Grice: *Studies in the Way of Words*, loc. cit., p. 294.

75.   Schiffer: *Meaning*, loc. cit., p. 118.

76.   Schiffer: *Meaning*, loc. cit., p. 119.

77.   Schiffer: *Meaning*, loc. cit., p. 122.

78.   Schiffer: *Meaning*, loc. cit., p. 122.

79.   Habermas has the following critical comment to Schiffer's example (an objection with which I obviously agree): "Damit S die Äußerung 'x' mit der bestimmten Intention, seinen Ärger zu zeigen, verbinden kann, muß also ein von S und A intersubjectiv geteiltes Wissen vorausgesetzt werden, nämlich des Inhalts, daß 'x' die Nachahmung einer Hundeknurrens ist, daß Hunde knurren, wenn sie ärgerlich sind, and daß 'x' infolgedessen *natürlicher* weise Ärger bedeuten kann. . . . Diese Formulierung widerspricht jedoch der Voraussetzung des ganzen Modells, demzufolge das 'was gemeint wird' in keiner Weise durch das 'was gesagt wird', also durch den Wert von 'x' bestimmt sein darf." (Habermas: *Vorstudien und Ergänzungen zur Theorie des kommunikativen Handelns*, loc. cit., p. 345).

80.   Schiffer: *Meaning*, loc. cit., p. 122-23.

81.   Schiffer: *Meaning*, loc. cit., p. 123.

82.   Schiffer: *Meaning*, loc. cit., p. 123.

83.   Schiffer: *Meaning*, loc. cit., p. 123.

84.   Insofar as we are talking about language's self-constitution, the first word would necessarily have to be purely inspirational, born out of chance and good luck. This explanation is admittedly completely empty, but I suggest it deliberately as the only possible explanation of self-constitution. Alternative

explanations must invariably count on origins predating the origin to be explained, such as ancestors knowing the meaning of certain noises before they have been uttered for the first time, or certain primary-primary ancestors living before our conversing ancestors, informing them on the meanings of certain noises—thus in both cases repeating the problem. Both explanation-models are invalid and are in fact as replete with chance and good luck than my deliberately empty explanation model. Here, it is a fair assumption that any kind of self-constitution of language at t_1 *a priori* cannot be understood and/or represented; t_1 is too ambitious a project for any philosophy and any philosopher. Philosophy cannot press its inquiries down to t_1. Theories can at best only understand t_2, which, on the other hand, leaves any theorist frustrated, unsatisfied, and starving to understand the desirable t_1.

NOTES TO 'A DESIRE FOR REASON'

1.   Beckett, Samuel: *Waiting for Godot* (London: Faber and Faber, 1956/65) p. 62.

2.   Communicative rationality rests on the relationship between (a) the normative set of conditions that validates a speech-act, (b) the speaker's tacit pledge that he is satisfying these conditions, and (c) the speaker's credibility; his willingness to provide further reasons to discursively vindicate his claims. "The speaker would like the addressee to accept what is said as valid; this is decided by the addressee's 'yes' or 'no' to the validity claim for what is said that the speaker raises with his speech act. What makes the speech-act offer acceptable are, ultimately, the reasons that the speaker could provide in the given context for the validity of what is said. The rationality inherent in communication thus rests on the internal connection between (a) the conditions that make a speech act valid, (b) the claim raised by the speaker that these conditions are satisfied, and (c) the credibility of the warranty issued by the speaker to the effect that he could, if necessary, discursively vindicate the validity claims." (Habermas, Jürgen: *The Theory of Communicative Action,* vol. 1 (Boston: Beacon Press, 1984), p. 317).

3.   Habermas: "Further Clarifications of the Concept of Communicative Action," in: *On the Pragmatics of Communication* (Cambridge: MIT Press, 1998), p. 310.

4.   Habermas: "Further Clarifications of the Concept of Communicative Action," in *On the Pragmatics of Communication,* loc. cit., p. 315.

5.   Habermas: "What is Universal Pragmatics?" in *On the Pragmatics of Communication,* loc. cit., p. 26.

6.   Habermas: "What is Universal Pragmatics?" in *On the Pragmatics of Communication,* loc. cit., p. 47.

7.   Habermas: "What is Universal Pragmatics?" in *On the Pragmatics of Communication,* loc. cit., p. 49.

8.   Habermas: "What is Universal Pragmatics?" in *On the Pragmatics of Communication,* loc. cit., p. 21.

9.   Habermas: "Actions, Speech Acts, Linguistically Mediated Interactions, and Lifeworld" in *On the Pragmatics of Communication*, loc. cit., p. 227.

10.   "The aim of reaching understanding (*Verständigung*) is to bring about an agreement (*Einverständnis*) that terminates in the intersubjective mutuality of reciprocal comprehension, shared knowledge, mutual trust, and accord with one another." (Habermas: "What is Universal Pragmatics?" in: *On the Pragmatics of Communication*, loc. cit., p. 23).

11.   Unless, one might object, I perceive myself as a heterogeneous, decentered subject where multiple conflicting voices struggle to come to terms with each other. But this theoretical dimension is not part of the semantic content of *Einverständnis*.

12.   In the weak sense of understanding the interlocutors do not need to reach agreement on the issue in question; it is enough that the hearer understands that the speaker is sincere and have reasons for her statement. A dialogue like, *A*: "It is unhealthy to smoke, and it ought to be banned." *B*: "I understand why you think so, but I don't agree," might indicate an example on *Verständigung* where *B* understands *A*'s opinion, but don't agree. *Einverständnis* would transpire, if *B*—in addition to understanding *A*'s reasons—shares the same opinion.

13.   Habermas, "Some Further Clarifications of the Concept of Communicative Rationality" in: *On the Pragmatics of Communication*, loc. cit., p. 321.

14.   Habermas: *The Theory of Communicative Action*, loc. cit., p. 308.

15.   Habermas: "What is Universal Pragmatics?" in *On the Pragmatics of Communication*, loc. cit., p. 42.

16.   Habermas: "Questions and Counterquestions" in *On the Pragmatics of Communication*, loc. cit., p. 407.

17.   Habermas: "Questions and Counterquestions" in *On the Pragmatics of Communication*, loc. cit., p. 408.

18.   Habermas: "What is Universal Pragmatics?" in *On the Pragmatics of Communication*, loc. cit., p. 37.

19.   However, this concept of truth would stand in stark contrast to Habermas' general defense of a consensualist concept of truth as developed in the essay "Wahrheitstheorien." (In: Habermas, Jürgen: *Vorstudien und Ergänzungen zur Theorie des kommunikativen Handelns* (Frankfurt: Suhrkamp Verlag, 1984/95)). Habermas cannot mean that the truth of deep-structural competency-rules relies on the dominant consensus in a scientific community.

20.   "Rational reconstructions necessarily make an 'essentialist' claim: If they are true they must correspond to precisely those rules that are operative in the object domain, i.e., that actually determine the production of surface structures." (McCarthy, Thomas: *The Critical Theory of Jürgen Habermas* (Cambridge, Mass.: The MIT Press, 1981), p. 283).

21.   Habermas: "Wahrheitstheorien" in *Vorstudien und Ergänzungen zur Theorie des kommunikativen Handelns*, loc. cit. See also, Swindal, James: *Reflection Revisited—Jürgen Habermas's Discursive Theory of Truth* (New York: Fordham University Press, 1999).

22.   It is also my firm conviction that Habermas' project—to establish the rules for communicative competency, domination-free dialogue, and democratic legitimacy—is both absolutely sympathetic, and, regarding its content and theme, one of the most pertinent having been developed over the last century. The urgency of *the theme* in Habermas' 'play' is not here in question, but the mechanisms of 'play' are.

23.   One notices these indicators when beginning to think the immanent logic of Habermas' theory; thinking the 'immanent logic' of a theory means approximately to start thinking it inwardly or from the inside. It is always too difficult to see everything on the textual surface alone. There is always-already too much information on the textual surface. In this sense the Deconstructive slogan, 'back to the text,' although pertinent in some polemical contexts, has certain empirical limitations; better is perhaps, 'thinking with the text'—a slogan being also in good accordance with what Derrida is usually doing.

24.   Habermas: "What is Universal Pragmatics?" in *On the Pragmatics of Communication*, loc. cit., p. 23.

25.   Habermas: *The Theory of Communicative Action*, loc. cit., p. 328.

26.   The distinction between the ideal and the standard McCarthy takes for granted as a dogma, and, consequently, perceives it as being obvious: "To put it roughly, understanding is the immanent telos or function of speech. This does not, of course, mean that every actual instance of speech is oriented to reaching understanding." . . . "Although this 'supposition of responsibility' is frequently (perhaps even usually) counterfactual, it is of fundamental significance for the structure of human relations that we proceed as if it were the case." (McCarthy: *The Critical Theory of Jürgen Habermas*, loc. cit., pp. 287 & 291). This supposition is described also as an 'unavoidable fiction.' Such language serves (unwittingly) my thesis that principles for rational communication are suggested not in complete seriousness, but in a kind of hybrid *playful seriousness*, according to which they become, precisely, 'fictions'—but 'serious fictions,' 'unavoidable fictions,' or something of that order.

27.   Habermas: "What is Universal Pragmatics." *On the Pragmatics of Communication*, loc. cit., p. 22.

28.   Gripp, Helga: *Jürgen Habermas — Und es gibt sie doch – Zur kommunikationstheoretischen begründung von Vernunft bei Jürgen Habermas* (Paderborn: Ferdinand Schoningh, 1984), p. 51.

29.   Habermas: "What is Universal Pragmatics?" in *On the Pragmatics of Communication*, loc. cit., p. 23

30.   It is easy to imagine the response by dedicated habermasians: 'Of course, we don't speak rationally!' they might emphatically counter my objections, affirming them in the process, but by their emphasis making them trivially true, and therefore false.

31.   Derrida has, in an essay on Saussure (see Derrida, Jacques: *Of Grammatology* (Baltimore: Johns Hopkins University Press, 1978)) two consecutive sections called respectively, *The Outside and [et] the Inside* and *The Outside is [est] the Inside*. We cannot hear the difference, but we see it; it is both there and not there. The 'and' equals 'is' equals 'is.' When Derrida talks about

inside and outside, it is here and elsewhere in terms of the metaphorical couple, Voice vs. Writing. *Voice* is *inside, Writing* is *outside*. However—after Derrida's demonstration of a deconstructive reversal—the voice "is" writing in the sense that writing is always-already inscribed in the 'voice.' In other words, the positions, inside/outside, cannot be sustained. In the metaphysical text they are unstable and flow—much against the explicit intention of the author—into each other, thus destabilizing and blurring the initial distinction. Since *Writing* is a differential principle that cannot assert a unified notion of being, the "is" in the equation has to be crossed out. This description of the futile attempt to separate and segregate an 'inside' from an 'outside' precisely diagnoses a struggle universally carried out in the metaphysical text. According to this description, Derrida implies that the metaphysical text tends to suggest two distinct core notions, which the text, in its logical progression, has exceptional difficulties keeping apart. Subjected to scrutiny, the two distinct notions begin to look like one another, or they start to carry the same qualities. It becomes difficult to identify the distinguishing mark separating them, and the line that was meant to keep them apart becomes blurred. This situation arises much to the frustration and regret of the metaphysical writer, who feels that his theory depends on the purity of the suggested distinction, and who is therefore evoking a considerable arsenal of rhetorical disclaimers to convince himself and his recipient of the purity of a distinction that in its logical progression becomes fatally impure.

32.   These thoughts started out from some considerations over Jacques Derrida's philosophy, and since everybody who has read an introduction to Derrida knows that he allegedly represents a certain 'difference-thinking,' it would be tempting to conclude that my conclusion is in complete contradiction to Derrida. In my opinion, not the least. In Derrida's 'difference-thinking,' an analysis of difference is performed, as this difference is represented in various texts, typically in order to deconstruct the founding difference. That is, the difference falls apart, becomes indeterminable or undecidable (or in some other ways unstable). It has, in other words, no solidity. We can therefore conclude that in some 'last analysis,' difference is non-existent. In conclusion, I paraphrase Derrida's *The Outside* ~~is~~ *the Inside* (see also note above), and appropriate it as my own formula, but with the significant modification that in my version the 'is' is not crossed out; rather, it ought to be underlined, written in bold, or in some other way highlighted, in order to emphasize 'is' as a logical copula.

33.   Habermas: "What is Universal Pragmatics?" in *On the Pragmatics of Communication*, loc. cit., p. 49 & 54.

34.   Structural Linguistics, in its emphasis on the language-system, suffers allegedly from neglecting the pragmatic active language-use, with this also ignoring the active and creative role of the subject, which Habermas' Pragmatics rehabilitates: "By elevating anonymous forms of language to a transcendental status, it [Structural Linguistics] downgrades the subjects and their speech to something merely accidental. How the subjects speak and what they do is supposed to be explained by the underlying system of rules. The individuality and creativity of subjects capable of speaking and acting . . . now become

residual phenomena." (Habermas: "Themes in Postmetaphysical Thinking." In Habermas, Jürgen: *Postmetaphysical Thinking* (Cambridge: MIT Press, 1993), p. 47).

35.   Austin, J. L.: *How to Do Things with Words* (Cambridge, Mass.: Harvard University Press, 1975), pp. 109, 110, & 121.

36.   Searle, John R.: *Speech Acts* (Cambridge: Cambridge University Press, 1969), p. 25.

37.   Austin: *How to do Things with Words*, loc. cit., p. 128.

38.   Austin: *How to do Things with Words*, loc. cit., p. 121.

39.   Habermas: *The Theory of Communicative Action*, loc. cit., p. 292. Elsewhere the same idea is repeated: "Austin concluded that illocutionary success stands in a conventionally regulated or internal connection with the speech act, whereas perlocutionary effects remain external to the meaning of what is said. The possible perlocutionary effects of a speech act depend on fortuitous contexts." (Habermas: "Social Action, Purposive Action, and Communication" in *On the Pragmatics of Communication*, loc. cit., p. 125).

40.   Habermas: *The Theory of Communicative Action*, loc. cit., p. 289.

41.   To illustrate a Habermasian perlocution, we can imagine the following situation. At a business meeting, B (the younger female employee) is giving a lengthy defense of an important decision in her company, which A (the older male manager) irritatingly brush aside, responding: "maybe you could make us some coffee!" The request for coffee (with the apparent illocutionary aim that the female employee leaves the boardroom and makes coffee) glides in the background for the much more significant perlocutionary aim, to denigrate and humiliate the female employee. Following Habermas, we can understand this type of situation as 'instrumental' or 'strategic' uses of language. Language is used 'non-conventionally'—that is, what is said by conventional means is no longer the perlocutionary aim of the utterance. The perlocutionary aim is implicit and its deciphering depends on fortuitous context (notice that I have to elaborate my example in some detail before the reader has a chance to understand the implicit perlocutionary aim that I want to illustrate). It is therefore *possible* that the perlocutionary effect is a 'manipulation,' a 'perversion,' or an 'abuse' of speech. But it is not *necessary*. A variation over the same example makes this clear. The older manager asks his younger female protégé in a jovial manner, "maybe you could now make us some coffee," and intends to convey the perlocutionary effect that she has done a brilliant job and it is time to relax. Whatever one might think of the sexism still implicit in the example, the strategic and manipulative intentions have disappeared from the speech-act.

42.   Habermas: *The Theory of Communicative Action*, loc. cit., p. 292. The same passage is found in, "Social Action, Purposive Action, and Communication" in *On the Pragmatics of Communication*, loc. cit., p. 125-26. The distinction based on the principle of 'openness' is problematic, and as typical in much philosophical writing, the *writing* of Habermas reveals that he is aware of the problem. However, his awareness manifests itself only on the surface of the text; it is not consciously reflected, has no consequences for the theory, and is ultimately pushed aside in favor of the desired state of affairs, the

radical demarcation between illocution and perlocution. The two 'may' in the quotation above, indicate that Habermas is in fact *writing* about a *possibility*, but it is also clear that Habermas intends us to ignore the 'may' and to focus on the clear-cut distinction between illocution and perlocution as between what is openly declared and what is secretly held back. Also elsewhere Habermas demonstrates that he knows that his account of perlocution is different from Austin's: "Austin did not keep these two cases [illocutionary aims and perlocutionary effects] separate as different types of interaction, because he was inclined to identify speech acts . . . with the linguistically mediated interactions themselves." (Habermas, "Social Action, Purposive Action, and Communication" in *On the Pragmatics of Communication*, loc. cit., p. 129). However, Habermas *also* refers to Austin when seeking support for a radical distinction.

43.   We notice the parallel to Kant's ethics. Habermas is applying Kant's moral theory to speech-acts—whether consciously of not. To Kant, a morally worthy act cannot have a purpose external to itself. The 'good will' must be an end in itself, it cannot be performed for the sake of achieving something; and in order to emphasize the distinction, Kant suggests his two different imperatives, the categorical and the hypothetical imperative. Actions must be performed for their own sake, not as means to an end. An action inscribing an 'if-then' relation between an action and its consequences (if I do x, then I get y) constitutes a hypothetical or 'problematic' imperative. It invalidates itself as a moral imperative. Habermas' rigorous distinction between illocutionary and perlocutionary acts reflects this original distinction from Kant. Illocutionary understanding-oriented language is an end in itself, but as soon as it is performed as a means to an end, it degenerates to perlocution—with this, becoming purpose-rational, instrumental, or strategic. *Understanding* (in Habermas' emphatic sense) is thus established in the instance of enunciation itself. Any utterance that points beyond itself and its own instance of enunciation taints the possible *Understanding* (capitalized-anasemic) between interlocutors.

44.   Habermas: "Social Action, Purposive Activity and Communication" in *On the Pragmatics of Communication*, loc. cit., p. 122 & 126.

45.   Habermas: "Actions, Speech Acts, Linguistically Mediated Interactions, and Lifeworld" in *On the Pragmatics of Communication*, loc. cit., p. 224.

46.   Cf.: Encarta 98 Desk Encyclopedia & 1996-97 Microsoft Corporation.

47.   For such a classical distinction, one may recall Glaucon's distinction between *seeming just* and *being just* in Plato's *The Republic*.

48.   Karl-Otto Apel: "Openly strategic uses of language: a transcendental-pragmatic perspective." In: Dews, Peter (ed.): *Habermas: A Critical Reader* (Oxford: Blackwell Publishers, 1999), p. 274.

49 .   For example: 'If we have sex tonight, I will love you forever.' Any gnawing doubt about the 'forever' would make the utterance manipulative, and speaker and hearer would reach agreement on false grounds.

50.   This point would be identical to Karl-Otto Apel's criticism of Habermas: "Habermas has already loaded the concept of understanding normatively, so that a consensual-communicative solution to the problem of rational communication,

and thus to the problem of linguistic understanding in the broader sense, tends to be anticipated." (Apel: "Openly strategic uses of language: a transcendental-pragmatic perspective." In: Dews: *Habermas*, loc. cit., p. 276).

51.   An example might illustrate this. A wife has decided that she wants to get a job. Her husband provides strong and rational reasons going against her decision: they don't need an extra income, the job would exhaust her, she has more freedom to pursue her hobbies without a job, (etc.). In Habermas' theory of communicative action, he *is* sincere because he *believes* that he is sincere. The theory cannot address unconscious motives behind apparent rationally pursued communicative action. Thus, superficially, the husband is or might be sincere, but as soon as we introduce unconscious motives into the dialogue, this appearance is quickly proven naïve. Unconscious motives for avoiding the wife taking up a job could be: fear of the wife gaining independence, of her out-competing her husband on the job-market, of her interaction with other men, (etc.). If his rational objections to his wife's wishes are motivated by these fears, where is now his sincerity? In the dialogical situation, he believes that he is sincere and rational, but we would tend to say that he is not.

52.   An example of such plain misunderstanding: 'Why does he say that the lamb is *bleeding*—is this something religious?' uttered by a hearer that didn't hear the difference between bleating and bleeding.

53.   "A bank robber's cry of 'Hands up!' while pointing a gun at a cashier whom he orders to hand over money demonstrates in a drastic fashion that, in such a situation, the conditions of normative validity have been replaced by sanction conditions. The acceptability conditions for an imperative that has been stripped of any normative backing must be supplemented by such sanction conditions." (Habermas: "Actions, Speech Acts, Linguistically Mediated Interactions, and Lifeworld" in *On the Pragmatics of Communication*, loc. cit., p. 225).

54.   Karl-Otto Apel: "Openly strategic uses of language: a transcendental-pragmatic perspective." In: Dews: *Habermas*, loc. cit., p. 274.

55.   Habermas: "Comments on Searle's *Meaning, Communication, and Representation*" in *On the Pragmatics of Communication*, loc. cit., p. 265.

56.   Habermas: "Comments on Searle's *Meaning, Communication, and Representation*" in *On the Pragmatics of Communication*, loc. cit., p. 266.

57.   The claim made here is different from, but roughly concordant with, a claim I made in a previous work on Habermas (written several years ago). I wrote in these early days: "In scientific discourse one continuously exposes language to control, and in certain scientific societies and communities one employs the validity-basis Habermas has proposed. Thus, in scientific and academic institutions, Habermas' validity-basis is typically prescriptive and the norm for the language employed. Therefore, within this pragmatic, institutional perspective, it could be suggested that Habermas' validity-claims have validity. Here, his validity-claims are true. Habermas' 'serious speech-offer' corresponds to the demand for seriousness, sincerity, and openness in the scientist. Thus, *validity claims are not everyday-speech-typical*. If they function as the basis of a long line of different and competing interpretive communities, then their truth is

to be *institution-specific*, and typical of the meta-communicative language-usage of theoretical communities. Consequently, they are typical of schematizing and scriptural non-spontaneous discourse. Rationality is not, therefore, an intrinsic quality of the communicative act, but a possible product of written (or reflective or self-reflective) systems." Bornedal, Peter: *Speech and System* (Copenhagen: MTP—University of Copenhagen, 1996), p. 327-28.

58.   Habermas: "What is Universal Pragmatics" in *On the Pragmatics of Communication*, loc. cit., p. 75.

59.   Habermas: "What is Universal Pragmatics" in *On the Pragmatics of Communication*, loc. cit., p. 82.

60.   Habermas: "What is Universal Pragmatics" in: *On the Pragmatics of Communication*, loc. cit., p. 84.

61.   Habermas: "What is Universal Pragmatics" in: *On the Pragmatics of Communication*, loc. cit., p. 85.

62.   Habermas: "What is Universal Pragmatics" in: *On the Pragmatics of Communication*, loc. cit., p. 85.

63.   Habermas: "What is Universal Pragmatics" in: *On the Pragmatics of Communication*, loc. cit., p. 85.

64.   Habermas: *The Philosophical Discourse of Modernity* (Cambridge, Mass.: MIT Press, 1992).

65.   Habermas: *The Philosophical Discourse of Modernity*, loc. cit., p. 185.

66.   Habermas: *The Philosophical Discourse of Modernity*, loc. cit., p. 188.

67.   Habermas: *The Philosophical Discourse of Modernity*, loc. cit., p. 188.

68.   Perelman and Olbrechts-Tyteca represent such hierarchical oppositions as term I/term II relationships, and I am here following this simple and artless labeling. See Perelman, Ch. & Olbrechts-Tyteca, L.: *The New Rhetoric—A Treatise of Argumentation*. Translated by J. Wilkinson & P. Weaver (Notre Dame: The University of Notre Dame Press, 1969).

69.   Norris, Christopher: "Deconstruction, Postmodernism and Philosophy: Habermas on Derrida" in d'Etrèves & Benhabib (eds.): *Habermas and the Unfinished Project of Modernity* (Cambridge, Mass: MIT Press, 1997).

70.   Habermas: *The Philosophical Discourse of Modernity*, loc. cit., p. 190.

71.   Habermas: *The Philosophical Discourse of Modernity*, loc. cit., pp. 205 & 207.

72.   Habermas: *The Philosophical Discourse of Modernity*, loc. cit., p. 188. In a footnote to one of the essays in *Limited Inc.* (see Derrida: *Limited Inc.* (Evanston: Northwestern University Press, 1972), Derrida responds to this critique of himself launched by Habermas. The major problem of this critique, says Derrida, is that Habermas has not demonstrated any readiness to read him, that, in effect, he does not encounter Derrida's texts, but reduces them to a few arguments, which are then refuted. With this, Habermas, the theoretician of communication, has avoided communication. Habermas is guilty of what he accuses Derrida, namely the so-called 'performative contradiction.' Derrida objects to this strategy in the following rejoinder: "Everywhere, in particular in the United States and in Europe, the self-declared philosophers, theoreticians, and ideologists of communication, dialogue, and consensus, of univocity, and

transparency, those who claim ceaselessly to reinstate the classical ethics of proof, discussion, and exchange, are most often those who excuse themselves from attentively reading and listening to the other, who demonstrate precipitation and dogmatism, and who no longer respect the elementary rules of philology and of interpretation, confounding science and chatter as though they had not the slightest taste for communication or rather as though they were afraid of it, at the bottom. Fear of what, at bottom? Why? . . . They even dare to accuse the adversary, as Habermas does me, of 'performative contradiction.' Is there a 'performative contradiction' more serious than that which consists in claiming to discuss rationally the theses of the other without having made the slightest effort to take cognizance of them, read them, or listen to them?" (Derrida: *Limited Inc.*, loc. cit., p. 157-58.) Derrida's reading of Habermas in this citation is slightly inaccurate. Derrida does not notice that Habermas, in the particular excursus where he develops his critique, does not so much criticize Derrida's employment of 'performative contradiction,' as he criticizes the specific strategy Derrida employs to *escape* it. Habermas is, in fact, a little disappointed in Derrida's evasion of this particularly strong refuting argument, which he and Karl-Otto Apel successfully have aimed at skeptical, irrational, and postmodernist discourses.

73.   Habermas: *The Philosophical Discourse of Modernity*, loc. cit., p. 210.

74.   Habermas: *The Philosophical Discourse of Modernity*, loc. cit., p. 210.

75.   Habermas: *The Philosophical Discourse of Modernity*, loc. cit., p. 210.

76   It is from other contexts in *The Philosophical Discourse of Modernity* clear that non-cognitivist skeptics like Heidegger and Derrida are still regarded as guilty in 'performative contradiction' or so-called 'self-referential critique of reason': "No matter whether Heidegger and Derrida evade the obligation to provide the grounds by fleeing into the esoteric or by fusing the logical with the rhetorical: There always emerges a symbiosis of incompatibles. . . . Things are only shifted to a different place if we change the frame of reference and no longer treat the same discourse as philosophy or science, but as a piece of literature. That the self-referential critique of reason is located everywhere and nowhere, so to speak, in discourses without a place, renders it almost immune to competing interpretations. Such discourses unsettle the institutionalized standards of fallibilism; they always allow for a final word, even when the argument is already lost." (Habermas: *The Philosophical Discourse of Modernity*, loc. cit., p. 336-37).

77.   See Christopher Norris' "Deconstruction, Postmodernism and Philosophy" and David Couzens Hoy's "Splitting the Difference," both in d'Etrèves & Benhabib (eds.): *Habermas and the Unfinished Project of Modernity*, loc. cit. Rorty addresses Habermas' critique in "Habermas and Lyotard on postmodernity" in *Philosophical Papers* vol. 2 (Cambridge: Cambridge University Press, 1993). Stanley Fish has an incisive essay on Habermas, "Critical Self-Consciousness," in *Doing What Comes Naturally* (Durham: Duke University Press, 1989). In *Speech and System* (Copenhagen: MTP-University of Copenhagen Press, 1996), I have a chapter on Habermas' reading of Derrida.

78.   See   Habermas: "Themes   in   Postmetaphysical   Thinking"   in: *Postmetaphysical Thinking*, loc. cit.,

79.   Habermas: *The Philosophical Discourse of Modernity*, loc. cit., p. 409.

80.   Habermas: *The Philosophical Discourse of Modernity*, loc. cit., p. 312.

81.   Habermas: "Richard Rorty's Pragmatic Turn" in: *On the Pragmatics of Communication*, ibid. p. 364.

82.   The schism filters down to Habermas' commentators. Thus Meave Cooke introduces both of the two positions in singular passages: "A fallibilistic (as opposed to foundationalist) understanding of validity takes into account that claims to validity are raised in actual, historical contexts which do not remain stationary but are subject to change. . . . The theory of communicative action relies in particular on a reconstructive theory that seeks to identify the universal presuppositions of everyday communication of modern societies." (Cooke, Meave: *Language and Reason* (Cambridge: MIT Press, 1994), p. 2-3.) We notice the double-bind in action: although validity-claims are subject to change, they are also universal presuppositions of communication. Or, what does a passage like the following actually say? "This dialogical-fallibilist perspective should not be misunderstood as the thesis that any given claim can be called into question at any given time: it merely asserts that we can never know when new evidence may cast doubt on what now appear to be true or established facts." (Meave Cooke: *Language and Reason*, loc. cit., p. 109). It seems to me that the passage asserts two contraries simultaneously. A claim cannot be questioned at any given time, but one does not know at which time a claim can be questioned. If we do not know at which time a claim can be questioned, it seems that it can be questioned at 'any given time.' To "call into question" and to "cast doubt on" is surely the same thing. In another of Habermas' commentators, the oscillation between universalistic and contingent positions (in this writer, universalistic and individualistic) is again apparent: "It may be true that the universalistic dimensions of Habermas' pragmatic theory lie closer to the surface of his writing; but this should not obscure the fact that this theory accords a role to the individual that is at least as significant as the role it attributes to universal validity claims." (William M. Hohengarten: "Translators Introduction" in Habermas: *Postmetaphysical Thinking*, loc. cit., p. xii).

83.   I ignore for now that this is, on a content-level of his theory, exactly what Habermas does. I notice that also Karl-Otto Apel is aware of this dilemma in Habermas. Apel lists in an essay some of the advocates of non-foundationalism, and includes in his list Habermas—however, Apel adds the following parenthesis: "(In fact Habermas seems more concerned to avoid the term *ultimate foundation* than to avoid what the term actually refers to. After all, he seeks a 'normative foundation ' for ethics. . . . In other words, he seeks a foundation.)" (Karl-Otto Apel: "Can an ultimate foundation of knowledge be non-metaphysical" in Apel: *From a Transcendental-Semiotic Point of View* (Manchester: Manchester University Press, 1998), p. 81).

84.   I am aware that Popper himself, in at least one essay, tries to adopt to philosophy the principle of falsifiability in form of the general idea that one ought to critical examine assumptions and resolutions in philosophical systems.

However, in the same work he also realizes that, "the solution of a philosophical problem is never final. It cannot be based upon a final proof or upon a final refutation: this is a consequence of the irrefutability of philosophical theories." (Karl Popper: "Conjectures and Refutations." Quoted from *Popper Selections* (Princeton: Princeton University Press, 1985), p. 219).

85.   Habermas is especially well-protected by his erudition. As it is exercised, in both breadth and depth, it is plainly difficult for even professional scholars and philosophers to keep up and, with this, enter on equal terms a discussion, and counter him in debate. Stating this, however, should not give rise to the misunderstanding that I am *criticizing* Habermas for being erudite. Obviously not. Habermas' erudition continues to impress, as it should, but this admission does not contradict the claim that erudition is or may be a form of self-protection.

86.   "The skeptic may reject morality, but he cannot reject the ethical substance (*Sittlichkeit*) of the life circumstances in which he spends his waking hours, not unless he is willing to take refuge in suicide or serious mental illness. In other words, he cannot extricate himself from the communicative practice of everyday life in which he is continually forced to take a position by responding yes or no. As long as he is still alive at all, a Robinson Crusoe existence through which the skeptic demonstrates mutely and impressively that he has dropped out of communicative action is inconceivable, even as a thought experiment." (Habermas: "Discourse Ethics" in *Moral Consciousness and Communicative Action* (Cambridge, Mass: MIT Press, 1996), p. 100).

87.   Samuel S. Wheeler: *Deconstruction as Analytic Philosophy* (Stanford: Stanford University Press, 2000).

88.   Especially three essays of Karl-Otto Apel are here essential: "The *A Priori* of the Communication Community and the Foundations of Ethics" in *Towards a Transformation of Philosophy* (London: Routledge & Kegan Paul, 1980); "The Problem of Philosophical Foundations Grounding in Light of a Transcendental Pragmatics of Language" in Baynes/Bohman/McCarthy (eds.): *After Philosophy* (Cambridge, Mass., MIT Press, 1987); and "Can an Ultimate Foundation of knowledge be non-Metaphysical" in Apel: *From a Transcendental-Semiotic Point of View* (Manchester: Manchester University Press, 1998).

89.   Habermas: "Discourse Ethics" in *Moral Consciousness and Communicative Action*, loc. cit., p. 80.

90.   René Descartes: *The Philosophical Writings of Descartes*, vol. 1 (Cambridge: Cambridge University Press, 1985), p. 194-5.

91.   This *school-book skeptic* that is compulsively—on all possible and impossible occasions—conjured up by everybody with a foot in analytic philosophy. 'Does non-belief refute belief?' The question is tirelessly repeated, and its predictable answer force-fed into the listeners to prevent them from forgetting the ringing 'No!'

92.   This redefinition does not seem to include the cases explicitly discussed in "Discourse Ethics," where Habermas discusses unavoidable universal assumptions in ethical judgments. It is hard to see how my formula for

performative fallacy, *I doubt that x (x being included in the instance of enunciation)*, applies to 'I doubt the universal validity of ethical principles.' How could meta-ethical principles be already presupposed in 'I doubt'? Referring to an argument of Apel, Habermas is convinced that this is in fact the case: "The proponent [of universal meta-ethical judgments] asserts the universal validity of the principle of universalization. He is contradicted by an opponent relying on the Münchhausen trilemma. On the basis of this trilemma the opponent concludes that attempts to ground the universal validity of principles are meaningless [I my reformulation, the opponent '*doubts that x*']. . . . But the opponent will have involved himself in a performative contradiction if the proponent can show that in making his argument, he has to make assumptions that are inevitable in any argumentation game aiming at critical examination and that the propositional content of those assumption contradicts the principle of fallibilism [in this context, the notion 'fallibilism' is approximately synonymous to *skepticism* or *anti-Foundationalism*]. This is in fact the case, since in putting forward his objection, the opponent necessarily assumes the validity of at least those logical rules that are irreplaceable if we are to understand his argument as a refutation. In taking part in the process of reasoning, even the consistent fallibilist has already accepted as valid a minimum number of unavoidable rules of criticism." (Habermas: "Discourse Ethics" in *Moral Consciousness and Communicative Action*, loc. cit., p. 80-81).

93.   Habermas: "What is Universal Pragmatics?" in *On the Pragmatics of Communication*, loc. cit., p. 81.

94.   Habermas: *The Theory of Communicative Action*, loc. cit., p. 308.

95.   Benveniste: *Problems in General Linguistics* (Coral Gables: University of Miami Press, 1971).

96.   Whether Derrida has actually ever uttered anything like this statement (even, whether he has ever meant it), I will have to ignore. Obviously, I am not at this point addressing what Derrida actually says, means, or writes, but only the interpretation he gets in Habermas.

97.   One might, as an example of another evocation of performative contradiction, recall the typically objection to Nietzsche's thinking: 'If Nietzsche claims that there is no truth, then Nietzsche's statement itself cannot be true, and we don't need to heed the statement in the first place.' (We find an interesting presentation and refutation of this objection in Heidegger's Nietzsche lectures, vol. III: "The Will to Power as Knowledge").

NOTES TO "THE USES AND ABUSES OF PLEASURE"

1.   Goethe, Johann Wolfgang von: *Faust* vol. I. Translated by D. Luke (Oxford: Oxford University Press, 1994), pp. 60 & 80.

2.   I refer to the following works: Berger, Fred R.: *Happiness, Justice, and Freedom* (Berkeley: University of California Press, 1984), Crisp, Roger: *Mill on Utilitarianism* (London: Routledge, 1997), Ryan, Alan: *The Philosophy of John Stuart Mill* (London: Macmillan, 1970), and Skorupsky. John: *John Stuart Mill*

(London: Routledge, 1989). For other cooperating accounts: Kerner, George C.: *Three Philosophical Moralists—Mill, Kant, Sartre* (Oxford: Clarendon Press, 1990), Donner, Wendy: "Mill's Utilitarianism," in: *The Cambridge Companion to Mill*, ed.: Skorupsky (Cambridge: Cambridge University Press, 1998).

3.   I refer to: Bradley, F. H.: *Ethical Studies*, 2nd ed. (Oxford: Oxford University Press, 1962), Sidgwick, Henry: *The Methods of Ethics*, 7th ed. (London: Macmillan, 1907), Moore, G. E.: *Principia Ethica*, revised ed. (Cambridge: Cambridge University Press, 1993), and Russell, Bertrand: *A History of Western Philosophy*, ch. XXVI (New York: Simon & Schuster, 1945). For other critical assessments, see also, Anschutz, R. P.: *The Philosophy of J. S. Mill* (Oxford: The Clarendon Press, 1953), Copleston, Frederick: *A History of Philosophy* vol. VIII (New York, Image Books, 1994), and Stephen, Leslie: *The English Utilitarians, vol. III, John Stuart Mill* (New York: Peter Smith, 1950).

4.   As just one example on apologetic commentary, "*Happiness is the supreme good* is not, as its grammatical form suggests, a statement at all, but an imperative—[it means] *Seek happiness.*" (Alan Ryan: *The Philosophy of John Stuart Mill*, loc. cit., p. 190).

5.   Knocking on the table with clever irony, Derrida's critics are only too eager to teach the exotic philosopher that 'outside the text' there is a real world. (The objections usually never get much beyond Dr. Johnson's famous 'I refute you thus,' kicking a stone in the direction of a devastated Bishop Berkeley.) Reading these critics is a feast one should never deny oneself. One of Derrida's cleverest critics, Raymond Tallis, is tireless in his mockery of the famous statement, and has written a book about it. (See Tallis: *Not Saussure* (New York, St. Martin's Press, 1995).) One gets a sense of the work from a look at the title. It already tells us something about the author: *Not Saussure*, intended to mean 'not so sure' about Derrida &co. —It is a mere detail that the witty title contradicts the work's general defense of Saussure against Derrida, and that 'so sure' is not pronounced 'Saussure.'

6.   Moore: *Principia Ethica*, loc. cit., p. 118.

7.   Cf. Mill: "Utilitarianism" in *On Liberty and Other Essays* (Oxford: Oxford University Press, 1991), p. 137.

8.   Mill refers to Kant's categorical imperative, the idea that the so-called maxim of an action should correspond to universal law, formulated by Kant: "I should never act except in such a way that I can also will that my maxim should become a universal law." (Kant: *Grounding of a Metaphysics of Morals* (New York: Hackett Pub. Co., 1993) p. 14). This implies that actions whose maxim cannot be raised to universal law are contrary to reason. They can be rejected on logical grounds, since moral acts have to be in accordance with universal law. To give an example "when I am in distress, may I make a promise with the intention of not keeping it." (Kant, ibid., p. 15). Is it under some circumstances justified to make an insincere promise? The maxim of the action, *insincere promise*, we call *lying*; in other words, can I want *lying* to become universal law, can I *will* a universal law to lie? The answer to this must be *No*, because if I *will* a universal law to lie, then all promise-making breaks down: "I immediately become aware that I can indeed will the lie but can not at all will a universal law to lie. For by

such a law there would really be no promises at all, since in vain would my willing future actions be professed to other people who would not believe what I professed." (Kant, ibid., p. 15). If I cannot will a universal law to lie, I must admit that neither do I will my first proposal justifying occasional lying. I can no longer want my maxim to become universal law without involving myself in a logical contradiction, because if I want *lying* to become universal law, I can no longer lie, since universally everybody lie and are obligated to lie. Mill is right in criticizing this principle for being so abstract and super-rigid in its emphasis on logical contradiction (between maxim and law) that it would include only a few acts as immoral, while it does not root out several actions that intuitively seem immoral. For example: A man who cares only of himself and scoffs at other people's hardship could still pass for a moral man, because his maxim, *everybody for himself*, could correspond to his universal law, a social Darwinism where the survival of the fittest is seen as beneficial to society. But Mill's understanding of Kant is here 'abbreviated,' since also Kant sees this problem and therefore amends his categorical imperative by introducing a so-called 'consistency of the will' as another test of the morally worthy act. The selfish man above may pass the categorical imperative, but he could not pass the 'consistency of will'-test, because, simultaneously, he wants to be taken care of and does not want other people to be taken care of. He wills, at the same time, his own prosperity and other people's poverty. He is not involved in a logical contradiction, but he is involved in an *inconsistency of his will*.

9.   Mill: "Utilitarianism," loc. cit., p. 136.

10.   Jeremy Bentham: *Introduction to the Principles of Morals and Legislation* (New York: Doubleday, Doran & Company, 1935). p. 7-8, note.

11.   "The chief reason for adopting the name 'Utilitarianism' was, indeed, merely to emphasize the fact that right and wrong conduct must be judged by its results—as a means, in opposition to the strictly Intuitionistic view that certain ways of acting were right and others wrong, what ever their results might be." (Moore: *Principia Ethica*, loc. cit., p. 157).

12.   Mill: "Utilitarianism," loc. cit., p. 136.

13.   Mill: "Utilitarianism," loc. cit., p. 136.

14.   Mill: "Utilitarianism," loc. cit., p. 136.

15.   From a footnote we learn, surprisingly, that Mill understands himself as the originator of this new term: "The author of this essay has reason for believing himself to be the first person who brought the word utilitarian into use." We also learn that Mill considers his use of the term innovative and neologistic: "As a name for one single opinion . . . the term supplies a want in the language." (Mill: "Utilitarianism," loc. cit., p. 137, note). Mill is thus engaged in a polemic against those that do not understand his neologistic semi-private language.

16.   Mill: "Utilitarianism," loc. cit., p. 137.

17.   Several cooperating Mill-scholars reproduce this logic of illogicality. They share Mill's attempt to qualify the emphasis of utilitarianism as a pleasure-theory. They typically starts out quoting with appreciation Mill's famous creed, actions are good insofar as they promote happiness, wrong insofar as they produce the opposite of happiness—by 'happiness' we imply the promotion of

pleasure, etc. But at this point, qualifications are being introduced. By 'pleasure,' Mill does not mean pleasure exactly; his argument is far more 'subtle,' 'sophisticated,' 'rich,' or 'complex'; we are talking about more *complex* experiences. Even if this stands to reason, as we read on, there is typically no clear and communicable presentation of what this alleged 'complexity' consists—part of the problem being that in these 'complex experiences,' pleasure must not be blatantly absent. Cooperating commentators thus reproduce Mill's double-bind; on the one hand, the term 'pleasure' regulates and ought to regulate human utility/well-being, but on the other and in another sense, it does not and ought not to regulate human utility. The problem is, as in Mill, to avoid an interpretation of utilitarianism as a hedonism 'worthy only of swine.' When, e.g., Wendy Donner comments: "Good resides in internal mental states of pleasure or happiness." (Donner: "Mill's Utilitarianism," in Skorupski (ed.): *The Cambridge Companion to Mill* (Cambridge: Cambridge University Press, 1998), p. 257), one believes that to be in an 'internal mental state of pleasure' is equal to 'feeling pleasure,' but this is not the case; it is again far more 'complex': "But while for Bentham these mental states are sensations of pleasure, for Mill they are *far more complex states* of experience." (Donner, ibid., p. 257). Within the next few pages, it is emphasized about ten times that we are dealing with something 'complex.' While Mill's theory "is a *sophisticated kind of* hedonism because of the role that pleasure and pains play in generating *complex pleasurable experiences, it would be a mistake* to view his theory as *primarily* focused on the evaluation of pleasures." (Donner, ibid., p. 259). This supposed 'sophistication' is produced by the following formula: on the one hand, x, but on the other hand, not-x. A primitive hedonism considers non-complex pleasurable experiences; Mill's Utilitarianism considers complex pleasurable experiences; but what is Mill's theory of complex pleasurable experiences about? If I haven't misread Donner, this theory is about 'the meaningful life.' The theory stimulates the moral agent to promote self-development and to pursue *a meaningful life.* "Mill's fundamental purpose is to promote human self-development and so he is centrally occupied with exploring the forms of character that allow humans to pursue meaningful lives." (Donner, ibid., p. 259). Complex pleasurable experiences must then be experiences of meaningfulness, and, correlatively, actions are considered good insofar as they promote meaningfulness, wrong insofar as they produce the opposite of meaningfulness. Mill's anasemic 'x' is in Donner interpreted as 'meaning.' This is the term that can fulfill the difficult condition of being both a pleasure and a non-pleasure. However, in this reformulation, Donner has merely built another fragile house of cards on top of Mill's already fragile construction, and it falls apart under the simple question, What is *a meaningful life?* The theory must be able to outline the conditions of satisfaction for the good, the satisfying, and the meaningful life *in principle,* the conditions for the *universally* meaningful life, and this is impossible.

18.　　Mill: "Utilitarianism," loc. cit., p. 137.

19.　　We may assume that since Mill's essay is a reaction to critics of utilitarianism, it must be a reaction not so much to criticisms of himself (since he is presenting utilitarianism consistently for the first time) as to criticisms of

Bentham and especially his father, James Mill's writings. The indignation over these willful misunderstandings is likely to be a defense of his father's word. Critics never understood, and maliciously continue to misunderstand, his father.

20.   Mill: "Utilitarianism," loc. cit., p. 138.

21.   Mill: "Utilitarianism," loc. cit., p. 138.

22.   Mill: "Utilitarianism," loc. cit., p. 138-139.

23.   Bradley, Moore, Copleston, and other commentators, notice the incongruence between Bentham and Mill's utilitarianism, and Mill's apparently lacking awareness of this fact. Here, Copleston asserts: "He [Mill] does not appear to understand the extent to which he is subjecting the original Benthamite framework of his thought to acute stresses and strains. . . . It is the fact that he grafts on to Benthamism a moral theory which has little or nothing to do with the balancing of pleasures or pains according to the hedonistic calculus of Bentham. . . . He trends to slur over the difference between them [Mill and Bentham], especially, of course, when it is a question of writing against what they would consider reactionary forces." (Frederick Copleston: *A History of Philosophy*, vol. VIII, loc. cit., p. 31-32).

24.   Mill: "Utilitarianism," loc. cit., p. 139.

25.   Let us quote Moore's acute objection to this alleged test of the superior qualities of pleasures: "It will be seen that Mill's test for one pleasure's superiority in quality over another is the preference of most people who have experienced both. A pleasure so preferred, he holds, is more desirable. But then, as we have seen, he holds that 'to think of an object as desirable and to think of it as pleasant are one and the same thing.' He holds, therefore, that the preference of experts merely proves that one pleasure is pleasanter than another. But if that is so, how can he distinguish this standard from the standard of quantity of pleasure? Can one pleasure be pleasanter than another, except in the sense that it gives *more* pleasure?" (G. E. Moore: *Principia Ethica*, loc. cit., p. 130).

26.   Mill: "Utilitarianism," loc. cit., p. 139.

27.   Mill: "Utilitarianism," loc. cit., p. 140.

28.   Mill: "Utilitarianism," loc. cit., p. 140.

29.   Mill: "Utilitarianism," loc. cit., p. 140.

30.   Moore: *Principia Ethica*, loc. cit., p. 131.

31.   Mill: "Utilitarianism," loc. cit., p. 140.

32.   Mill: "Utilitarianism," loc. cit., p. 141.

33.   Mill: "Utilitarianism," loc. cit., p. 142.

34.   Mill: "Utilitarianism," loc. cit., p. 142.

35.   Mill: "Utilitarianism," loc. cit., p. 143.

36.   Mill: "Utilitarianism," loc. cit., p. 147 & 148.

37.   Mill: "Utilitarianism," loc. cit., p. 143.

38.   It is equivalent to the so-called 'ego-instinct,' according to one of the topologies of Freud, who regards it as diametrically opposed to pleasure in the form of the 'object instinct.'

39.   Mill: "Utilitarianism," loc. cit., p. 147-48.

40.   Jacques Derrida: *Of Grammatology*, part III (Baltimore: Johns Hopkins University Press, 1976).

41.   Mill: "Utilitarianism," loc. cit., p. 148.

42.   Mill: "Utilitarianism," loc. cit., p. 148-49.

43.   The term we find often in Nietzsche's writings; however, it has been canonized especially in Rodolphe Gasché. cf.: *The Tain of the Mirror* (Cambridge: Harvard University Press, 1986).

44.   Mill: "Utilitarianism," loc. cit., p. 174.

45.   Mill: "Utilitarianism," loc. cit., p. 174.

46.   Bentham: *Introduction to the Principles of Morals and Legislation,* loc. cit., p. 24-25.

47.   Mill: "Utilitarianism," loc. cit., p. 159.

48.   Mill: "Utilitarianism," loc. cit., p. 161.

49.   Mill: "Utilitarianism," loc. cit., p. 161.

50.   Mill believes that he by this reference to subjective feelings in the performance of duty is criticizing Kant—he believes that Kant's 'duty' is a 'thing in itself': "There is, I am aware, a disposition to believe that a person who sees in moral obligation a transcendental fact, an objective reality belonging to the province of 'Things in themselves,' is likely to be more obedient to it than one who believes it to be entirely subjective, having its sat in human consciousness only. But whatever a person's opinion may be on this point of ontology, the force he is really urged by is his own subjective feeling." Mill: "Utilitarianism," loc. cit., p. 162.

51.   Mill: "Utilitarianism," loc. cit., p. 163.

52.   Mill: "Utilitarianism," loc. cit., p. 163.

53.   Mill: "Utilitarianism," loc. cit., p. 164.

54.   Mill: "Utilitarianism," loc. cit., p. 163.

55.   Mill: "Utilitarianism," loc. cit., p. 168.

56.   Mill: "Utilitarianism," loc. cit., p. 168.

57.   Bertrand Russell: "John Stuart Mill, in his Utilitarianism, offers an argument which is so fallacious that it is hard to understand how he can have thought it valid. He says: Pleasure is the only thing desired; therefore pleasure is the only thing desirable. He argues that the only things visible are things seen, the only things audible are things heard, and similarly the only things audible are things heard, and similarly the only things desirable are things desired. He does not notice that a thing is 'visible' if it can be seen, but 'desirable' if it ought to be desired. Thus 'desirable' is a word presupposing an ethical theory; we cannot infer what is desirable from what is desired." (Russell: *A History of Western Philosophy* (New York: Simon & Schuster, 1945) p. 778).

58.   Mill: "Utilitarianism," loc. cit., p. 168.

59.   Mill: "Utilitarianism," loc. cit., p. 168.

60.   Mill: "Utilitarianism," loc. cit., p. 169.

61.   Mill: "Utilitarianism," loc. cit., p. 168-69.

62.   It is beyond my analytical scope, but in another context there is something to be said about the relationship between Mill's childhood and his adult writings. Mill has given us an account of his childhood in the first chapter of his *Autobiography*. The most striking about this account is that his childhood is in fact absent. Mill was a 'manufactured man'—his own words later in the

autobiography—subjected by his father to an experimental education that effectively robbed him of all childhood. He started learning Greek and Latin at three, math and algebra at six, history and philosophy at eight, etc. His autobiography reflects this lack of childhood by being a commented listing of books. All he has to tell us about his childhood is what books he read when, in what order, and with what amount of excitement. Mill's 'childhood' is a reading-list, the most exciting on that list being Homer, whom he therefore read (in Ancient Greek) frugally and never overdid (excitement is only good in carefully measured portions; pleasure is a scarce commodity and is therefore economized in order to last longer). Other highlights were the daily walks he and his father enjoyed where little Mill summarized yesterday's readings for father, and was duly corrected. After such an effective indoctrination, it is completely understandable that the adult Mill believes that he ought to prefer higher, intellectual pleasures to lower one's. It is maybe also understandable why he cannot come to grips with why he finds them so strangely dissatisfying, even unbearable.

63.   Mill: "Utilitarianism," loc. cit., p. 169. We notice that, often, cooperating commentators of Mill adopt his ambiguities. An authoritative and erudite commentator as John Skorupski also defends several different interpretations of utilitarianism. He starts out defending the official utilitarian doctrine: "He [Mill] tries to show that happiness is the *only thing* desired, and hence the only criterion of morality." . . . "What Mill wants to establish is the desirability of happiness *as such*. He thinks that there is such a thing as a person's objective good, and he wants to establish that it consists *exclusively* in that person's happiness." . . . "Not only does Mill appeal to the *fact* that people desire happiness, in order to show that happiness is desirable—he also devotes a good deal of space to show . . . that happiness is the *only* thing desired, in order to show that it is the *only* thing desirable [my emphases]." (John Skorupski: *John Stuart Mill* (London: Routledge, 1989) pp. 285, 289, & 291). But Skorupski is also ready to defend Mill's remedial version of utilitarianism: "He concedes that in the ordinary sense in which people desire happiness, they desire other things too." . . . "The case for happiness as the sole end cannot then rest as straightforwardly on the fact that it alone is desired." . . . "Happiness is not the only organizing idea, or categorical end, under which we want things." . . . "Neither happiness, not even 'internal satisfaction,' is the only desirable end." (Skorupsky, ibid. p. 295, 295, 300, & 307). Compare these letter statements to the above: "happiness is the *only* thing desired." Cooperating commentators are dangerously exposed to the infectious Mill-disease: like Mill, they defend opposite positions; like Mill, while writing under the influence of 'reasonableness' and goodwill, they become indifferent to inner consistency.

64.   Mill: "Utilitarianism," loc. cit., p. 170.
65.   Mill: "Utilitarianism," loc. cit., p. 171.
66.   Mill: "Utilitarianism," loc. cit., p. 172.
67.   One of Mill's cooperating commentators writes at one point: "one could dismiss Mill as essentially a muddled man." (Alan Ryan: *The Philosophy of John Stuart Mill*, loc. cit., p. 188). Indeed one could, and I would agree in this

statement was it not because Ryan by his remark is defending Mill. That kind of constructions usually mean, *one could but shouldn't*. It is assumed that something seemingly obvious is mere appearance. One could dismiss him as a 'muddled man,' but this would be too easy, simple, or trivial. However, as I have here ventured, sometimes the obvious is in fact true, and sometimes—instead of looking for a truth beneath an appearance—it is shrewder to doubt one's search for profundity, and *restore* appearance beneath the supposed truth. It is sometimes the case that someone that *seems* like a muddled man, *is* a muddled man.

68.   Mill: "Utilitarianism," loc. cit., p. 168-69.
69.   Mill quoted from Roger Crisp: *Mill on Utilitarianism*, loc. cit., p. 78.

LIST OF LITERATURE

Aarsleff, Hans: *From Locke to Saussure* (Minneapolis: University of Minnesota Press, 1982).

Alston, William P.: *Philosophy of Language* (Englewood-Cliffs: Prentice-Hall, 1964).

Anschutz, R. P.: *The Philosophy of J. S. Mill* (Oxford: The Clarendon Press, 1953).

Apel, Karl-Otto (ed.): *Sprachpragmatik und Philosophie* (Frankfurt: Suhrkamp Verlag, 1982).

Apel, Karl-Otto: "Openly strategic uses of language: a transcendental-pragmatic perspective." In Dews, Peter (ed.): *Habermas: A Critical Reader* loc. cit.

Apel, Karl-Otto: "The Problem of Philosophical Foundations Grounding in Light of a Transcendental Pragmatics of Language." In: Baynes, et al: *After Philosophy*, loc. cit.

Apel, Karl-Otto: *From a Transcendental-Semiotic Point of View* (Manchester: Manchester University Press, 1998).

Apel, Karl-Otto: *Towards a Transformation of Philosophy* (London: Routledge & Kegan Paul, 1980).

Aristotle: *Ethica Nicomachea. In The Basic Works of Aristotle*, edited by R. McKeon. (New York: Random House, 1941).

Aristotle: *Metaphysics. In The Basic Works of Aristotle*, edited by R. McKeon. (New York: Random House, 1941).

Austin, J. L.: *How to Do Things with Words* (Cambridge, Mass.: Harvard University Press, 1975).

Baynes/Bohman/McCarthy (eds.): *After Philosophy* (Cambridge, Mass., MIT Press, 1987).

Beckett, Samuel: *Waiting for Godot.* (London: Faber and Faber, 1956).

Bentham, Jeremy: *The Principles of Morals and Legislation* (Amherst: Prometheus Books, 1988).

Benveniste, Emile: *Problémes de linguistique gènèrale.* (Paris: Editions Gallimard, 1966).

Benveniste, Emile: *Problems in General Linguistics.* Translated by M. E. Meek (Miami: University of Miami Press, 1971).

Berger, Fred R.: *Happiness, Justice, and Freedom* (Berkeley: University of California Press, 1984).

Booth, Wayne C.: *Critical Understanding—The Power and Limits of Pluralism* (Chicago: The University of Chicago Press, 1982).

Bornedal, Peter: *Speech and System* (Copenhagen: Museum Tusculanum Press-University of Copenhagen, 1996).

Bornedal, Peter: *The Interpretations of Art* (Lanham/New York: University Press of America, 1996).

Bradley, F. H.: *Ethical Studies*, 2nd ed. (Oxford: Oxford University Press, 1962).

Cassirer, Ernst: *The Philosophy of Symbolic Forms, vol. I: Language* (New Haven: Yale University Press, 1955).

Cooke, Meave: *Language and Reason* (Cambridge: MIT Press, 1997).

Copleston, Frederick: *A History of Philosophy* vol. VIII (New York, Image Books, 1994).

Crane, Ronald S.: *The Language of Criticism and the Structure of Poetry* (Chicago: The University of Chicago Press, 1953).

Crisp, Roger: *Mill on Utilitarianism* (London: Routledge, 1997).

Culler, Jonathan: *On Deconstruction—Theory and Criticism after Structuralism* (Ithaca: Cornell University Press, 1982).

D'Entréves/Benhabib (eds.): *Habermas and the Unfinished Project of Modernity* (Cambridge: MIT Press, 1997).

Davidson, Donald: "A Nice Derangement of Epitaphs." In Grandy/Warner (eds.): *Philosophical Grounds of Rationality*, loc. cit.

Davis, Wayne A.: *Implicature, Intention, Convention, and Principle in the failure of Gricean Theory* (Cambridge: Cambridge University Press, 1998).

Deleuze, G. & Guattari, F.: *What is Philosophy?* Translated by H. Tomlinson & G. Burchell. (New York: Columbia University Press, 1994).

Derrida, Jacques: *Limited Inc.* (Evanston: Northwestern University Press, 1988).

Derrida, Jacques: *Of Grammatology*. Translated by G. Spivak (Baltimore: Johns Hopkins University Press, 1974).

Derrida, Jacques: *The Postcard—From Socrates to Freud and Beyond.* Translated by A. Bass. (Chicago, The University of Chicago Press, 1993).

Derrida, Jacques: *Writing and Difference*. Translated by A. Bass (Chicago: The University of Chicago Press, 1978).

Descartes, Rene: *Meditations on First Philosophy*, in *The Philosophical Writings of Descartes*, vol. I, loc. cit.

Descartes, Rene: *Principles of Philosophy*, in *The Philosophical Writings of Descartes*, vol. I, loc. cit.

Descartes, Rene: *Objections and Replies*, in *The Philosophical Writings of Descartes*, vol. II, loc. cit.

Descartes, Rene: *The Philosophical Writings of Descartes*, vol. I & II. Translated by J. Cottingham et al, (Cambridge: Cambridge University Press, 1984).

Dews, Peter (ed.): *Habermas: A Critical Reader* (Oxford: Blackwell Publishers, 1999).

Donner, Wendy: "Mill's Utilitarianism." In Skorupski, John: *The Cambridge Companion to Mill*, loc. cit.

Dosse, Francois: *History of Structuralism*, vol. I & II. Translated by D. Glassman (Minneapolis: University of Minnesota Press, 1997).

Dryzek, John S.: "Critical Theory as a Research Program." In White, Stephen K. (ed.): *The Cambridge Companion to Habermas*, loc. cit.

Duclot & Todorov: *Encyclopedic Dictionary of the Sciences of Language*. Translated by C. Porter (Baltimore: The Johns Hopkins University Press, 1979).

Dux, Günter: "Kommunikative Vernunft und Interesse." In Honneth/Joas (eds.): *Kommunikatives Handeln*, loc. cit.

Fish, Stanley: *Doing What Comes Naturally* (Durham: Duke University Press, 1989).

Fish, Stanley: *Is There a Text in This Class?* (Cambridge, Mass.: Harvard University Press, 1980).

Fish, Stanley: *The Trouble with Principle* (Cambridge, Mass.: Harvard University Press, 1999).

Fish, Stanley: *There is No such Thing as Free Speech and It Is a Good Thing Too* (Oxford: Oxford University Press, 1994).

Freud, Sigmund: *On Metapsychology* (London: Penguin Books, 1991).

Freud, Sigmund: *The Interpretations of Dreams* (London: Penguin Books, 1990).

Gadamer, Hans-George: *Truth and Method* (New York: Seabury Press, 1975).

Gasché, Rodolphe: *The Tain of the Mirror* (Cambridge: Harvard University Press, 1986).

Geoffrey Hartman: *Criticism in the Wilderness* (New Haven-London: Yale University Press, 1980)

Geoffrey Hartman: *Saving the Text* (Baltimore: The Johns Hopkins University Press, 1981).

Goethe, Johann Wolfgang von: *Faust* vol. I & II. Translated by D. Luke (Oxford: Oxford University Press, 1994).

Grandy/Warner (eds.): *Philosophical Grounds of Rationality* (Oxford: Clarendon Paperbacks, 1986).

Grandy/Warner: "Paul Grice: A View of his Work." In Grandy/Warner (eds.): *Philosophical Grounds of Rationality,* loc. cit.

Greimas, A. J.: *On Meaning. Selected Writing in Semiotic Theory* (Minneapolis: University of Minnesota Press, 1994).

Greimas, A. J.: *Structural Semantics. An Attempt at a Method* (Lincoln-London: University of Nebraska Press, 1983).

Grice, Paul: "Reply to Richards." In Grandy/Warner (eds.): *Philosophical Grounds of Rationality*, loc. cit.

Grice, Paul: *Studies in the Way of Words* (Cambridge: Harvard University Press, 1989).

Gripp, Helga: *Jürgen Habermas — Und es gibt sie doch – Zur kommunikationstheoretischen begründung von Vernunft bei Jürgen Habermas* (Paderborn: Ferdinand Schoningh, 1984).

Habermas, Jürgen: *Moral Consciousness and Communicative Action* (Cambridge: MIT Press, 1989).

Habermas, Jürgen: *On the Pragmatics of Communication*. Edited by M. Cooke. (Cambridge: MIT Press, 1998).

Habermas, Jürgen: *Postmetaphysical Thinking* (Cambridge: MIT Press, 1993).

Habermas, Jürgen: *The Philosophical Discourse of Modernity* (Cambridge: MIT Press, 1988).

Habermas, Jürgen: *The Theory of Communicative Action,* vol. 1 & 2 (Boston: Beacon Press, 1984).

Habermas, Jürgen: *Vorstudien und Ergänzungen zur Theorie des kommunikativen Handelns* (Frankfurt: Suhrkamp Verlag, 1984/95).

Harris, Roy: *Reading Saussure* (La Salle: Open Court, 1987).

Hawkes, Terence: *Structuralism and Semiotics* (Berkeley: University of California Press, 1977).

Heidegger, Martin: *An Introduction to Metaphysics*. Translated by R. Manheim (New Haven/London: Yale University Press, 1987).

Heidegger, Martin: *Basic Writings*. Edited & translated by D. F. Krell (San Francisco: HarperSanFrancisco, 1993).

Henrich, Dieter: "What is metaphysics—What is modernity?" In Dews, Peter (ed.): *Habermas: A Critical Reader* loc. cit.

Herder: *On the Origin of Language*. Translated by Moran & Gode (Chicago: The University of Chicago Press, 1966).

Hjelmslev, Louis: *Prolegomena to a Theory of Language* (Madison: The University of Wisconsin Press, 1963).

Hohengarten, William M.: "Translators Introduction." In Habermas: *Postmetaphysical Thinking*, loc. cit.

Holdcroft, David: *Saussure—Signs, System, and Arbitrariness* (Cambridge: Cambridge University Press, 1991).

Honneth/Joas (eds.): *Kommunikatives Handeln* (Frankfurt am Main: Suhrkamp Verlag, 1988).

Horster, Detlef: *Habermas: An Introduction* (Philadelphia, Pennbridge Books, 1992).

Hoy, David C.: "Splitting the Difference." In: D'Entréves/Benhabib (eds.): *Habermas and the Unfinished Project of Modernity* loc. cit.

Husserl, Edmund: *Logical Investigations* (London: Routledge & Kegan Paul, 1970).

Ingarden, Roman: *Vom Erkennen des literarischen Kunstwerks* (Tübingen, Niemeyer, 1968).

Ingram, David: *Habermas and the Dialectic of Reason* (New Haven: Yale University Press, 1987).

Iser, Wolfgang: *The Act of Reading—A Theory of Aesthetic Response* (Baltimore/London: The Johns Hopkins University Press, 1978).

Iser, Wolfgang: *The Implied Reader* (Baltimore/London: The Johns Hopkins University Press, 1974).

Joas, Hans: "Die unglückliche Ehe von Hermeneutik und Funktionalismus." In Honneth/Joas (eds.): *Kommunikatives Handeln*, loc. cit.

Kafka, Franz: *The Castle*. Translated by M. Harmon (New York: Schochen Books, 1998).

Kant, Immanuel: *Critique of Pure Reason*. Translated by W. S. Pluhar (Indianapolis: Hackett Publishing Company, 1996).

Kant, Immanuel: *Grounding of a Metaphysics of Morals*. Translated by J. W. Ellington (New York: Hackett Publishing Company 1993).

Kant, Immanuel: *Prolegomena to Any Future Metaphysics*. Translated by P. Carus (Indianapolis: Hackett Publishing Company, 1977).

Kerner, George C.: *Three Philosophical Moralists—Mill, Kant, Sartre* (Oxford: Clarendon Press, 1990).

Koreng, Christine: *Norm und Interaktion bei Jürgen Habermas* (Düsseldorf: Patmos Verlag, 1979).

Kortian, Garbis: *Metacritique—The philosophical argument of Jürgen Habermas* (Cambridge: University of Cambridge Press, 1980).

Lorenzen, Paul: *Constructive Philosophy* (Cambridge, Mass.: MIT Press, 1987)

Lyons, John: *Semantics* vol. I & II (Cambridge: Cambridge University Press, 1977).

McCarthy, Thomas: *The Critical Theory of Jürgen Habermas* (Cambridge, Mass.: The MIT Press, 1981).

Mill, John Stuart: *Autobiography* (London: Penguin Books, 1989).

Mill, John Stuart: *On Liberty.* In: *On Liberty and Other Essays*, loc. cit.

Mill, John Stuart: *On Liberty and Other Essays*, edited by J. Gray (Oxford: Oxford University Press, 1991).

Mill, John Stuart: *System of Logic* (New York: Classic Books, 2001).

Mill, John Stuart: *Utilitarianism.* In: *On Liberty and Other Essays*, loc. cit.

Moon, J. Donald: "Practical Discourse and Communicative Ethics." In White, Stephen K. (ed.): *The Cambridge Companion to Habermas*, loc. cit.

Moore, G. E.: *Principia Ethica – Revised Edition* (Cambridge: Cambridge University Press, 1993).

Moran, Dermot: *Introduction to Phenomenology* (London/New York: Routledge, 2000).

Morick, Harold (ed.): *Challenges to Empiricism* (Indianapolis: Hackett Publishing Company, 1980).

Nietzsche, Frederich: *The Will to Power.* Translated by Holllingdale & Kaufmann (New York: Random House, 1967).

Nietzsche, Friedrich: *Beyond Good and Evil.* Translated by J. Norman (Cambridge: Cambridge University Press, 2002).

Nietzsche, Friedrich: *Sämtliche Werke Kritische Studienausgabe.* Edited by G. Colli & M. Montinari (Berlin/New York: Walter de Gruyter, 1967-77).

Nietzsche, Friedrich: *The Gay Science.* Translated by W. Kaufmann (New York: Vintage Books—Random House, 1974).

Norris Christopher: "Deconstruction, Postmodernism and Philosophy." In d'Etrèves & Benhabib: *Habermas and the Unfinished Project of Modernity*, loc. cit.

Norris, Christopher: *Against Relativism* (Oxford: Blackwell, 1997).

Norris, Christopher: *Deconstruction and the Interest of Theory* (Norman: University of Oklahoma Press, 1989).

Perelman, Ch. & Olbrechts-Tyteca, L.: *The New Rhetoric—A Treatise of Argumentation.* Translated by J. Wilkinson & P. Weaver (Notre Dame: The University of Notre Dame Press, 1969).

Pettit, Philip (ed.): *Consequentialism* (Aldershot: Dartmouth, 1993).

Plato: *The Republic of Plato.* Translated by F. M. Cornford (Oxford: Oxford University Press, 1945).

Popper, Karl: *Popper Selections.* Edited by D. Miller (Princeton: Princeton University Press, 1984).

Popper, Karl: *The Logic of Scientific Discovery* (London/New York: Routledge, 1992).

Rehg, William: *Insight and Solidarity—A Study in the Discourse Ethics of Jürgen Habermas* (Berkeley: California University Press, 1994).

Ricoeur, Paul: *Hermenutics and Social Sciences* (Cambridge: Cambridge University Press, 1981).

Ricoeur, Paul: *Interpretation Theory* (Austin: Texas Christian University Press, 1976).

Ricoeur, Paul: *The Conflicts of Interpretations* (Evanston: Northwestern University Press, 1974).

Rorty, Richard: *Philosophical Papers* vol. 2 (Cambridge: Cambridge University Press, 1993).

Rorty, Richard: "Is Derrida a Transcendental Philosopher." In Wood, David (ed.): *Derrida—A Critical Reader*, loc. cit.

Rorty, Richard: *Consequences of Pragmatism* (Minneapolis: University of Minnesota Press, 1982).

Rorty, Richard: *Contingency, Irony, and Solidarity* (Cambridge: Cambridge University Press, 1989).

Rousseau, Jean Jacques: *On the Origin of Language.* Translated by Moran & Gode. (Chicago: The University of Chicago Press, 1966).

Russell, Bertrand: *A History of Western Philosophy* (New York/London: Simon & Schuster, 1972).

Ryan, Alan: *The Philosophy of John Stuart Mill* (London: Macmillan Press, 1970).

Saussure, Ferdinand de: *Cours de Linguistique Générale.* Edited by C. Bally & A Sechehaye (Paris: Payot, 1975).

Saussure, Ferdinand de: *Course in General Linguistics.* Translated by W. Baskin (New York: McGraw Hill, 1966).

Schiffer, Stephen R. : *Meaning* (Oxford: The Clarendon Press, 1972).

Schiffer, Stephen R.: "Compositional Semantics and Language Understanding." In Grandy/Warner (eds.): *Philosophical Grounds of Rationality,* loc. cit.

Schiffer, Stephen R.: *Remnants of Meaning* (Cambridge, Mass: The MIT Press, 1989).

Schnädelbach, Herbert: "Transformation der Kritischen Theorie." In Honneth/Joas (eds.): *Kommunikatives Handeln,* loc. cit.

Searle, John R.: *Intentionality* (Cambridge: Cambridge University Press, 1983).

Searle, John R.: "Meaning, Communication, and Representation." In Grandy/Warner (eds.): *Philosophical Grounds of Rationality,* loc. cit.

Searle, John R.: *Meaning and Expression* (Cambridge: Cambridge University Press, 1979).

Searle, John R.: *Speech Acts* (Cambridge: Cambridge University Press, 1969).

Seel, Martin: "Die zwei Bedeutungen kommunikativen Rationalität." In Honneth/Joas (eds.): *Kommunikatives Handeln*, loc. cit.

Sidgwick, Henry: *The Methods of Ethics* (London: Macmillan Press, 1962).

Skorupski, John: *John Stuart Mill* (London: Routledge, 1989).

Skorupski, John (ed.): *The Cambridge Companion to Mill* (Cambridge: Cambridge University Press, 1998).

Starobinski, Jean: *Jean Jacques Rousseau* (Chicago: The University of Chicago Press, 1988).

Stephen, Leslie: *The English Utilitarians, vol. III, John Stuart Mill* (New York: Peter Smith, 1950).

Swindal, James: *Reflection Revisited—Jürgen Habermas's Discursive Theory of Truth* (New York: Fordham University Press, 1999).

Tallis, Raymond: *Not Saussure* (New York, St. Martin's Press, 1995).

Taylor, Charles: "Sprache und Gesellschaft." In Honneth/Joas (eds.): *Kommunikatives Handeln*, loc. cit.

Taylor, Kenneth: *Truth and Meaning* (Oxford: Blackwell, 1998).

Tugendhat, Ernst: *Vorlesungen zur Einführung in die sprachanalytische Philosophie* (Frankfurt: Suhrkamp Verlag, 1976/94).

Warnke, Gorgia: "Communicative Rationality and Cultural Values." In White, Stephen K. (ed.): *The Cambridge Companion to Habermas*, loc. cit.

Werth, Paul (ed.): *Conversation and Discourse* (London: Crom Helm, 1981).

Wheeler, Samuel S.: *Deconstruction as Analytic Philosophy* (Stanford: Stanford University Press, 2000).

White, Stephen K. (ed.): *The Cambridge Companion to Habermas* (Cambridge: Cambridge University Press, 1995).

White, Stephen K.: *The Recent Work of Jürgen Habermas* (Cambridge: Cambridge University Press, 1988).

Wilden, Anthony: *System and Structure: Essays in Communication and Exchange* (London: Tavistock Publications, 1972).

Wilson, Fred: "Mill on Psychology." In Skorupski, John (ed.): *The Cambridge Companion to Mill*, loc. cit.

Wilson/Sperber: "On Grice's Theory of Conversation." In Werth, Paul: *Conversation and Discourse*, loc. cit.

Wittgenstein, Ludwig: *On Certainty* (New York: Harper Torchbooks, 1969).

Wittgenstein, Ludwig: *Philosophische Untersuchungen/Philosophical Investigations* (Oxford: Blackwell, 1997. Re-issued 2nd ed.).

Wood, David (ed.): *Derrida—A Critical Reader* (Oxford: Blackwell, 1992).

INDEX

Peter Bornedal is Associate Professor at American University of Beirut. He is Dr. Phil. from The University of Copenhagen, with a specialization in contemporary theory of interpretation, language-theory, and semiotics, and Ph.D. from The University of Chicago, with a specialization in aesthetics and literary theory. His previous publications include: *Speech and System* (1997); *The Interpretations of Art* (1996); *Rekonstruktioner* (1990); & *Skrift og Skribent* (1986). Forthcoming is *The Surface and the Abyss—Nietzsche as Philosopher of Mind and Language*. He can be reached for comments and suggestions at bornedal@hotmail.com.